WITHDRAWN
WRIGHT STATE UNIVERSITY LIBRARIES

A PRIMER OF CLINICAL HYPNOSIS

Barbara DeBetz, M.D.
Gérard Sunnen, M.D.

PSG PUBLISHING COMPANY, INC.
LITTLETON, MASSACHUSETTS

Library of Congress Cataloging in Publication Data

Main entry under title:

DeBetz, Barbara.
A primer of clinical hypnosis.

Includes bibliographies and index.
1. Hypnotism—Therapeutic use. I. Sunnen, Gérard.
II. Title. [DNLM: 1. Hypnosis. WM 415 D286p]
RC495.D44   1985   615.8'512   84-18932
ISBN 0-88416-486-1

Published by:
PSG PUBLISHING COMPANY, INC.
545 Great Road
Littleton, Massachusetts 01460

Copyright © 1985 by Barbara DeBetz and Gérard Sunnen

All rights reserved. No part of this publication may be reproduced or transmitted in any form or by any means, electronic or mechanical, including photocopy, recording, or any information storage or retrieval system, without permission in writing from the publisher.

Printed in the United States of America

International Standard Book Number: 0-88416-486-1

Library of Congress Catalog Card Number: 84-18932

To Herta, Ingrid and Harald with love and gratitude.
BHD

To my parents André and Wanda for their openness, love and wisdom.
GVS

ABOUT THE AUTHORS

Barbara DeBetz received her medical degree from the University of Miami, School of Medicine. She did her internship and residency in psychiatry at Bellevue Psychiatric Hospital in New York City.

Dr. DeBetz is a practicing psychiatrist and an assistant clinical professor of Psychiatry at Columbia University, College of Physicians and Surgeons. Before joining the teaching faculty at Columbia University, she was on the faculty at New York University Medical Center. She is a diplomate of the American Board of Neurology and Psychiatry.

Dr. DeBetz is a member of the American Psychiatric Association, American Medical Association, American Medical Women's Association, American Society of Clinical Hypnosis, Society of Experimental and Clinical Hypnosis, and a fellow of the New York Academy of Medicine, among others.

Dr. DeBetz has lectured extensively and has written several articles on hypnosis and a self-help book on sexual disorders. By her colleagues she is considered an expert in the clinical uses of hypnosis. She has participated and taught hypnosis in numerous post-graduate courses given throughout the country, and she has supervised psychiatric residents, psychologists, medical students and various other mental health practitioners.

Among her many areas of interest are the use of hypnosis as applied to habit disorders, sexual dysfunction and pain management.

Gérard Sunnen received his medical degree from the State University of New York, Downstate Medical Center, and following an internship in medicine and surgery, he became resident and chief resident at Bellevue Psychiatric Hospital, New York City. He has practiced psychiatry in the Air Force, in forensic, acute care and general hospital liaison settings, and is currently in private practice and a consultant to several corporations and agencies.

Dr. Sunnen has for many years applied hypnosis to patient care. Both in the United States and his native France, he has lectured extensively on the theoretical and practical aspects of hypnotic treatment as well as on related topics including newer methods of psychotherapy, states of consciousness, the creative process, and future directions in psychiatry. He is also interested in the connections between art and the dynamics of imagination and he has shown his own artwork in New York.

A diplomate of the American Board of Psychiatry and Neurology, Dr. Sunnen is an assistant clinical professor at the New York University Medical Center and a member of the American Psychiatric Association and of the American Society of Clinical Hypnosis.

CONTENTS

Introduction vii

PART I. THEORETICAL ISSUES

1. **Historical Developments** 1
   Barbara DeBetz
2. **Current Concepts of Hypnosis and Future Directions** 7
   Gérard Sunnen
3. **Hypnotic Phenomena** 25
   Barbara DeBetz and Gérard Sunnen

PART II. INDUCTION TECHNIQUES

4. **General Considerations** 41
   Gérard Sunnen
5. **Illustrated Method for Self-Hypnosis** 53
   Barbara DeBetz
6. **Hypnotic Rating Scales and Induction Techniques** 67
   Barbara DeBetz

PART III. THERAPEUTIC APPLICATIONS

7. **Anxiety** 85
   Gérard Sunnen
8. **Habit Disorders** 101
   Barbara DeBetz
9. **Pain Control** 113
   Barbara DeBetz
10. **Hypnosis in the Hospital Setting** 127
    Gérard Sunnen

11	**Hypnotic Approaches in the Cancer Patient** 137 Gérard Sunnen	
12	**Hypnosis in Psychosomatic Medicine** 151 Gérard Sunnen	
13	**Hypnosis and Sex Therapy** 163 Barbara DeBetz	
14	**Hypnosis in Psychotherapy** 179 Gérard Sunnen	
15	**Psychotherapy of the Highly Hypnotizable Individual** 197 Barbara DeBetz	
16	**Miscellaneous Medical Applications of Hypnosis** 221 Gérard Sunnen	

Index 237

INTRODUCTION

Hypnosis is a useful instrument in medicine and psychiatry and has a wide range of therapeutic applications. It offers the clinician an opportunity to make systematic use of an individual's psychological resources for change. Everything done in therapy with hypnosis can also be done without it, but hypnosis offers the advantage of facilitating and accelerating the impact of the therapeutic intervention.

Hypnotic phenomena occur all the time with or without formal induction. When individuals with trance capacity act with high motivation, concentrate intensely, or find themselves in stress situations, they tend to shift into spontaneous trance states. Therefore it is useful for the clinician to learn to recognize such trance phenomena even if he does not plan to use hypnosis in the formal sense.

The word "hypnosis" is unfortunately misleading, especially in view of our current knowledge about the nature of hypnosis. The word hypnosis is derived from the Greek root *hypnos* and means sleep. Hypnotic phenomena have very little to do with sleep. Hypnosis is a complex process of attentive, receptive concentration. Although peripheral awareness is reduced both in sleep and in the hypnotic trance, focal awareness, which is totally diffused in sleep, is at an optimal level during hypnosis.

Hypnosis is an altered state of consciousness, characterized by an increased ability to respond to treatment strategies that can effect changes in habit patterns, motivations and attitudes, self-image, anxiety, and stress conditions. There may also be changes produced in physiological functions, such as pain perception, and those illnesses that are of psychosomatic origin such as functional colitis, asthma, and ectopic dermatitis, just to mention a few.

Hypnotic phenomena have occurred in one form or another all along, but they were interpreted and used differently at different periods. A large portion of the general population has a certain degree of hypnotic trance capacity, and it is generally agreed upon that 65% to 70% of all people are able to shift into a trance state. There are different levels and not everybody has the capacity to experience the same depth of hypnosis; even within each individual the depth of the trance experience can fluctuate depending on a variety of factors.

In spite of its great utility, hypnosis has been a stepchild in the scientific medical community for a long time. It is only fairly recently that hypnosis has gained more professional attention and prestige, and there is a rapid growth of clinicians who are eager to use hypnotic treatment modalities as part of their professional armamentarium. Among the reasons why hypnosis has taken such a back seat in medicine and psychiatry are the many misleading myths about hypnosis and its indiscriminate use for entertainment purposes such as stage, TV, the movie industry, and other public media. However, with clarification of these misconceptions, we can open the way to greater professional acceptance of the clinical uses of hypnosis.

While all hypnosis is in essence self-hypnosis, when an individual allows the trance experience to be structured by another (hypnotist), then the hypnotic experience is also characterized by an intense and sensitive interpersonal relatedness between the subject and the operator with the relative suspension of critical judgment on the subject's side. This capacity can be actively tapped by the operator and used towards a specific therapeutic goal. Hypnosis in a clinical context is only of value if done in a therapeutic setting. There are no hypnotists per se, there are only clinicians of whatever specialty who use hypnosis as a tool to implement a specific treatment strategy.

Another important reason hypnosis has not received the clinical attention it deserves has been the unscientific and often unprofessional way of inducing and testing for trance capacity. In order to use hypnotic trance capacity in a clinical setting, the clinician has to first evaluate the clinical situation and measure the patient's level of hypnotizability. Then he must have available an easy and relatively quick method to induce the trance. Our busy schedules do not allow us to take an hour or more to induce a trance, but nowadays there are tests and induction techniques available which can be suited to any clinician's schedule, busy as he may be. Any clinician can learn to test and induce a trance in a relatively short period of time. Trance induction is teachable and learnable. There are no special personality traits required of the person who wants to administer hypnosis other than his own clinical judgment, and there is no special setting necessary.

Hypnosis is remarkably safe when used with good clinical judgement in a goal-directed setting. Its use entails far fewer side effects than even the most benign medications and surgical procedures. However, if it is used unethically or therapeutically in the wrong situation, then the mistake or harm is the result of the clinician's bad judgement rather than the hypnosis itself.

This book is intended for those clinicians and practitioners who practice medicine, psychiatry, clinical psychology, surgery, dentistry, or any other specialty involved with any kind of anxiety conditions and chronic and acute pain conditions. It is also intended for other health practitioners who work under the guidance of a physician such as nurses, clinical social workers, and paramedics: in short, for all those who desire a fundamental knowledge of the principles and clinical applications of hypnosis. This book reviews the different leading theories about the nature of hypnosis in a historical way as well as up-to-date information in regard to current theories about hypnosis. It does not endorse one theory or method in particular but rather gives a neutral overview of the field.

However, the bulk of the book will be dedicated to reviewing the therapeutic uses of hypnosis in a concise and brief form, yet sufficiently comprehensive for the reader to feel confident that he is aware of the wide range of situations in which hypnosis might be of value to the patient. We do not expect the reader to have any previous knowledge of the subject of hypnosis nor do we expect him to have a vast understanding of the psychological aspects of illness. This is a "primer" which means a "first" or "basic" book in the field of hypnosis. The approach we are taking in this book places great weight on simplicity of expression without diminishing the depth and integrity of the subject.

A final comment should be made regarding the scope and purpose of this primer. Hypnosis, like surgery or dentistry, cannot be learned fully from textbooks. This book is meant to give the beginner a broad and full understanding of the field of hypnosis and, with some additional practical experience, one can learn to apply hypnosis to one's own area of specialty.

This book has a unique section on self-hypnosis. And those who follow the instructions to induce self-hypnosis will find it easy to use those instructions as a take-off to induce a hypnotic trance in others. With the new interest and acceptance of hypnosis in the professional community, it should not be difficult for anyone interested to perfect and complete the ability to learn to induce a hypnotic trance, learn to construct proper treatment strategies, and teach patients the use of self-hypnosis.

PART I. THEORETICAL ISSUES

1

Historical Developments

Barbara DeBetz

Hypnotic phenomena have occurred all along, although they were not always recognized as such or called that. Since antiquity, hypnotic techniques have been used by priests in ancient Egypt and Greece. For instance, there are hieroglyphic descriptions of the Egyptian Pharaoh Imhotep who allegedly had such an impact on the sick that his mere presence could banish disease. The Ebers Papyrus, an ancient scroll, mentions the "laying on of hands" as a practice to reduce fever, inflammatory disease, and cure pain and a variety of other physical and emotional ailments.

Between 400 and 100 BC, there were several hundred Aesculapian "sleep temples" in Greece and Rome where the primary form of treatment consisted of inducing a hypnotic sleep and initiating the healing process through posthypnotic suggestions.

With the dawn of Christianity, suggestive healing was regarded as a miraculous working of the deity. One can find in the Bible numerous examples of Christ's power to heal the ill and deranged. During the early period of Christianity, disease was ascribed to demonical possession, and therefore the religious healer directed his suggestive efforts towards expelling the demons from the body of the possessed. In addition to the healing powers of religious faith — still existing in the miraculous cures of places such as Lourdes — royalty, king's touch in particular, had also special healing powers. Less effective powers were ascribed to a queen's touch and the touch of lesser nobility.

Around 1530, the German physician Theophrast Paracelsus

postulated that the human body and mind were influenced by emanations of a magnetic fluid from the stars and the moon. His theory was followed by numerous other theories and cures for diseases, but all of them were based either on divine or celestial influences on mind and body. Remnants of some of these beliefs are still found in many parapsychology theories as well as astrology.

The simple country priest Johann Joseph Gassner (1727 to 1779) attracted much public attention because of his "healing powers" and ability to "exorcise" evil spirits causing illness. The Austrian physician Franz Anton Mesmer (1734 to 1815) practiced in France at the time of the Enlightenment and the American Revolution. Mesmer is often identified with the term "animal magnetism," although he neither originated the term nor the concept. He believed that he was gifted with some kind of "fluid" that he had circulating within him and that he could transfer this "fluid" to others and heal them. Initially he had used magnets that were passed over the patient's body, effecting a cure. He also led group sessions (seances) where several patients sat around a tub with protruding magnets. Some of these patients would develop a "crisis," a kind of hysterical seizure, lapse into sleep, and awaken cured or at least improved. Mesmer later found that magnets were not crucial and all that was needed was the touching of the patient.

A follower of Mesmer, the nobleman Amand-Marie-Tasques de Chastenet de Puysegur (1751 to 1825) magnetized a tree on his estate, at which his peasants would obtain relief from their ailments. He also found that the "mesmeric crisis" was unnecessary and that he could mesmerize a person just by talking to him and giving him specific suggestions.

The notoriety that followed Mesmer's spectacular therapeutic claims led to the appointment of a panel of scientists, including the American diplomat Benjamin Franklin, then living in Paris, to investigate Mesmer's methods and claims of the healing properties of animal magnetism. This panel concluded that no magnetic fluid existed and that Mesmer's cures were attributable to the imagination of the patients.

In 1813, a Portuguese priest by the name of Abbe Faria established himself in Paris and postulated that the essential process of magnetism was due less to the magnetizer than to the subject. He also claimed that certain individuals were more "susceptible" to magnetism than others. His technique consisted in seating the patient in a comfortable chair, having him fix the eyes on a certain point, and raising one hand. Then he would command in a loud voice "Sleep!," upon which the subject would fall into a magnetic sleep. While in that state, he would give him posthypnotic suggestions. Although he was not the most important person in the history of hypnosis, his name survived mainly because Alexandre Dumas used it for a character in his classic novel *The Count of Monte Cristo*.

The revival of magnetism in France is usually ascribed to J.P.F. Deleuze. He gave public courses and published a clear and well-organized textbook. He declared that the era of "prodigious healings" had gone and now the time of elaborate and methological techniques had set in.

In the middle of the last century, hypnosis was used extensively during surgery. John Elliotson (1791 to 1868), an English surgeon, reported several cases of painless surgery due to "mesmeric sleep." James Esdaile (1808 to 1859), also an English surgeon living in India, performed over 3000 operations using the mesmeric process of inducing somatic anesthesia. He was able to create insensibility to pain and allegedly reduce the post surgery mortality rate from 50% to 5%. His operations included amputations, cataract removals, tumor surgery, and orthopedic procedures. He used mesmeric methods by stroking in a specific manner over the patient's body. Supposedly, his induction procedures took an average time of 20 to 30 minutes but could also last as long as several hours. Towards the end of the nineteenth century, chemical anesthesia was discovered and with it the use of hypnoanesthesia was almost totally abandoned.

Even though hypnosis had lost its importance in surgery, it continued to be of interest to other specialties. A Manchester physician, James Braid (1785-1860), coined the term "hypnotism," derived from the Greek word hypnos, sleep. Ever since that time, this name has remained although we know now that hypnosis is quite different from sleep. Although Braid believed initially that hypnosis was a physiological event, his experiments convinced him that it was a psychological rather than physiological phenomenon. He also stressed the importance of suggestion as a major factor.

In the period from 1860 to 1880, magnetism and hypnotism had fallen into such disrepute that a physician working with these modalities would have gotten himself into serious difficulties regarding his scientific career. Among the few who dared to use hypnosis openly was August Ambroise Liébeault (1823 to 1904). Liébeault thought that hypnosis was identical with natural sleep except that hypnotic sleep was induced by suggestion. He saw a large number of patients free of charge and enjoyed widespread fame, especially among the many peasants who were his patients.

Hippolyte Bernheim (1840 to 1919), a well-known and highly respected professor from Alsace and a strong French patriot, heard about Liébeault's successes and went to see him and learn from him. They became good friends, and Bernheim introduced hypnosis in his university medical hospital. Because of Bernheim's endorsement of hypnosis, Liébeault suddenly rose to fame in the medical community. Bernheim became the leader of the School of Nancy and, after a considerable amount of investigation and research, came to the conclusion that hypnosis was not a pathological condition but was the effect of suggestion. However, as time went by, Bernheim made less and less use of hypnosis, claiming that the effects obtained by this method were as easily obtained by suggestion alone and with the patient in the waking state. This form of treatment was from that time on called "psychotherapy" at the School of Nancy. Bernheim considered himself the original founder of psychotherapy.

While Bernheim was doing his work at the School of Nancy, the famous neurologist Jean-Martin Charcot (1825 to 1893) also got involved with hypnosis at the Salpêtière Hospital in Paris. Charcot was mainly interested in working with hysteria, and he postulated that hypnosis could only be effective in people with pathological conditions. This view was different from that of Bernheim, who felt that in order to be hypnotized the subject had to have a relatively intact nervous system. As a consequence, a violent quarrel developed between the followers of Bernheim and those of Charcot. The disagreement was eventually settled to Charcot's satisfaction. Even though Charcot was wrong in his assumptions, he did a service to hypnosis by confirming its value in treatment with patients. Because of the controversy that had developed, many other respected clinicians became interested in hypnosis; among them eminent names such as Richard von Krafft-Ebing (1856 to 1939), Pierre Janet (1859 to 1947), and Sigmund Freud (1856 to 1939) can be found.

Sigmund Freud was interested in hypnosis early in his career and went to study hypnotic techniques and methods in Paris with Charcot and in Nancy with Bernheim. He was impressed with the therapeutic potential of hypnosis for neurotic disorders, especially hysteria. Much of his work in hysteria was done together with his friend and colleague Joseph Breuer (1842 to 1925). Freud and Breuer came to the conclusion that hypnosis was able to alleviate hysterical symptoms immediately but they would return after the trance was terminated. The symptom would only disappear permanently if the basic cause was discovered. Therefore, Breuer would have the patient regress in the hypnotic trance and have him recall events that led to the development of the symptom. The importance of Breuer's work was in the change of emphasis of the hypnotic intervention. Instead of simply trying to remove the symptom, he tried to get at the roots and causes through hypnosis. Freud, as he began to develop his psychoanalytic theories, gave up the formal use of hypnosis in favor of his method of free association.

The introduction of magnetism in North America took place mostly via New Orleans, which at the time was a French city and where flourishing mesmeric societies quickly developed. In the other parts of the United States magnetism only grew slowly but steadily increased after 1840. Two names deserve special mention.

One was Phineas Parkhurst Quimby (1802 to 1866). He understood quickly that the main ingredient of magnetism was suggestion, and he practiced what he called "mind cure." One of his patients was Mary Baker Eddy (1821 to 1910), who was to become the founder of the Christian Science movement. The other name to remember is Andrew Jackson Davis, who used some form of daily self-hypnosis and, while in the trance dictated an enormous book about the world of the spirits. His book gained great popularity and opened the way for the propagation of spiritualism.

Morton Prince (1854 to 1929) suggested that dissociation of mental symptoms was common both to the neurotic disorder called multiple personality and to the phenomenon of hypnosis. Pierre Janet came to a similar conclusion at about the same time in France.

Clark L. Hall (1884 to 1952), an experimental physiologist, attempted to give hypnosis scientific validity and set up a series of controlled laboratory experiments. In 1933, he came to the conclusion that hypnosis can best be understood as a state of hyper-suggestibility. Milton Erickson's (1901 to 1980) pioneering work in clinical hypnosis has helped keep hypnosis alive as a valid therapeutic tool. In 1960 the American Medical Association and the American Psychiatric Association accepted the use of hypnosis as an important aid in therapy.

SUGGESTED READING

Darnton R: *Mesmerism and the End of the Enlightenment in France.* New York, Schocken Books, 1970.

Ellenberger HF: *The Discovery of the Unconscious.* New York, Basic Books, 1970.

Orne TM, Hammer AG: *Hypnosis Encyclopaedia Brittanica.* Chicago, Helen Hemingway Benton, 1974, pp 133-140.

Spiegel H: Hypnosis: myth and reality *Psychiatr Ann* 1981;11:9.

Wolberg L: *Hypnosis—Is It For You?* New York, Harcourt Brace Jovanovich, 1972, pp 22-45.

2

Current Concepts of Hypnosis and Future Directions

Gérard Sunnen

Although there is fairly good agreement concerning hypnotic phenomena, there is a lot of disagreement about explaining them. Observed throughout history, hypnotic phenomena have been interpreted in different ways through the tinted glass of each culture's ideology. In Grecian sleep temples, for example, hypnosis was seen as a sleep state facilitating communication with deities; in Mesmer's time, it was conceptualized as an agitated condition resulting from an absorption of cosmic forces.

Today, even with the great advances in the understanding of psychological mechanisms made during the last century, theories of hypnosis, it is observed, are found to be remarkably numerous and divergent. The search for a unified theory has been elusive. To be integrated, it would have to explain the multitude of disparate hypnotic phenomena, from age regression to anesthesia, from catalepsy to hallucination; to account for the wide ranges of its individual manifestations; and to show the reasons for the striking subjective experiences that are often induced.

Since theories are approximations, it is possible that several of them may be concurrently valid, each seeing a piece of a complex process involving both psychological and physiological mechanisms. In any case, it is obvious that not enough is known about the nature and the workings of the mind and that our current degree of sophistication is not as yet sufficient to define hypnosis. However, we can look at the following theories to help us structure our clinical observations, keeping our minds open for new and better-fitting conceptualizations.

HYPNOSIS AS AN ALTERED STATE OF CONSCIOUSNESS

The view that hypnosis is an altered state of consciousness finds many followers who point out that individuals often report experiencing during the trance significant differences from their usual state of mind. This, in fact, is true. Many deeply hypnotized subjects describe how incredibly relaxed or peaceful their experience was and how differently they perceived the flow of time or the feel of their body image. The usual waking state has a familiar experiential quality. We know it to be there most of our waking hours and, it is argued, we would know of any significant deviations from it.

This subjective alteration in the personal field of awareness or aliveness during hypnosis is correlated, by state theorists, to depths of hypnosis. To determine how "deeply" a subject had experienced the trance state we would, in this system, ask for an introspective report, usually with reference to an arbitrary scale. Zero could represent the usual waking state, and ten, let us say, the deepest trance the subject estimates he could attain.

The state theorists posit quantitative (in, for example, the tonus of consciousness) as well as qualitative changes (certain mental processes may be more or less operational, ie, shift to primary process thinking, alterations in ego mechanisms, shift to introspective orientation).

A strong support for the state theory is said to be the occurrence of "trance logic," which refers to the ability of deeply hypnotized subjects to be comfortable with the coexistence of logically inconsistent perceptions or ideas. This, it is pointed out, cannot be done by imitators. Trance logic is, of course, also found in dreams, in manifestations of primary process thinking, and in schizophrenia. How much is it part and parcel of hypnosis? If the waking state is one state of consciousness and the hypnotic state another, we may then ask, how many states are there? Is there a spectrum of states? If so, how does hypnosis fit into it? The school of states of consciousness develops many of its concepts from Eastern philosophies, which have a much longer tradition of interest in these areas. In the Western tradition, states of mind are often equated with states of consciousness, ie, sedation, stupor, light coma, deep coma, and part of the problem in defining hypnosis may be semantic — we may not have developed the words to describe complex higher mental phenomena.

Although theorists often put themselves in state or nonstate camps, these divisions may, in the end, be unnecessarily polarizing. A more integrated view would see hypnotic phenomena as occurring more strongly in the context of certain mental sets (state theory), and as capable of being intensified or shaped by many environmental influences (nonstate theory).

PHYSIOLOGICAL THEORIES

Those who correlate states of consciousness with changes in the central nervous system, or those who hold that physiological events precede all phenomena (the materialist view), look for physical reasons for hypnosis — variations in the EEG or in evoked potentials, cerebral metabolism, cerebral blood flow, or changes in neurotransmitter dynamics. More recently, work has been done with positron emission tomography and magnetic resonance imaging (MRI). Difficulties with this approach have to do partly with the different manifestations of hypnotic states. In passive or neutral hypnosis, for example, where subjects are physiologically slowed down, we would expect readings in all the above tests to be different from those in active hypnosis where the subject, eyes open and alert, may be very task-oriented.

Investigators interested in the neurophysiology of hypnosis look for signs of either increased or decreased activity of certain nuclear formations or pathways or for alterations in regional blood flow. Increases in blood flow, however, do not lead to heightened awareness, and decreases usually lead to drowsiness, stupor, and coma. Hypnosis is none of these. Investigations into the function of the reticular activating system, the diffuse thalamic projections, the frontal lobes, and the limbic areas have been inconclusive. We still do not know enough about these areas of the brain as they relate to normal consciousness or hypnosis.

There are investigators who share Charcot's concepts that hypnosis is based on physiological disturbances or Pavlov's ideas of cortical alterations of function. For some, the right hemisphere, with its connectedness to imagery and feeling states, is more involved with hypnotic phenomena. Others have been impressed by more behavioral manifestations (eye roll), as an indicator of deeper physiological mechanisms.

Since body and mind meet at some yet unknown stratum of brain function, it is conceivable that hypnosis must, at some level, have neurophysiological correlates. The question remains: if a particular neurophysiological constellation proves to be characteristic of hypnosis, is it an effect or a cause?

Hypnosis as a form of sleep Early magnetists were fooled by the resemblance of the hypnotic state to sleep. They assumed, since a subject was in a state of torpitude, that hypnosis was a form of sleep. Yet they could not resolve the apparent contradiction that their subjects behaved more as if awake.

In recent years, sleep has been increasingly studied and has become more equated with a state of aliveness than with one of suspended animation. It has been divided and subdivided into stages, correlated with varieties of dream activities, chronobiological cycles, neurohumoral mechanisms, and neurotransmitter metabolism. Sleep is a dynamic, phasic process, whose ultimate purpose still continues to elude us. Could hypnosis be one of the sleep stages? Or a sleep stage with some degree of added awareness?

Pavlov termed hypnosis "partial sleep." In his view, both sleep and hypnosis resulted from the inhibition of some cerebral areas.

However, in hypnosis, the preservation of "sentinel points" accounted for limited reactivity to the environment. Some investigators point out that light sleep can be made to shift into hypnosis with its characteristics of rapport and response to suggestion and that hypnotized subjects, at times, when left alone or given appropriate suggestions, have gone to sleep.

Some investigators have postulated the existence of hypnotic centers in the subcortical sleep-regulating centers adjoining the third ventricle (Schilder and Kanders, 1926). More modern research points out the importance of the pontine nuclei, reticular formation, and the neural transmitter serotonin. Whether these structures are actively involved in hypnosis is unknown. When global physiological measures are taken, hypnosis is found to be very close to wakefulness. Reflexes are not altered in hypnosis, whereas in sleep, the knee jerk, for example, is diminished or absent. Moreover, sleep is accompanied by modifications in the output of consciousness as it is channeled to the outside world, while in hypnosis, responsiveness to outside stimuli is preserved. In the final analysis, hypnosis appears to be a condition which is neither the usual waking state nor any one of the sleep stages.

Hypnosis as an atavistic phenomenon This theory states that hypnosis represents an archaic form of mentation, a return to more primitive mental functioning where suggestion plays an important role. This primitive mental state is postulated to be superceded, but not replaced, by logical, intellectual, and critical faculties. In this model, humans, during the early period of their mental evolution, functioned much more fully in modes of thought where nonverbal communication and "hypnotic" rapport with friendly authority figures were present.

In the perspective of this theory, several facets of hypnosis are explained: in many hypnotic inductions, critical faculties are dulled by giving monotonous, repetitive suggestions. The prestige of the hypnotist is important, perhaps in the same way as that of tribal leaders a long time ago. Nonverbal communications occur much more frequently in hypnosis; the subject is able to draw from many subliminal cues and is aware of being much more sensitive to the facial, gestural, and tonal communications of the hypnotist. Hypnosis favors amnesia, because in this model ego control is lessened, and amnesia protects the ego from awareness of this relative loss.

In the atavistic hypothesis, depth of hypnosis can be equated with completeness of regression, and spontaneous pseudo-trance or daydreams could represent a mixture of logical and atavistic processes. Posthypnotic suggestion phenomena — the remarkable event in which instructions given during hypnosis are carried out seemingly automatically at some point in the future, sometimes in the distant future — is explained by a mechanism of introjection, where the subject accepts the hypnotist's messages as his own and carries them out as self-fulfilling time-released personal expressions.

The atavistic theory is attractive, but it does not adequately account for hypnotic phenomena such as anesthesia and hallucinations.

PSYCHOANALYTIC THEORIES OF HYPNOSIS

Somewhat similar to the atavistic theory, but much more centered on stages of personal development, are psychoanalytic theories of hypnosis which see the subject as regressing to an infantile ego state, with the hypnotist acting as a parent. The concept of rapport becomes imbued with notions of transference — the process by which feelings, attitudes, and wishes originally linked with an important figure in one's early life are channeled onto others.

Freud had difficulty integrating hypnosis into his psychoanalytic theories. He was strongly influenced by the ideas of both Charcot and Bernheim, but came to see hypnotic phenomena through the perspective of transference. We may ask whether transference, like suggestibility, is a surface manifestation of hypnosis or a primary ingredient?

Ferenczi believed that hypnosis recapitulated the Oedipal situation. If induction was of the authoritarian or commanding type, the subject would associate the hypnotist with a strong father and, if permissive, with the mother. Implied in this view is a sexual element in the hypnotic condition which, barring some claims by occasional subjects who experience erotic feelings in a trance, is not borne out by clinical observations.

Hypnosis, in the psychoanalytic view, implies a regressed condition where magical expectations, dependency strivings, and primitive wishes and fears are operational. Because, seen from this perspective, the hypnotist is placed in an omnipotent position, many psychoanalysts have stayed away from its use; others, however, pointing out the rich potential of the transference condition implied in hypnosis, have integrated it in the psychotherapeutic context (Chapter 14).

Hypnosis as a dissociative condition To Janet, the concept of dissociation was central to hypnosis. In this process, a system of ideas, emotions, and behaviors could split off from the personality and exist with a certain degree of autonomy in the unconscious. This dissociated material could be brought into consciousness through the use of hypnosis.

Automatic handwriting provides a superb illustration of this phenomenon—the subject, conscious and alert, can watch his hand write out answers to questions or long narratives as if detached from the supervision of the self. In this model, there is an observing ego, and a dissociated ego which is perceived by the observing ego as acting independently. In clinical situations, this is seen when the subject, during induction, is quite amazed—and often amused—to see his arm come up, seemingly by itself, to touch his face.

Although we do not know the nature of the mechanisms of dissociation either in the central nervous system or in psychological realms, this theory describes some, but by no means all, of the characteristics of the hypnotic trance. It does not, for example, explain suggestibility (and vice versa).

Behavioral approaches to hypnosis (nonstate theories) This viewpoint runs counter to state theories of hypnosis and seeks to strip the hypnotic trance of its status as a separate entity or as a special condition of consciousness. To bring home their arguments, some authors point out that all the phenomena said to happen in hypnosis can be produced in nonhypnotized subjects. If, side by side, we observe a hypnotized subject and a simulator responding in the best of their abilities to the suggestions of a hypnotist, we may have cause to wonder who is who. Using this behavioral perspective, it is true that there may be little way of telling them apart because responses to instructions can be so convincing in both. Is hypnosis a more or less consciously determined simulation? A role play? A complex behavior gleaned from perceptions of social cues?

To cut through the argument of outright mimicry, we could, as amply documented by historical examples (the work of Esdaille in particular), perform a major operation on the hypnotized subject without anesthesia. It is likely that the simulator, on approach of the scalpel, will quickly give up the charade. Nor can simulation fake the appearance of a Babinski reflex during age regression or the experience of a visual hallucination.

Simulation is a conscious maneuver. On a more unconscious level, it is felt by some theorists that hypnosis derives from deep motivations to behave like a hypnotized person should. The definition of what constitutes hypnotic behavior can be overtly or subtly communicated by the culture (radio, TV, magazines), or by the hypnotist who presents cues, verbal and nonverbal, to this effect. This would explain the varied manifestations of hypnosis in different cultures, but it would not explain the deeper intrapsychic mechanisms presumably needed for their creation.

The drive to behave in ways suggested by the hypnotist is related, in this model, to the completeness of the hypnotic rapport. The strength of the motivations to please the hypnotist and his symbolic representations (task motivation) has been proven to be remarkably strong in some individuals. It is felt that the role-taking behavior of the subject may be so complete, so profound, and so intense, that there is a total belief in its validity. For the hypnotized individual, his behavior becomes completely congruent with self-image, and the perception of altered reality becomes so self-syntonic, that phenomena—even phenomena involving the deepest mechanisms of perception or the participation of the autonomic nervous system — are allowed to happen.

Ego state theory Ego state theory is closely allied to dissociation theory and even to concepts dealing with the phenomena of multiple personalities. Rather than seeking to be a comprehensive theoretical approach to hypnosis, it proposes to explain phenomena which occur regularly in hypnoanalysis.

Ego state theory postulates the existence of networks of personality traits, experiences, feelings and behaviors, which in a more or less connected form, are bound by common principles in the context of the whole personality (Watkins, 1954). Several ego states may coexist as fairly distinct entities within the same person; their boundaries are thought to be loosely defined, in contrast to the more rigidly marked boundaries found in multiple-personality syndromes. In the hypnotic trance, different ego states may be communicated with for the purpose of bringing about a more global integration (ego state therapy).

HYPNOSIS — FUTURE DIRECTIONS

The many unresolved issues concerning the nature of hypnosis, and the growing sophistication of its applications, make its future promising in several areas — from research to clinical practice. At the same time — and this is seen in the increasing volume of papers dealing with hypnosis — there is expanding medical and public acceptance of its therapeutic potential. Since its birth as a science, hypnosis has had a cyclical evolution with fluctuating levels of interest from the scientific community. Today, however, hypnosis appears to be firmly implanted as a medical tool, and its future is likely to see ongoing progress in the areas of research and practice discussed below.

Hypnosis as an altered state of consciousness Basic questions, still with us, have to do with hypnosis as a special state of consciousness. We will, unfortunately, not be able to answer these questions adequately until we clarify issues concerning the normal state of consciousness and the nature of consciousness itself.

(Only by knowing what normal states of consciousness are will we be able to put altered states in proper perspective).

Experimental approaches to these questions may be physiological or psychological. There is, as regards the latter, active interest in the subjective experiences of hypnosis and especially very deep hypnosis. Scales are being developed to describe more accurately the experiential components of the hypnotic trance. Perhaps, with this type of investigation, we may be more able to differentiate hypnotic states from meditative or autogenically induced ones. As research moves forward, our vocabulary to describe these special conditions of consciousness may become as rich as that found in some Eastern cultures.

Physiological changes in hypnosis Physiological changes in hypnosis can, with newer technologies, be measured more accurately and sensitively. For example, techniques which allow for the noninvasive mapping of neurotransmitter activity in the brain may provide knowledge about correlations between mental states and neurophysiological parameters.

Research into psychodynamics Even with discoveries of psychological defenses and adaptation mechanisms made during the last century, much remains unknown. Somewhat like the population of identified neurotransmitters which is steadily growing in number, the dynamics of mental processes continue to yield ever greater evidence of their complexity, variety, and plasticity.

Since the early work of Breuer and Freud, hypnosis has found a place in the study of repression, conversion, catharsis, and psychogenic amnesia, among other preconscious and unconscious processes. While relatively abandoned for decades in favor of free association and dream interpretation, hypnosis has recently been "rediscovered" for the experimental investigation of conflicts and their solutions, for the study of ego homeostasis, primary process thinking and imagery, and more generally, for the study of the dynamic interface separating the conscious from the unconscious.

Applications of hypnosis to medical problems Hypnosis is greatly underutilized in its applications to medicine. In the hospital setting especially, where patients are so prone to experience fear, stress, discomfort, and pain, hypnosis has the potential to offer remarkable relief.

However, practically speaking, when a hypnotherapist is invited onto a medical or surgical unit for a consultation, the staff is likely to respond with some skepticism mixed with cautious interest. This bias works to the patient's detriment. The problem is partly due to the vestiges of hypnosis' historical associations, to lack of information and also in part derives from a general defensive posture toward all unfamiliar states of consciousness.

The future of hypnosis, shaped by the demands of patient care, will see greater utilization in all medical settings.

Integration of hypnosis into other psychotherapies There is currently a tendency to integrate different therapeutic modalities in the hope of achieving more efficient individual change. The future of hypnosis will likely witness studies of its usefulness as a facilitator to other therapies, much as hypnobehavioral approaches have already been applied to systematic desensitization, aversion, flooding, assertiveness training, and imagery techniques.

Newer psychotherapies designed to keep pace with the style and demands of modern life, such as short-term dynamic or time-limited psychotherapies may, in the future, incorporate the use of the hypnotic trance to facilitate insight and the working through of conflicts.

Hypnosis and creativity While creativity has traditionally been assumed to be a gift bestowed on fortunate individuals, it is now more correctly seen as a malleable mental process subject to many psychological influences; as such, it can be facilitated, enhanced, or repressed.

Interest in creativity enhancement comes from several sources. As one of the highest mental functions, creativity, when expressed to its fullest, provides a special source of personal satisfaction. To be maximally creative, for some people, is to be maximally fulfilled. Innovation and invention and the individual's creative expression, as they benefit society's needs, are increasingly in demand.

One of several difficulties for creativity research concerns shing proper definitions. What is creativity? What are the mental mechanisms which allow totally new ideas to be formed? Is there a unitary creative process in each individual, or does every endeavor require its own creative substrate?

Most investigators agree that creativity involves a process of seeing things in a novel way and of grasping solutions to problems or conflicts through new perspectives (Jackson and Messick, 1965). In 1926, Wallas, expanding on the contributions of Helmholtz, Poincaré, and others, described the creative process in its well-known sequence of preparation, incubation, illumination, and verification. In the prelude of the creative process, the individual experiences an intimation, a yearning to create in a particular field of endeavor. The stage of preparation involves gathering data, facts, opinions, and impressions, to serve as the potential building blocks for the coming creation. The stage of incubation is largely unconscious; much of creativity happens below the level of awareness. In illumination, the solution to the problem is brought to full awareness. In verification, the creative solution is applied to reality or is communicated to others.

Kris (1952) theorized a capacity and tolerance for forms of thinking and experience that were not logical, structured, or programed as an integral part of creativity. He called the ability to do so regression in the service of the ego. The ability to experience and integrate primitive as well as mature styles of thought—the mixing of primary and secondary processes—is commonly found in creative individuals. Creativity implies a psychological set of openness to the new, a condition of balance between the unstructured and the structured, as well as a dynamic interaction between the intellect and the emotions.

Clinical applications of creativity enhancement have made use of cognitive strategies, relaxation, hypnosis, and related states. Cognitive techniques may involve looking at other aspects of the problem, stimulating imagination or visualization, removing blocks or negative attitudes, and freeing structured thinking. Is creativity enhanced by hypnosis? Once sufficient energy has been applied to the preparation stage—the fact-finding preliminaries to creativity—can the incubation stage be shortened or the illumination stage ignited with hypnotic use?

A common finding in hypnosis research is that experimenters in the laboratory setting attempt and often fail to replicate findings observed in the clinical setting. It is true that clinical and experimental situations may, in their context, be vastly different. Creativity, as a complex, sensitive, highly individualized and variable ability, follows a similar pattern. In the experimental situation, results have yet to be conclusive. In the clinical setting, however, there is ample anecdotal evidence that hypnosis is helpful for facilitating the flow of creativity by providing optimal state of mind conditions and by guiding and stimulating unconscious processes.

An attempt to accelerate creative solutions in a hypnotized patient is illustrated by the following example: "As you sit here in a deep hypnotic trance, we will ask your subconscious mind to find creative solutions to your problems. We have already talked at length and in detail about the dilemmas you are facing. The only thing that remains is to find constructive answers to them. The answers you come up with may involve new ways for you to see things, new ways for you to experience things, or ways for you to change what you do. In any event, your subconscious mind can help you even more than it has until now, and you can help it to give you constructive answers by keeping your outlook open and receptive . . ."

Hypnosis, by all available evidence, does not enhance human performance by direct action; rather, it does so indirectly by allowing mental mechanisms already present to develop or express themselves more freely. In this regard, creativity—like equally complex higher functions such as learning and memory—can be facilitated by providing it with optimal mental environments. Because of the increasing importance of creativity in modern life, hypnosis and related techniques will find more sophisticated applications to this end.

Hypnosis and space medicine The possibility of applying hypnosis to the problems of space mission crews continues to be explored. Nausea and vomiting associated with prolonged weightlessness are debilitating problems, poorly controlled by medications. Self-hypnosis has clear potential to modify and, in some cases, abolish these symptoms. It can also help in the adjustment to new circadian rhythms and the attainment of deep relaxation states to fit short rest periods. While current space crews are on a busy, compartmentalized schedule, it is conceivable, in future missions requiring long travel time, that crew selection will be based in part on the ability to induce prolonged trances.

Hypnosis and hemispheric laterality The brain has long been assumed to be an organ whose symmetry implied an equal sharing, by each hemisphere, of its many functions. For centuries, the contributions made by the brain to the workings of the whole person were not realized; yet the Ebers Papyrus (2500 BC) tells of a man who, as a result of head injuries "lost his ability for speech without paralysis of his tongue." Later, Roman physicians were to describe deficiencies in consciousness, perception, cognition, and behavior due to cerebral traumas incurred by gladiators. In 1861, Broca described a patient who had lost the "faculty for articulated speech" as a result of a left hemispheric lesion. Wernicke in 1874 described a different syndrome—loss of verbal comprehension, preservation of speaking capacity, and writing impairment—as a sequela of a lesion in the posterior portion of the first temporal gyrus.

Since these early findings, the brain "localizationists" have worked to find discrete locales for each of man's many faculties. While successful for purely sensory or motor modalities—sight, touch, hearing, etc—this compartmentalizing approach has had many difficulties with the mapping of associational areas and still more with complex abstract psychological dimensions such as emotionality and intelligence. As much as providing some notion of the location of function in the central nervous system, this line of research has provided an appreciation for the intricacies and the plasticity of the brain (as seen in its adaptation to injury, especially at an early age), and the dynamic interrelatedness of both hemispheres as they complement each other.

Studies were initially made of patients who, for purposes of seizure control, underwent severance of the corpus callosum and the anterior commissure, thus completely separating the right from the left hemisphere. Information—sensory, verbal, emotional, musical, gestalt, conceptual, and abstract—can, in these patients, be presented to the hemispheres separately to determine how differently it is processed in each.

Sketching some global differences, the left hemisphere in most individuals has more jurisdiction over expressive speech, syntax, reading, writing, arithmetic, and rhythm; and the right hemisphere, with processing visual patterns, spatial configurations, holistic analysis, tone and melody, imagery, and the interpretation of special meanings and metaphors.

Future directions in laterality research will include the elucidation of its relationship to mental illness. Can schizophrenia or manic-depressive illness be better understood as dysfunctions in the right or left hemisphere or as abnormalities in interhemispheric interaction? Research is also pointing to laterality as it applies to communication, not only verbal, but gestural, symbolic, emotional, and intuitive.

It is in this area that hypnosis and hemispheric function meet. Can resistances to induction be considered manifestations of logical, left hemispheric function? By what neurophysiological mechanisms do techniques such as confusion, paradox, doublebind (the simultaneous communication of conflicting messages) or reframing (changing a person's perspective of events or situations in order to change their meaning) work to circumvent them? What is the importance of other forms of communication in induction? How can abilities inherently present in the right hemisphere be tapped for more effective hypnotic communication through the use of metaphor, humor or imagery?

SUGGESTED READING AND REFERENCES

Barber TX: *Hypnosis: A Scientific Approach.* New York, Von Nostrand Reinhold, 1969.
Bowers K, Bowers PG: Hypnosis and creativity: A theoretical and empirical rapprochement, in Fromm E, Shor R (eds): *Hypnosis, Research*

Developments and Perspectives. Chicago, Aldine/Atherton, 1972, pp 255-291.

Carter B, Elkins G, Kraft S: Hemispheric asymmetry as a model for hypnotic phenomena: A review and analysis. *Am J Clin Hypn* 1982; 24(3): 204.

Coe WC, Buckner LG, Howard ML, et al: Hypnosis as role enactment: Focus on a role specific skill. *Am J Clin Hypn* 1972;15:41-45.

Ellenberg H: *The Discovery of the Unconscious.* New York, Basic Books, 1970.

Esdaille J: *Mesmerism in India.* Hartford, England, S. Andrus and Son, 1850.

Ferenczi S: Introjecktion und Vebertragung. *JB Psychoanalyse* 1909;1:422.

Fromm E: Quo vadis hypnosis? Predictions of future trends in hypnosis research, in Fromm E, Shor R (eds): *Hypnosis, Research Developments and Perspectives.* Chicago, Aldine/Atherton, 1972, pp 575-586.

Fromm E: A ego psychological theory of altered states of consciousness. *Int J Clin Exp Hypn* 1979;25:372.

Frumkin LR, Ripley HS, Cox GB: Changes in cerebral hemispheric lateralization with hypnosis. *Biol Psychiatry* 1978;13(6):741.

Gill MM, Brenman M: *Hypnosis and Related States.* New York, Hallmark Press, 1977.

Guze H: The Phylogeny of hypnosis. *J Clin Exp Hypn* 1953;1:41.

Janet P: *Major Symptoms of Hysteria* New York, Macmillan, 1920.

Jayres J: *The Origin of Consciousness in the Breakdown of the Bicameral Mind.* Boston, Houghton Mifflin, 1976.

Kris E: *Psychoanalytic Explorations in Art.* New York, International Universities Press, 1952.

Levin LA, Harrison RH: Hypnosis and regression in the service of the ego. *Int J Clin Exp Hypn* 1976;24:400.

Levitt EE, Chapman RH: Hypnosis as a research method, in Fromm E, Shor RE (eds): *Hypnosis: Research Development and Perspective.* Chicago, Aldine/Atherton, 1972, pp 85-113.

Ludwig AM: Altered states of consciousness. *Arch Gen Psychiatry* 1966; 15:225.

Meares A: *A System of Medical Hypnosis.* New York, Julien Press, 1972.

Orne MT: The nature of hypnosis: Artifact and essence. *J Abnorm Soc Psychol* 1959;58:277.

Prince GM: *The Practice of Creativity.* New York, Harper & Row, 1970.

Sacerdote P: On the pscyho-biological effects of hypnosis. *Am J Clin Hypn* 1967;10:10-14.

Sarbin TR, Coe WC: *Hypnosis: A Social Psychological Analysis of Influence Communication.* New York, Holt, Rhinehart & Winston, 1972.

Schilder P, Kanders O: *The Nature of Hypnosis,* Part II. New York, International Universities Press, 1956, pp 45-184.

Stein M, in Flach F (ed): *Creativity: The Process and its Stimulation.* The Life Science Advisory Group. Geigy Pharmaceuticals, 1975.
Sperry, RW: Hemispheric deconnection and unity in conscious awareness. *Am Psychol* 1968;23:723-733.
Tart C: *States of Consciousness.* New York, EP Dutton, 1975.
Wallas G: *The Art of Thought.* New York, Harcourt Brace, 1926.
Watkins JG: Trance and transference. *J Clin Exp Hypn* 1954;2:284-291.
Wernicke C: *Der Aphasische Symptomkomplex.* Weigert, Breslau, 1874.
Wexler B: Cerebral laterality and psychiatry: A review of the literature *Am J Psychiatry* 1980;137(3):279-291.

3

Hypnotic Phenomena

Barbara DeBetz
Gérard Sunnen

PHYSIOLOGICAL CHANGES OBSERVED IN HYPNOSIS

The literature contains many accounts of physiological changes associated with hypnosis. However, it is important to add that no physiological variable has been shown to be systematically or regularly associated with hypnosis. Most experiments that purportedly show a systematic relationship to physiological variables fail on replication or are methodologically unsound. Keeping the above statement in mind, here are some of the commonly described physiological changes that have been observed.

Cardiovascular System

It is common to observe tachycardia during the initial period of the hypnotic trance. Irregularities in the heart beat have been measured on ECG tracings during the trance when suggestions of anger or fear were given. The heart and blood vessels are indirectly influenced by emotions evoked in the trance. Longitudinal studies on blood pressure reduction through hypnosis have not proven to be effective. Reduced bleeding time has been reported in patients undergoing surgical procedures with the help of hypnoanesthesia. Vasodilatation and increased circulation to otherwise poorly circulated areas have also been reported in patients in the trance in response to instructions to that effect.

Respiratory System

A decrease in breathing rate can be observed in subjects who are in a deep hypnotic state. Respiratory rate was found to increase when thoughts of fear, anger, pain, or muscular activity were introduced.

Gastrointestinal Functions

The changes that have been reported in the gastrointestinal tract, range from increased salivation to vomiting, increased gastric secretion and motility, as well as diarrhea and constipation.

Genitourinary Functions

The majority of reports regarding genitourinary functions are anecdotal and in the form of case histories. Few controlled studies have been carried out in this area. Examples of hypnotic control of menstrual cramps, fertility, impotence, changes in menstrual cycles and painless childbirth have been reported.

Endocrine Functions and Metabolism

A number of metabolic changes have been reported to take place following hypnotic suggestions. Among them are changes of blood glucose levels, basal metabolic rate, and calcium metabolism. There are also reports that the body temperature may be raised or lowered depending on the suggestion. Few endocrine studies have been done other than those related to gastric secretions, digestion, circulation, and respiration. Release of ACTH by the pituitary can be affected directly by emotional stimuli. A drop in plasma cortisol titers to significantly low levels shortly after hypnotic induction has been reported by some researchers.

Cutaneous Functions

Skin blisters and wheal formation Their cure and exacerbation have been attributed to hypnotic suggestions.

Dermal excretion Little or no experimental work has been done on this subject. There are a few anecdotal case reports where people learned hypnotically to control their sweat gland secretions.

Skin temperature There have been several studies done in regard to changes in skin temperature, either to increase or to reduce skin temperature through vasoconstriction and dilation.

Electrodermal changes Some studies have shown a reduction in spontaneous electrodermal activity during hypnosis as compared to a waking condition. This means that there was a significant decrease in basal skin resistance.

Central Nervous System Functions

Evoked potentials A sudden change in brain voltage that is initiated by an external stimulus is referred to as "evoked potential." Experiments have not given support that hypnosis in itself is able to produce any spontaneously evoked potentials other than those produced through stimuli in the waking as well as hypnotically induced states.

Spontaneous EEG activity Numerous studies have been done to find correlates between sleep and hypnosis as measured on the electroencephalogram. In some reports, EEG recordings after hypnotic induction have been claimed to be indistinguishable from waking patterns while other workers have found the postinduction EEG to resemble "light sleep." Some researchers have found increases in alpha-wave activity, others increases in beta activities, and others yet increases in delta activities. In view of the many contradictory findings relating hypnosis to changes in EEG patterns, it is safe to say that there is no one particular brain wave activity that can be exclusively identified with the hypnotic trance state.

Eye Movements

Rapid eye movements   It has been demonstrated that rapid eye movements (REMs) are concommitant with dreaming. One interpretation of this phenomenon is that the dreamer is scanning visual changes. Another interpretation is that REMs are a nonspecific correlate of attentive activity. In relation to hypnosis, some investigators have attempted to test these two different hypothesis. Hypnotized subjects showed a reduced REM rate, if hypnotized by a "sleep model" induction technique, as well as increased alpha EEG activity. REM increased when hypnotic dreams were produced.

Optokinetic nystagmus   If a person with normal vision gazes at a rotating drum that has alternating black and white lines, he will show horizontal optokinetic nystagmus. A person with true blindness will not show it, but a person with hysterical blindness will. There is one case report in the literature where a hypnotized person did not show optokinetic nystagmus when gazing at the drum. The hypnotic suggestion had been that he (the hypnotized subject) would not see any drum in front of his eyes.

Ocular anatomy   One theory of hypnosis postulates that hypnotizability is associated with a person's upgaze and eyeroll. It has been found that the higher a person's upgaze and eye roll, the higher this person's hypnotic trance capacity. This eye roll sign seems to be a biologically fixed trait and remains relatively stable throughout life, being slightly higher during childhood and somewhat lower above the age of 60.

Effects on Sensation of Touch and Pain

Paresthesias and alteration of pain have been observed. Among the most common ones are numbness, tingling, itching, prickling, burning, coldness, or warmth. An increase or decrease in sensitivity to pain, pressure, temperature, and touch have been reported.

Pain perception is processed in the brain, and it has been postulated that the pain experience can be psychologically altered to a certain degree. In hypnotized people, suggestions can produce a loss of the sense of touch, pain, and temperature. Often this loss is relative, and the subject will describe a diminished rather than a total absence of sensation. However, with proper training, highly hypnotizable individuals can learn to have complete sensory loss enabling them to undergo dental, obstetrical, and other minor and major surgical procedures. Whether the sensory loss and anesthesia is real or merely role playing on the patient's part is a question of controversy with different interpretations of the phenomenon.

Effect on Vision, Hearing, Taste, and Smell

Hypnosis can produce alterations in the perception of the special senses of vision, hearing, taste, and smell. Visual hallucinations occur in the form of flashing lights, dark spots, altered colors, and even objects that are not there or that are there and not seen. For example, a subject may see a nonexistent clock on the wall and even read the time if instructed to do so.

Taste, smell, and auditory hallucinations, both pleasant and unpleasant may also be induced. A subject may smell an imaginary rose or listen to an imaginary orchestra playing his favorite symphony. In addition to these sensory hallucinations, hypnotized subjects may exhibit an increased degree of acuity in vision, hearing, touch, taste, and smell. In hypnotically induced blindness or deafness, the subjects appear as if they had a real hearing or vision loss but tests do not detect a real organic loss. The hypnotically blind person will avoid obstacles while walking and his pupils will react to light stimuli. Hypnotic deafness probably represents a decrease or blocking of auditory stimuli.

PSYCHOLOGICAL PHENOMENA OF HYPNOSIS

When an individual is hypnotized, a variety of responses may be observed or elicited. These may be physiological, psychological, or both, and may manifest differently depending on the subject. Because of their variety and range, hypnotic phenomena pose some difficulties for a unified theory of hypnosis: How can hypnosis, as one process, produce such a multiplicity of effects? For the practitioner, the question is made even more interesting by the fact that individuals vary considerably in both the kind and intensity of effects shown. Where one person, for example, easily achieves deep relaxation yet is unable to achieve pain control, another will demonstrate the opposite. The practitioner therefore needs to approach hypnosis in its proper context: The unique individual in whom it happens, with all due consideration given to the personality structure, aptitudes, defenses, and treatment goals in that person. It is important also to have knowledge of the kinds of hypnotic phenomena available to a particular patient, so that one may use them for maximal therapeutic gain.

The following is an overview of the clinically relevant manifestations of the hypnotic trance.

The Subjective Experience of Hypnosis

Whenever an individual is hypnotized in front of a group for demonstration purposes, the first questions from the floor usually center on finding out about the experience. How did "it" feel? Although subjects vary greatly in their experiences during hypnosis, certain feelings stand out as commonly encountered, while others remain idiosyncratic and rare. In clinical situations, some people exit from the hypnotic state astonished to have felt a state of mind so different from their normal waking state; others talk as if nothing had happened. In the former case, the impact of the experience will serve to facilitate further hypnotic work. In the latter, in spite of the lack of trancelike sensations, individuals often show clear-cut hypnotic phenomena. Apparently, the feelings of trance are not necessary conditions for the manifestations of trance.

While in the deeper stages of trance, a subject may be asked if he or she would like to talk about or to notice how they feel. The answers are usually, but not always, spoken in a monotone, slowly, and with pauses. Such a query, asked during hypnosis, even if not answered, will make it easier for detailed reports to be shared afterwards, because some degree of self-awareness will have been mobilized. The following experiences comprise the bulk of these reports.

Psychomotor slowdown The motions and the internal workings of the body feel slowed. There is a sense of inertia, a feeling of not desiring to move; or, if movements are made, they are less frequent and have less range than in the normal state. Although the sense of presence is maintained, thought flow is slowed. There is a lessened tendency to think about anything in particular and a shift towards experiencing the feel of the body in the present moment. Concerns about the past or the future are at bay.

Time slowdown The sense of time is shifted from external to internal events. Consequently, it is stretched, since internal events are less geared to the clock. Time feels less insistent, and it is not uncommon for a subject to estimate the span of a hypnotic session to be 20 minutes when it has, in fact, been five.

Body image changes The experience of how the body feels during the normal waking state is often changed during hypnosis. Without directive suggestions, the body may feel heavier and pushing into the cushions of the chair; or lighter as if floating. At times, the body will feel larger, expanded, as if filling the entire room; more rarely, it will feel smaller.

Intensification of rapport In hypnosis, some individuals report feeling a heightened sense of awareness of the verbal and nonverbal transactions with their therapist. Knowing this, the therapist may feel under some pressure to shape his communications carefully.

Changes in thinking While the flow of thought may be slowed, its structure is also likely to be changed. Trance logic refers to mental mechanisms in deep trance where incongruous ideas or perceptions can coexist without clashing. The same processes are commonly manifested in dreams.

Alterations in consciousness Aside from and beyond the effects mentioned above, the global experience of awareness can show alterations. These experiences are the most difficult to describe, in part for semantic reasons, in part for their ineffable qualities. Rarely, on emergence from the trance, an individual will describe the hypnotic experience as transcendental or mystical.

Relaxation Relaxation has both physical and psychological components. In parallel with physiological parameters, the experience is one of repose and calm. Of all the hypnotic phenomena, relaxation is the most common and the most easily observed. In many subjects, it can be very pronounced, and it is not infrequent to have someone say that they have never been so completely relaxed.

This important global response is already present in neutral hypnosis, the suggestion-free trance state; and with the proper suggestions it can be amplified. Once experienced by the patient, it can, through techniques of self-hypnosis or posthypnotic suggestion, be applied to many previously stressful situations.

The feelings of relaxation in hypnosis can range from mild slowdown to deep peacefulness. In the latter instance, several areas of the mind normally contributing to anxiety are quieted. Anticipatory anxiety is a universal source of stress. Self-reproach, guilt, and dwelling on the past are also sidestepped. There is a moving away from the intricate complexities of the current life situation. It may be said, half in jest, that the frontal lobes of a hypnotized patient, as important agents for the mediation of these psychological processes, ie, concerns about the past and worry about the future, are taking a rest. Hypnosis is the most potent nonchemical relaxant of all therapeutic approaches.

Hypnotic Effects on Imagery

The ability to experience and create mental images is present to some degree in everyone. It is most pronounced, of course, in dreams, when the message flow of the senses is drastically reduced. In the waking state, the phenomenon surfaces in daydreams when the mind shifts attentiveness to the privacy of personal mental life. The imagery of daydreams is complex, under partial volitional control, and uniquely expressed in everyone; it may contain visual impressions, feelings, somesthetic sensations, the interplay of dialogue and scenarios. Daydreams can be so engrossing that coming back to "reality" feels like a small shock.

Clinically, it is important to know the style of imagery used by our patients. In hypnotic induction, as well as in treatment, the stimulation of imagery, in any one of its modalities, will provide the vehicle for progress. It makes little sense for example, to induce relaxation by suggesting a sense of heaviness in the body musculature, when someone much more naturally responds to suggestions of warmth, ie, lying down in heated sand, or to more visual suggestions, ie, seeing oneself on a peaceful beach or in a clear meadow.

The ability to create, intensify, and sustain images is enhanced in hypnosis. In certain subjects, this faculty can be activated to such a degree that the sense of reality recedes and imagery takes precedence; we then have a situation in which the processes of wakefulness coexist with the processes of dreaming. When this happens, imagery is so intense that it can be called an hallucination: With eyes open, the subject is able to see an object or a person as if it were there; or not to see an object that is there, a negative hallucination.

Imagery is turned into a therapeutic asset in clinical hypnosis. Personal images constructed by the patient can symbolize and point to growth and resolution. Through their influence, they have been found to exert continuous beneficial effects.

Hypnotic Effects on Perception

Each second in the uncharted leap of body to mind, billions of sensory inflow signals become actual sensations. A hand dipped in the icy water of a wintry lake, for example, will send signals via the lateral spinothalamic tract to nuclei in the thalamus, then on to the postcentral gyrus. Somewhere along the way, feelings of cold will be created. This raw sensation can, however, be modified by other areas of the mind. The sudden startle of a flight of birds in our wintry scene will shift patterns of perception, and the feelings in the cold hand will momentarily be overridden.

Hypnosis taps into this ability to move into or away from sensory experiencing. Sensations can be made to expand or recede; the process by which this is done can be learned by the patient for therapeutic gain. The stroke victim can be taught to hone in on awareness of the vestiges of sensory impressions in an affected limb in order to make it stronger with time. The child accident victim can be helped to veer away from the insistent annoyance of uncomfortable casts to aid in the quality and speed of recovery.

Effects on Emotions

Although the word emotion most directly conveys the idea of a feeling, it is, in fact, a conglomerate process involving the autonomic nervous system and many associational ramifications, in addition to an experiential state.

While it is possible in hypnosis to quell emotions as in deep relaxation, it is also possible to enhance feeling states. Sometimes, in a hypnotherapeutic situation, a solitary feeling may be presented to the patient for contemplation and amplification. A demoralized individual, for example, may be asked to center solely on a feeling of optimism. For some subjects, this is difficult because they may prefer a contextual milieu for the emotion. It can be suggested, then, that they are reexperiencing a life even which was happy, or a time when they were confident or in control; these feelings, once recreated, can be made to intensify.

An interesting feature of hypnotically induced feelings is that they tend to persist after the session, which makes one think of Papez's description of how emotional circuits reverberate in the limbic system.

Emotions such as anger or anxiety, when hypnotically induced, may be associated with a great deal of physiological activity. Others, like relaxation, have an opposite effect.

HYPNOTIC EFFECTS ON MEMORY

As dreams dramatically show, the distant and detailed remembrances of childhood years can be vividly brought back to us as adults. The nervous system stores every experience for future reference. New experiences are recorded in its substance, in a sequenced series of bioexperiential events, requiring, for their integrity, the proper functioning of short-, intermediate-, and long-term memory mechanisms.

Many memories, although indelibly present, do not gain entrance to consciousness because they are connected to too much fear or pain. Others are cast aside permanently because, in the priority of things, they have no relevance. Conversely, some memories impinge too much on daily experience and are disruptive or annoying. With effort one can ask for the retrieval of a forgotten detail; or, as in suppression, one can consciously overlook an uncomfortable fact.

The ability of the mind to modulate access to personal memory stores is itself a malleable quality. In the hypnotic state, the individual may be asked to move away from his present reality and rekindle the remembrances of an event. This phenomenon is called hypermnesia. In the context of supportive therapeutic intervention, he also may be shown that it is all right to let an event be relegated to the realms of the forgotten. Hypermnesia also includes the increased ability to learn and remember posthypnotically when suggestions are made to that effect.

In the phenomenon of posthypnotic amnesia, the subject forgets what has transpired during the trance state. This effect may occur on its own or may be encouraged by suggestions. In either case, the elements of the experience usually come back to the subject at some point in the future, sometimes days later. Posthypnotic amnesia is partially related to the individual's concept of hypnosis, ie, some connect it with an idea of "blanking out."

Posthypnotic Suggestions

For the sake of demonstration and as an added test of range capacity, a subject in deep trance is told that the following day he will be, for some unexplained reason, unusually interested and inquisitive about the weather. The next day comes and our subject goes about his usual business. But quite out of routine and character, he looks out of the window, asks a colleague about the temperature, and reads about the forecast in the newspaper; when asked, he does not remember the suggestion given to him, but it is there in his behavior, acting in a forceful and complex fashion.

The phenomenon of posthypnotic suggestion is intriguing for the automaticity of its expression in the context of clear consciousness. It is as if a timer had been set to trigger a response.

Posthypnotic suggestions can be programed so that the subject thinks certain thoughts, feels certain experiences, or performs certain actions at some future date. Some authors feel that a posthypnotic suggestion lasts longer and retains more strength if suggestions for amnesia are made at the same time; but a subject may be quite aware of the suggestion and still be pushed to act it through.

When a signal is used to activate a posthypnotic suggestion, it is referred to as a posthypnotic signal. A signal such as, for example, a touch on a shoulder combined with a willingness of the subject to go into a hypnotic state, will make subsequent inductions more rapid.

Let us suppose, for the sake of experiment, that we gave our deeply hypnotized subject a behavioral posthypnotic suggestion: that for the next several hours he will find himself doodling on a few occasions. Upon coming out of the trance, he does not remember what he was asked to do. At some later time, during a casual conversation, we find him picking up a pen and absent-mindedly drawing on a handy piece of paper. When attention is brought to this activity, he may respond that he does not usually doodle but now realizes that he may have some artistic leanings.

Prevention of the posthypnotic behavior may lead to some anxiety because the individual experiences it as a wish, need, or impulse. This combination of amnesia, compulsive acting out, and rationalization following a posthypnotic suggestion is known as a compulsive triad.

Dissociation

There is a phenomenon observed during hypnotic states where one part of the person expresses itself relatively independently of the rest. In automatic handwriting, for example, the subject is conscious and alert, yet at the same time moves his arm and writes, as if it were disconnected from volitional control. Subjectively, the arm feels as if it is moving by itself, and the subject may be unaware of what is written until it is subsequently read. This technique is sometimes used to clarify conflicts.

In specialized treatment approaches, as well as in age regression, different parts of the personality can manifest themselves, often as distinct entities. This dissociative phenomenon, which is related to the mechanisms underlying multiple personality syndromes, can be used effectively to treat unexplained behavioral patterns.

Age Regression and Revivification

While memory retrieval and hyperamnesia involve a coming to the surface of specific events and affects, age regression implies a more complex phenomenon: the reliving of a part of the past in the context of the developmental state of that time.

Let us take an example of an adult subject (and it usually has to be a hypnotically talented one) who is asked to travel backwards to relive some segment of adolescence ". . . You are now about 15. Can you talk about what you are doing and how you feel?" Our subject will probably initially pause, eyes closed, inwardly searching. One can imagine a memory tape going backwards. Then, he begins talking about an event with varying amounts of detail and affect. Why, of all possible remembrances, did our subject hone in on the one he chose? If the event is emotionally charged, the description may be made as an observer on the sidelines. But in true age regression, the episode is relived in all its immediacy and intensity. We are reminded of Penfield's patients who, when cortically stimulated, could actually re-experience segments of their past in their proper sequence. With further regression, the expressions, speech patterns, emotional responses of the time emerge, turning back the developmental clock. Regressed to infancy, there maybe drooling, monosyllables, and sometimes, amazingly, the Babinski reflex. Clinically, age regression and revivification find usefulness in the clarification and release of repressed affect, in preparation for conflict resolution.

SUMMARY

As pointed out at the beginning of this chapter, many physiological changes have been reported, but at this point, we do not know if they are due to the phenomenon of hypnosis or if they are due to other factors such as a person's motivation, role playing, or need to comply. Any improvement and change in intellectual, emotional, behavioral, and physiological functions are probably the result of changed attitudes in the subject rather than the result of new capacities induced by a hypnotic state.

SUGGESTED READING AND REFERENCES

Deikman AJ: Deantomatization and the mystic experience. *Pyschiatry* 1966;29:324-338.

Ellenberg H: *The Discovery of the Unconcious.* New York, Basic Books, 1970.

Fromm E, Shor R: *Hypnosis: Developments in Research and New Perspectives.* New York, Aldine, 1979.

Meares A: *A System of Medical Hypnosis.* Philadelphia, WB Saunders, 1961.

Naranjo C, Orenstein R: *On the Psychology of Meditation.* New York, Viking Press, 1971.

Papez JW: A proposed mechanism of emotion. *Arch Neurol Psychiatry* 1937;38:725.

Penfield W, Japsers HH: *Epilepsy and the Functional Anatomy of the Human Brain.* Boston, Little Brown, 1954.

Sarbin TR, Slagle R, Burrows GD, et al: Psychophysiological outcomes of hypnosis, in Burrows G, Dennerstein L (eds): *Handbook of Hypnosis in Psychosomatic Medicine.* Amsterdam, Elsevier/North-Holland Biomedic Press, 1980.

Shapiro D: Overview: Clinical and psychological comparison of meditation with other self-control strategies. *Am J Psychiatry* 1982;139(3): 267-274.

Singer JL: Navigating the stream of consciousness: Research in daydreaming and related inner experience. *Am Psychol* 1975;30:727-738.

Tart C (ed): *Altered States of Consciousness.* New York, John Wiley, 1969.

Udolf R: *Handbook of Hypnosis for Professionals.* New York, Van Nostrand Reinhold, 1981.

Walsh R: The consciousness disciplines and the behavioral sciences: Questions of comparison and assessment. *Am J Psychiatry* 1980; 1937:663-673.

Wolberg LR: *Hypnosis—Is It For You?* New York, Harcourt Brace Javanovich, 1972, pp 123-134.

Wolberg LR: *Medical Hypnosis,* 2 volumes. New York, Grune & Stratton, 1948.

PART II. INDUCTION TECHNIQUES

4

General Considerations

Gérard Sunnen

PATIENT SELECTION AND PREPARATION

The first task of the hypnotherapist in the initial interview is to determine whether hypnosis is indicated in that particular patient. Once the decision is made to use hypnotherapy, the next task is to prepare the patient for the induction, trance, and treatment process.

The decision to use hypnosis for treatment is determined by a variety of factors. The patient himself may present specific requests for hypnotic treatment. Whether these requests are reasonable or not needs to be evaluated early in the screening interview. At other times, it is the therapist who, either in the recommendations made at the end of the consultation or at some point during the course of therapy, brings up the possible advantages and appropriateness of adjunctive hypnotherapy. Whatever the circumstances, several questions should routinely be attended to for a proper hypnotherapy evaluation:

Is hypnotherapy indicated for this patient? Are other treatment modalities more appropriate at this time? The hypnotherapist needs to develop a balanced view of the indications and therapeutic value of hypnotherapy. Many patients ask for magical cures or demonstrate such psychopathology as to make hypnotic treatment unadvisable. The schizophrenic individual, for example, whose desire for hypnosis is to control hallucinations, or paranoid patients who wish to be hypnotized to destroy their persecutors, obviously need other treatment approaches. Depressed, especially endogenously depressed patients with active suicidal ideation, should not be offered hypnotherapy as a first line of treatment. For some, hypnosis leads to temporary help, enough perhaps to facilitate acting out. As mood and ego strength return through supportive and pharmacotherapeutic measures — preferably in a hospital setting — hypnosis may be integrated into the later phases of recovery.

There are also "fringe" uses of hypnosis which, in spite of some popular following, have no place in the clinical setting, ie, the patient who requests hypnosis for personal regression to past lives or for contacting the dead. Other requests derive from popular misconceptions of hypnosis, ie, the marathon athlete who does not want to feel any discomfort during coming events or the student who wants hypnosis to avoid work.

A second focus in the screening session involves the exploration of the personality, history, symptoms, dynamics, and motivations of the patient. Dynamics of the presenting symptoms need to be reasonably understood. For the patient who comes specifically for hypnotic treatment, it is important to determine how and when the idea of it originated. Was a referral made by a health practitioner? If so why? Are the practitioner's evaluations for hypnotic intervention realistic? Why does the patient come for consultation at this time? Has there been a recent worsening of symptoms, a sudden surge of "courage" to seek help which has been needed for a long time? Has the patient been influenced by friends or relatives who themselves have been helped by hypnotherapy?

Symptoms need to be understood in their context: the total patient at this point in time. Are symptoms habit patterns with few unconscious conflictual determinants? Are they manifestations of long-standing unresolved feelings? Are they part of a more global syndrome — early morning awakening or insomnia in depression; memory difficulties in organic brain syndromes; thought dispersal in schizophrenia; anxiety and agitation in hypomania? Are there any secondary gains? Are they self-destructive, originating in unconscious guilt; or the expressions of chronic dissatisfaction and anger? Is the patient ambivalent about getting rid of the symptoms, secretly wishing to retain them in the face of pressure to give them up by employers, friends, or family, ie, chronic lateness at work, intentional forgetfulness, alcoholism?

What are the conscious and unconscious motivations for hypnotic treatment? While this question may need several sessions to be clarified adequately, it is important to realize that the more surface, conscious, stated motivations may be different from the unconscious ones. The latter are, of course, more important, since they constitute the actual reason for the patient coming for treatment. Exploring motivations for symptom change implies a psychodynamic understanding of the patient which will have direct bearing on the hypnotic strategy; it may also result in a decision not to use hypnosis or to delay hypnotic treatment. Motivations may be very high, direct, and clearly understandable, ie, in the patient with cancer pain, or they may be poorly defined and difficult to extricate from complex unconscious dynamics.

What personality style does the patient demonstrate? This question may have a direct bearing on the choice of induction technique. The individual with obsessive tendencies will need more methodical explanations of hypnosis and an induction style geared to desires to maintain control. Patients who have marginal ego resources, poor frustration tolerance, poor impulse control—especially if manifested by alcohol or drug abuse—are usually poor candidates for hypnotherapy. They may show transitory gains and lack the motivational stamina to follow through with the entire treatment. Histrionic patients who show exaggerated expressions of emotion, while usually easily hypnotizable, may have difficulties integrating the gains derived from hypnosis into their personality structures. Paranoid patients usually will not seek hypnotic intervention unless they have incorporated the idea of it into their defense systems. As with obsessive patients, induction may have to be deferred until sufficient rapport and trust have developed.

Do presenting symptoms have an organic etiology? The importance of this question cannot be overestimated. Any patient—especially an older patient—who develops new symptoms, symptoms poorly understood in the context of their past history, or symptoms accompanied by physical change, should receive appropriate medical investigation. Many people with hypertensive headaches have been treated by psychotherapy alone when medical treatment should have received priority, as have those with anxiety due to cardiac problems, or with depression stemming from endocrine disturbances.

What is the quality of the rapport established with the patient? The interpersonal experience coming from the emotional communication — much of it unconscious — between patient and therapist can be positive, negative, or relatively nonexistent. While the absence of positive rapport is not a contraindication for starting hypnosis, it is nevertheless an important driving force for induction. With some patients, for example, a session can be spent in active conversation, where many facts are gathered, and yet we are left with a sensation of void — somehow a sense of mutual understanding has not been achieved. At other times, in the space of a few minutes, without much said, feelings of rapport are clearly established. The quality and intensity of rapport will change markedly from patient to patient, and within the same patient as treatment progresses. It is an interhuman bridge through which the hypnotherapist conveys a desire to be helpful to the patient, and the patient acknowledges a sense of trust in the hypnotist.

CONCEPTIONS AND MISCONCEPTIONS ABOUT HYPNOSIS

Could you tell me what you think hypnosis is, or tell me what you've heard about it? This is a useful question which brings out notions, experiences and, importantly, misconceptions. Misconceptions, like negative suggestions, can easily channel the whole procedure into an impasse. Underneath misconceptions are fears which, as the induction progresses, sabotage the creation of the trance.

Before starting, an examination of the cognitive sets of the patient toward hypnosis needs to be done; it ultimately saves time and effort. This phase of preinduction is often overlooked because, it is reasoned, the patient came to the office for hypnosis and therefore is clear on his intent.

Exploration of concepts and misconceptions need not be long. Most patients will say that they have heard good things about hypnosis or that they are at least neutral about it. Surprisingly, even educated patients may say that they know very little about it. Common negative perceptions about hypnosis include those discussed below.

Thoughts and fears of being controlled This is a universal fear connected to many issues of self-development, including separation and individuation. To alleviate these fears, the idea of permissive hypnosis is explained. The idea of patient and hypnotherapist working together as a team for the unique purpose of changing symptoms or improving functioning and happiness is stressed. "I do not put anybody in a trance; I do guide them there if they are willing to go. You are free to go into hypnosis as far as you want to, and are free to terminate it at any time."

In part, also, this fear results from semantic considerations. We talk of "being put under," and "to hypnotize." The therapist should be aware of the forms of expression he uses to explain hypnosis to the patient, so as not to convey innuendos of domination, control, or even coercion.

Some patients will use the idea of control to elaborate on the concept that hypnosis is a battle of the wills, with the patient pitted against the therapist: "No one has been able to hypnotize me even though they've tried very hard." Preinduction preparation aims at changing this oppositional attitude to a cooperative stance.

Issues of loss of control are, of course, very important to the obsessive patient. In a person with perfectionistic tendencies showing preoccupation with trivial details, order and organization, indecisiveness, marked conventionality, undue seriousness and restriction of feelings, the fear of losing a sense of mastery constitutes a major stumbling block to successful hypnosis.

The same issues, for different reasons can be observed in the patient who shows guardedness, secretiveness, expectation of trickery or harm, overconcern with hidden motives, pathological jealousy, and constriction of emotional expression. Preliminary psychotherapy is often needed to soften this extremely defensive stance in the patient with such a paranoid personality structure.

Fears and thoughts of acting irrationally or yielding secrets These concerns, often voiced by patients who have been experiencing sexual or aggressive feelings, mostly unconsciously, can be put at ease by supporting the controlling ego forces, explaining to the patient that acting out does not happen in hypnosis, and by pointing out that, quite the contrary, there are likely to be intense feelings of relaxation and a predominant wish to remain physically tranquil. Sometimes the notion of doing ridiculous things in hypnosis is gleaned from seeing or reading about the exploits of stage hypnotists. In this instance, the differences between stage hypnosis and medical hypnosis are stressed, medical hypnosis being solely geared to the patient's well-being.

Apprehensions of not remembering the trance experience This fear is connected to fears of losing control or of acting irrationally. Rather than giving some interpretations, it is usually best to respond to the surface concerns and tell the patient that memory functions in hypnosis are intact and that with deep relaxation there is sometimes lack of concern for their exact recall.

Concerns about "going unconscious" or falling asleep These concerns are connected to fears of being helpless, defenseless, and vulnerable. It is explained that hypnosis is neither sleep nor unconsciousness and that awareness of all surroundings is maintained, even though there may be, with relaxation, some lack of attentiveness paid to them. "You'll hear everything around you, and you'll certainly hear me."

Fears of not being able to come out of the trance These fears usually find their source in sensationalistic newspaper articles. One such article described a somnambulistic subject who, resisting all attempts at "awakening," stayed in a trance and was maintained in "suspended animation" by medical supportive measures for weeks before finally "coming to." Such articles tantalize readers, but at the same time may act as powerful barriers to induction. One patient who wanted very much to learn self-hypnosis had repeated difficulties until, two sessions later, she finally remembered having read a similar article two years before. Although forgotten, its content had erected a barrier against the trance experience.

Miscellaneous fears   Besides the common concerns above, the hypnotherapist will encounter a host of others, ranging from the novel to the bizarre. "What would happen to me if you had to leave the office on some emergency? What if I have a nightmare in hypnosis? Could you do something to me I didn't want done? Could I go crazy?" The hypnotherapist will use his common sense and creativity to answer and negotiate these queries.

Once the indications for hypnosis are established, and there has been clearing and at least partial resolution of misconceptions, the next phase centers on clarifying the goals of treatment and on enhancing motivations for change.

MOTIVATING THE PATIENT FOR CHANGE THROUGH HYPNOSIS AND CLARIFYING THE GOALS OF TREATMENT

As important as finding out the sources of the motivations for change, is clarifying the goals of treatment. The patient himself may be unclear about them and needs the investigative interchange of the initial session(s) to bring them into sharper focus. Arriving at a list of desired changes has a direct feedback on motivation: the patient able to state, verbally or in imagery, what he or she desires, can channel motivational energies more efficiently.

Are the goals realistic? If not, the task of the therapist is to make them more so. Can the goals be stated in specific rather than general terms? Many individuals, for example, want to feel more confident about themselves. This is a very general goal which needs to be broken down into subgoals connected to issues of anxiety control and assertiveness, as well as self-image. Distilling goals is helpful for the patient as well as for the therapist.

Motivation for treatment can be enhanced by supporting healthy goals and constructive adaptations and by discouraging static, regressive, or self-negating ones. With rapport, the patient can develop the extra push to effect positive transformations within himself.

Another important issue in the induction preparation is that of responsibility. Easily overlooked is the patient's notion that it is the therapist's responsibility to help him change. After all, he is remunerating the therapist, so should not everything be provided in the treatments? There are all shades of gray in this outlook, which have close ties to issues of dependency. To maximize treatment efficacy, the notion of responsibility needs to be brought out. In some cases this may take some time because dependency needs are strong; accordingly, clarification of these issues may prolong the preinduction phase.

Treatment works best, of course, if the patient accepts and incorporates the notion that ultimately he is the creator of his symptoms and, as such, has responsibility for their maintenance, modification, or disappearance. To round out this approach, professional expertise and rapport are offered as the medium for change and hypnosis as a tool for change. The patient who is comfortable with this view is much more likely to respond favorably to the induction and to derive maximal benefits from what hypnosis has to offer.

EXPLAINING THE HYPNOTIC PROCESS TO THE PATIENT

The last phase of the screening preparation process involves explaining the hypnotic induction to the patient. While many patients are anxious to start the hypnotic procedure, most are anxious about it. The therapist is likely to note some restlessness and some stiffness of expression as the patient begins to feel that the induction is imminent. It is a good idea to explain that such reactions are normal and that as the experience of hypnosis progresses, feelings of relaxation will dissolve anxiety.

How would you feel, sitting in this chair, deeply hypnotized? This is a question that seeks to elicit feelings rather than concepts (and misconceptions) about hypnosis. If sufficiently relaxed, patients will introspect and, in an exercise of emotive imagination, will fantasize about the kinds of feelings they are likely to experience. Since hypnosis has already been defined by the therapist — by overt as well as subliminal cues — as a state of mind that is pleasant, positive, healing, etc, the patient will gravitate toward these kinds of feelings. How they are described subsequently — what words are used to express them — are noted; because of their connections to desired feeling states in that individual patient, the therapist may use them to advantage during induction as well as in the deepening process.

Since, up to this point, patients are not likely to have a clear idea of the mechanics of the induction, it is often advisable to go through its motions, even if sketchily. This not only allays anxiety, but provides for the introduction of prehypnotic suggestions. The technique of preinduction rehearsal is an especially important strategy for hypnotizing obsessive compulsive patients who do not like surprises.

In addition to describing probable feelings encountered during the trance (see section on psychological alterations in hypnosis), the therapist may describe and even mime the sequences of a typical induction, including arm levitation.

Finally, the therapist may offer helpful hints designed to place the patient in a propitious mental set, ie, "As you listen to my talking, please don't feel pressed or hurried — we have plenty of time. If you have any questions that come up, save them for later; we'll have time to discuss them too. And don't try too hard. Let yourself ease into relaxation, not by trying, but by allowing it to happen."

THE SUCCESSFUL HYPNOTHERAPIST

Since hypnosis is facilitated by the therapist and so is connected to the interactions of two individuals, it is understandable that the therapist brings important elements into it. Hypnosis is intimately tied into a dynamic interchange.

It is appreciated that given a certain patient, one hypnotherapist may fail to induce hypnosis while another may succeed easily. Conversely, with another patient, the opposite outcome is possible. Beyond idiosyncratic, poorly understood interpersonal factors, however, there are hypnotherapists who are consistently more (sometimes much more) successful than others. What personal and professional characteristics do they have? What are the important ingredients in their special skills?

The qualities of a good hypnotherapist are basically the same as those of a good psychotherapist. Much has been written on important prerequisites such as empathy, sensitivity, and intuitive understanding existing in the context of professionalism. Respect for the patient is communicated in tangible and intangible ways, but if genuinely felt by the therapist it will be imparted automatically. The same applies to the therapist's genuine desire to help the patient through his dilemmas; if the patient feels this, many defenses are dropped.

Aside from these attributes, the successful hypnotherapist will have developed a sensitivity to rapport, to transference and countertransference reactions, and to nonverbal communication, as they happen from the time of the first patient contact and as they apply to hypnotic induction and working within the trance. Besides being adept at negotiating some of the issues discussed in this chapter, he or she is able to respond appropriately to the interplay between the patient's wishes for and defenses against entering the trance. Once the trance state has been arrived at, communications from the patient may be vastly different—quantitatively and qualitatively—from those seen in more conventional psychotherapies; the patient may be silent, expressing emotions through micromovements and autonomic responses, or talk and show patterns of thinking and imagery commonly manifested in dream states.

The successful hypnotherapist is comfortable with all these forms of communication and, ideally, possesses not only the ability to enter the patient's frame of reference, but has developed the craft and wisdom to assist the patient in finding creative solutions and positive personal transformations.

SUGGESTED READING AND REFERENCES

American Society of Clinical Hypnosis — Education and Research Foundation: *A Syllabus on Hypnosis and a Handbook of Therapeutic Suggestions.* Chicago, 1973.

Brenman M, Gill M: *Hypnotherapy.* New York, International Universities Press, 1947.

Cheek DB, LeCron LM: *Clinical Hypnotherapy.* New York, Grune & Stratton, 1968.

Crasilneck HB, Hall JA: *Clinical Hypnosis: Principles and Applications.* New York, Grune & Stratton, 1975.

Hartland J: *Medical and Dental Hypnosis.* London, Balliere, 1966.

Kroger WS: *Clinical and Experimental Hypnosis.* Philadelphia, JB Lippincott, 1977.

LeCron L (ed): *Experimental Hypnosis.* New York, Citadel Press, 1968.

Meares A: *A System of Medical Hypnosis.* Philadelphia, WB Saunders, 1961.

Udolf R: *Handbook of Hypnosis for Professionals.* New York, Van Nostrand Reinhold, 1981.

Weitzenhoffler AM: *General Techniques of Hypnotism.* New York, Grune & Stratton, 1957.

5

Illustrated Method for Self-Hypnosis

Barbara DeBetz

Self-hypnosis is an ability to enter voluntarily, at one's own suggestion, into a hypnotic trance state. In essence all hypnosis is self-hypnosis. If it occurs with a therapist, then the patient is guided into the trance. Depending on a person's hypnotic trance capacity, the depth of the self-hypnotic trance may vary from a light trance (hypnoidal) to a deep trance (somnambulistic). Although people have a more or less fixed level of trance capacity, depending on external as well as internal circumstances of that moment, the patient may experience subjective variations of trance levels.

In the course of every day we enter and leave various self-hypnotic, meditative states, states of intense concentration, or states of inattentiveness many times. All of these states have in common the spontaneous shifting back and forth between peripheral and focal attention. We usually do not refer to these states as hypnotic trance states, but that is exactly what they are. In addition, daydreaming can be regarded as a form of self-hypnosis. Everyone of us has experienced it for a variety of reasons, be it for relaxation, out of boredom, as a defense mechanism, or for any number of other reasons. The person is fully awake and in touch with his surroundings, but at the time he is emerged in vivid fantasies and imagery. The same phenomenon occurs in the so-called "highway hypnosis," a state of trance induced by the repetitiousness of long driving and the monotony of the highway. Frequently, a person who has experienced this form of highway hypnosis will arrive at the destination without remembering exactly how he got there. If asked about it, one frequently gets as an answer that there was a feeling of "automatic behavior," the way a car automatically shifts gear. This double awareness that a person can be here but at the same time somewhere else is typical of the hypnotic trance experience.

Some people shift spontaneously into trance states during waking hours in which they experience lapses of time that are inaccessible to them by conscious recall. During this dissociative state the individual may act as though he were a different person with no conscious awareness of his real identity. Sometimes there is even a feeling of being at a different place and in a different time period. This kind of spontaneous state is called a fugue. Fugue states are obviously an extreme and usually occur only in the highly hypnotizable individual. The foregoing are all examples of spontaneous, unstructured trance states.

In the context of this book, we would like you, the reader, to experience a structured self-hypnotic state. This very structure can also be used as an induction technique. In my extensive teaching of hypnosis to psychiatric residents, interns, psychologists, and other health professionals, I have found that hypnotic phenomena are much easier to understand if the student experiences the trance state himself. This eliminates many fears and anxieties about trying to induce the trance in a patient.

By following the simple step-by-step instructions accompanying the figure drawings here, any clinician can experience a self-hypnotic trance state.

SIMPLE INSTRUCTIONS FOR SELF-HYPNOSIS

Please read the directions slowly and carefully as you practice the exercise step by step the first time. Then read and practice again, going through the same motions as the figures in the drawings. After a few times, you will absorb and know the few steps easily.

As in learning anything else, do not give up after the first time or two; if you do not quite understand fully at once, you will very soon. If you do not get into the relaxed self-hypnotic "float" in the first run-through, do not be discouraged.

As with any learning process, it is easier for some people to get into a trance than others. It also depends on your inherent level of hypnotic trance capacity. However, be reassured that with repeated practice, you will grasp this simple technique which later on, with slight variations, you can use as an induction technique.

Just following the instructions will lead you quickly, smoothly, and naturally into a pleasurable floating state, your thoughts free, released, nongoal oriented. Later on, there are also instructions on how to use the hypnotic trance state for specific treatment goals.

To begin, select a time and place for relative privacy. The self-hypnotic exercise may be done either sitting in a comfortable armchair or lying on a couch or bed — whatever suits you personally, whatever is most relaxing and comforting.

(*NOTE:* Read through the instructions first, perhaps several times, as needed, checking along with the illustrations, before you practice the steps. It is vital that you understand thoroughly, of course, how to enter the trance state and how to exit from it.)

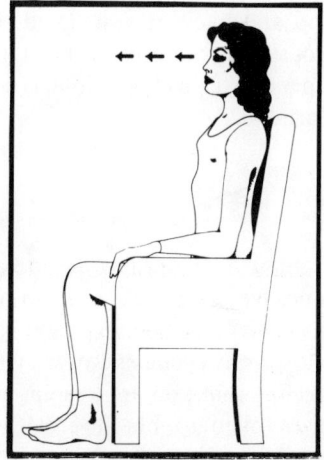

Step 1 If you are sitting up, keep your head straight but not stiff, and look directly ahead of you. Keep your body in a relaxed position.

If you are lying down, rest your head comfortably and look straight up at the ceiling, feeling at ease and unpressured. Your eyes should focus easily on the ceiling without any strong fixation or strain.

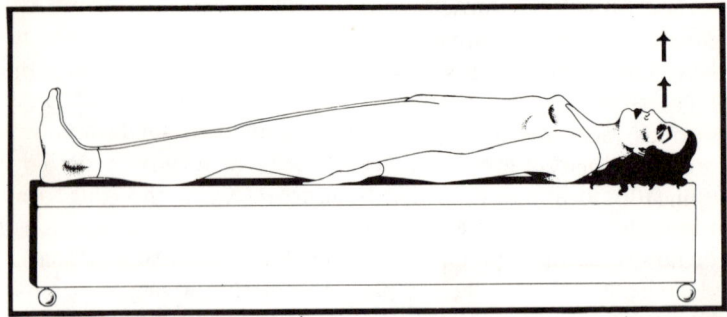

Step 2 Hold your head in the comfortable straight-ahead position (whether sitting or lying down) . . . now roll your eyes up and back, trying to look up past your eyebrows . . . and right over the top and back of your head. (Do not strain your eyes, just roll them up and back as far as it feels comfortable.

Step 3 Continue to look up and over and back . . . and now, as you are looking over and back, close your eyelids s-l-o-w-l-y (still feeling that you are keeping your eyes rolled up, but never with any strain or discomfort).

Step 4 Maintaining the eyelids-closed state . . . now take a deep breath through your nose, mouth closed . . . and keep breathing in deeply, deeply (but never straining) . . . and hold your breath for some seconds (according to your personal capacity, never overexerting).

Step 5 Then . . . slowly exhale through your slightly opened lips, and while you are exhaling, keeping your eyelids closed for this entire step . . . let your eyes come down, back into their normal straight-ahead position.

Step 6 Now . . . still with your eyelids closed . . . feeling very good, peaceful and pleasant . . . breathing easily at your normal rate . . . imagine your entire body is sinking deeper and deeper into the chair, couch or bed . . . feeling very comfortable and relaxed. You feel eased in mind and body, but at the same time focused and alert, a pleasant floating sensation.

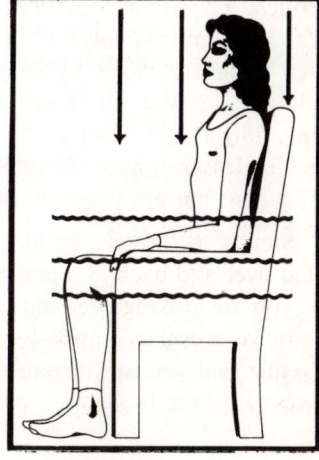

58

Step 7 Enjoy this feeling of floating . . . and now shift your attention to focus gently on your right or left hand and arm, as you choose . . . and imagine hand and arm, from hand to elbow, becoming very light and quite weightless . . . letting your hand and lower arm float upward slowly, easily and naturally (bending at the elbow, fingers and hand limp) . . .

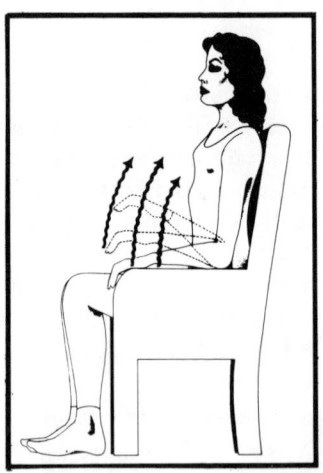

Step 8 You have reached your goal . . . as your hand and arm have floated upward easily to the upright position noted in the picture, elbow resting on the arm of the chair or the surface of the couch. You are now experiencing the buoyant, pleasurable state of self-hypnosis. Keep your eyes closed . . . mind and body floating, fully at ease. Your arm will remain pleasantly and effortlessly in this bent-upright position during the entire period.

This eight-step simple procedure, going along from step to step easily . . . and without any feeling of pressure or urgency whatsoever . . . will occupy only about 30 seconds once you have learned the progression thoroughly. You achieve the sequence smoothly and easily. Do not concern yourself at all with counting the seconds—a few more or less will not matter.

At first it may take you a little longer, but just go along at the pace which is most comfortable and unpressured for you personally. There is no need or advantage in timing your trance entry within 30 seconds exactly. You may proceed with the method more slowly if that suits you better.

It is desirable that you practice and train yourself to enter the state of self-hypnosis in as short a time as is possible and comfortable for yourself. Thus, if you want to use self-hypnosis to help treat and solve a specific problem in the future, it is advantageous to get in and out of the trance state as quickly as possible. Contrary to old beliefs, reaching the trance state does not have to be a long drawn-out process. The length of time you spend on each occasion in the trance state will depend on the particular treatment strategy you use. Even though it just takes about 30 seconds to enter, you may remain in this pleasant state of relaxation as long as you wish, according to what you feel is necessary to bring about a desired result. Now . . . once you have attained this pleasant state of buoyant repose, your body will be enjoying a wonderfully restful feeling of muscle relaxation (floating) . . . while your mind is clear and alert, not dulled or sleepy. Now, while in the trance state simply let your mind remain in neutral gear. That means keeping your mind "idling," relaxed, at peace, not concentrating on anything specific—just floating restfully, preferably with your eyes closed loosely, never squeezed tight, never frowning with strain. It is vital that you acquire the ability to float without mental or physical tension.

After you have mastered the skill to shift into "neutral" self-hypnosis, it will be very easy for you to also use the trance to restructure a specific problem that you may have. The person in a trance can focus much more clearly on formulating the problem and it is hoped, find new approaches in solving it. While in the trance, the person's mind is clear and responsive and new information can be assimilated and processed.

The human mind is probably the best, most efficient, and productive personal computer. It can provide proficiency in aiding to attain top performance, once you know how to "program" and use it in your own behalf—through the simple self-hypnosis technique you learn here.

Once you are in the hypnotic trance state (a mechanical computer might flash the signal: "ready"), your personal "brain computer" is all set for you to insert some new programing leading to the desired result. You are ready and able to erase old, blocking, perhaps misleading, and thus damaging responses. Then you can feed in new directions and attitudes.

EMERGING FROM THE SELF-HYPNOTIC TRANCE

It is as easy and simple to exit from the trance as it was to enter it. All you have to do is to reverse the process of entering the trance. Simply proceed as follows:

Step 1R (for "return") Your eyelids are still closed. Now, again, take a deep breath through your nose, keeping your mouth closed, holding your breath for a moment comfortably, never straining or overexerting yourself . . .

Step 2R As you are inhaling (in step 1R), eyelids closed, and then holding your breath . . . roll your eyes back up under your closed eyelids as far up and back as you can without stress . . .

Step 3R Exhale slowly through your mouth, pursing your lips a bit so air escapes gradually . . . and while the air is being breathed out, open your eyelids s-l-o-w-l-y . . .

Step 4R Easily, pleasantly, feeling relaxed and rested . . . eyes open . . . let your straight-ahead gaze come back into clear focus . . .

Step 5R Open and close the hand which is still in the upright position . . . repeat opening and closing the hand slowly and comfortably, no clenching . . . doing this a few times. . .

Step 6R Slowly, without any force or tension, let your elevated hand and arm return gently back down to its normal resting position . . .

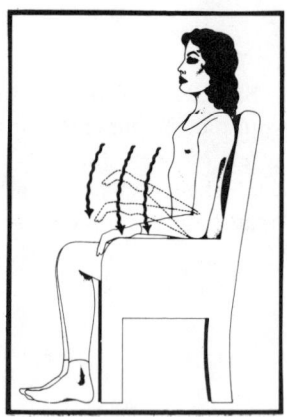

Step 7R Stay in the sitting or lying position for some leisurely seconds. You feel refreshed, at ease, and physically relaxed.

QUICK REFERENCE SUMMARY
Steps to Enter Self-Hypnosis

1. Sit in an armchair or lie on a horizontal surface, eyes straight ahead

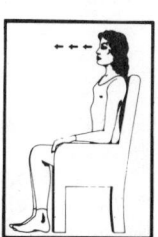

2. Roll your eyes way up and back

3. Keeping your eyes looking up, close your eyelids slowly

4. Take a deep breath through your nose, hold for a few seconds

5. Slowly exhale through slightly opened lips, letting your eyes roll back down under closed eyelids

6. Imagine your body sinking deeper and deeper into chair or couch

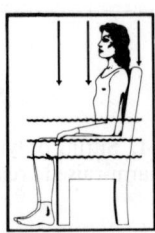

7. Eyes still closed, focus your mind on your right or left hand, let hand and arm become light and float upward

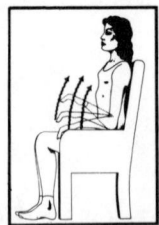

8. Keep eyes closed, elbow resting on arm of chair or surface of couch

QUICK REFERENCE SUMMARY
Steps to Emerge from Self-Hypnosis

1. Sitting or lying comfortably, in the arm-raised, relaxed position, eyelids closed, you now decide to emerge from the self-hypnotic trance (remember, you are in charge every instant)

2. Now take a deep breath, as in step 4 of entering the trance

3. Slowly exhale, as in step 5 of entering the trance

4. Roll up your eyes slowly, opening your eyelids, look straight ahead easily, pleasantly, no strain

5. Now make a fist (not too tight) with your raised hand, then open your fist and let your fingers and hand relax. Let your arm settle back into your starting position (in armchair or on horizontal surface) . . . and arise as you desire . . . to move about as usual.

You are now out of the hypnotic trance rested, refreshed, alert and invigorated.

NOTE: If you do not bring yourself out of the trance this way, it will leave naturally with sleep, or whenever you wish . . . you are always in charge.

The foregoing technique of self-hypnosis is only one way of reaching a trance state in a specifically structured way. This technique is based upon the Hypnotic Induction Profile which, in addition to being a way to reach a state of self-hypnosis, also is a clinical test for hypnotic trance capacity and trance induction. It is covered in detail elsewhere in this text. However, this is not the only way to reach a trance state. There are numerous other ways such as eye-fixation, progressive muscle relaxation techniques, meditation techniques, deep breathing techniques, etc. I like to consider them just different ceremonies to get to the same goal.

Many clinicians shy away from using any of those techniques because of some irrational fears and misconceptions about hypnosis. However, once the individual has gone through it with a technique as described above, many of these anxieties will have been alleviated. By having experienced a trance state personally, the clinician will also find it easier to explain the phenomenon to the patient.

6

Hypnotic Rating Scales and Induction Techniques

Barbara DeBetz

The use of hypnosis in the clinical setting calls for standardized, reliable, reproducible, and appropriate tests for hypnotizability as well as simple, effective methods of trance induction. Laboratory research findings have demonstrated that there is a fairly stable level of hypnotizability in the majority of individuals throughout adult life. Children are slightly more hypnotizable, while there seems to be a decline of trance capacity in the geriatric population. Although some clinicians have claimed that all persons are ultimately hypnotizable to the degree desired by their hypnotherapist, these claims have not been supported by valid research data.

It is now fairly universally accepted, however, that there are differences in levels of hypnotic trance capacity. Approximately 70% of the general population is hypnotizable; among those who are hypnotizable approximately 10% fall into the low range, 10% to 15% into the high range, and the remaining majority falls into the mid-range of hypnotic responsivity. There is some controversy regarding the relatively fixed nature of an individual's trance level. Some clinicians and researchers feel that depth or intensity varies depending on some other factors. Measurable trance responsivity should not be confused with the reported experience of the hypnotized subject. An individual may show a certain learning effect if a procedure is repeated several times, and the subjective individual experience may fluctuate considerably.

RATING SCALES

Standardized rating scales were developed initially in the context of laboratory research, and they have contributed immensely to the general understanding of hypnotic phenomena.

As an outgrowth of experimental laboratory research, we have also come to understand that no measurable physiological response has thus far been observed to be uniquely associated with hypnosis. For instance, alterations in blood pressure, blood flow, heart rate, respiratory rate, and electroencephalographic recordings might occur during a hypnotic procedure, but frequently these physiological changes are unrelated to the subject's level of trance capacity. In addition, many other procedures that induce a state of relaxation have been found to produce the same kinds of physiological responses. An essential aspect of hypnosis is the subject's subjective experience of an altered perception or altered state of awareness.

Until fairly recently the event of hypnotic responsivity was described clinically by the hypnotherapist's observations. Therapeutic success following the application of an induction procedure was frequently the only criterion on which the occurrence of hypnosis was assessed. For obvious reasons this kind of personalized assessment does not lend itself to systematic, valid, and reliable laboratory and clinical research. Out of this need, several research and clinical scales have been developed. The advantage of having standardized tests available and using them is that they permit the collection of norms and data that can be used in a meaningful and reliable way to communicate professionally.

Stanford Hypnotic Susceptibility Scales

The first of the Stanford scales, in two forms, the Stanford Hypnotic Susceptibility Scale, Form A and Form B (SHSS:A and SHSS:B) were essentially an outgrowth of the Friedlander-Sarbin Scale. Friedlander and Sarbin in 1938 had described a series of performances commonly recognized as belonging within the realm of hypnosis. Some of these items were suggested eye closure, items of motor inhibition such as arm catalepsy, finger lock, verbal in-

Table 6-1
Test Items

SHSSA:A and SHSS:B	SHSS:C
1. Postural sway	1. Hand lowering
2. Eye closure	2. Moving hands apart
3. Hand lowering	3. Mosquito hallucination
4. Arm immobilization	4. Taste hallucination
5. Finger lock	5. Arm rigidity
6. Arm rigidity	6. Dream
7. Moving hands	7. Age regression
8. Verbal inhibition	8. Arm immobilization
9. Hallucination	9. Anosmia to ammonia
10. Eye catalepsy	10. Hallucinated voice
11. Posthypnotic suggestion	11. Negative visual hallucinations
12. Amnesia	12. Amnesia

hibition, posthypnotic voice hallucination, and posthypnotic amnesia. The Stanford Hypnotic Susceptibility Scales altered some items and added some in order to have a broader distribution of hypnotic test items. Both the SHSS:A and the SHSS:B scales begin with the postural sway prior to hypnotic induction. Thus the subject is introduced to the meaning of involuntary response by receiving suggestions of falling backwards, to be caught by the hypnotherapist if the subject loses balance and falls. The postural sway test is one of the 12 items scored on the scale. After the postural sway test, hypnotic induction follows, modeled after that used by Friedlander and Sarbin, that is, suggested eye closure while looking at a small focusing target. This is followed by another ten tested score items (see Table 6-1). It was soon recognized that the SHSS:A and the SHSS:B scales used predominantly test items of motor functions, whether directly suggested movements or inhibitions of movement. In order to include other aspects of hypnotic phenomena, a test was necessary which included fantasy and cognitive distortion. Such a test was developed by Weitzenhoffer and Hilgard in 1962, the Stanford Hypnotic Susceptibility Scale Form C (SHSS:C) (see Table 6-1).

In addition to the three Stanford Hypnotic Susceptibility Scales, it was felt that another test was necessary to select out those subjects who were highly hypnotizable and had special hypnotic talents, such as positive and negative hallucinations in particular sensory areas. Such a test was developed by Weitzenhoffer and Hilgard (1963) called the Stanford Profile Scales of Hypnotic Susceptibility, Forms I and II (SPS:I and SPS:II) (see Table 6-2). A later version of the same test was restandardized by the same authors in 1967.

Because of the time required to administer the Stanford Profile Scale (SPS), another test emerged called the "tailored" SHSS:C in which one of the two items prior to the final amnesia item can be replaced by a special item to serve the purpose of the investigator. Let us assume an experiment is done on automatic writing, visual hallucinations, or hypnotic deafness; those with specially high hypnotic trance capacity can be selected from a large sample

Table 6-2
Test Item Content of Revised Stanford Profile Scales of Hypnotic Susceptibility, Forms I and II*

Adopted Name and Initials of Subscale	Functions Intended to be Tested	Item Content of Tests in Subscale
AG: Agnosia and cognitive distortion	Distortion of meaning and value, rather than of sense perception	I:7 Agnosia I: house I:8 Arithmetic impairment II:7 Agnosia II: scissors II:8 Personality alteration (reduced intelligence)
HP: Hallucinations: positive	The experiencing of sensory and perceptual phenomena in the absence of appropriate stimuli	I:2 Music hallucination I:5 Hallucinated light II:1 Heat hallucination II:3 Hallucinated ammonia
HN: Hallucinations: negative	Lack of awareness of stimulation that would normally be perceived	I:1 Hand analgesia to shock I:3 Anosmia to ammonia II:2 Selective deafness II:5 Missing watch hand (visual)

Table 6-2 (continued)

Adopted Name and Initials of Subscale	Functions Intended to be Tested	Item Content of Tests in Subscale
DR: Dreams and regressions	Memory revival and fantasy production, including fantasied "reliving" of events in the past	I:4 Recall of meal I:6 Dream I: general II:4 Regression to birthday II:6 Dream II: about hypnosis
AM: Amnesia and posthypnotic compulsions	Behavior suggested during hypnosis but carried out after arousal from hypnosis, usually with forgetting of the instructions	Amnesia: rescored from Form A I:9 Posthypnotic verbal compulsion II:9 Posthypnotic automatic writing
MC: Loss of motor control	Motor responses carried out automatically as a result of direct suggestion; loss of volitional control over movement as a result of suggestion	Motor pool (a) from Form A: 1. Postural sway 2. Eye closure 4. Arm immobilization 5. Finger lock Motor pool (b) from Form A: 6. Arm rigidity 7. Hands moving together 8. Verbal inhibition 10. Eye catalepsy

*Note that the last two subscales assume that the subjects were previously tested on SHSS:A.
Reprinted with permission from: Hilgard E: The Stanford Hypnotic Susceptibility Scales as related to other measures of hypnotic responsiveness. *Am J Clin Hypn* 1978/79;21(2 and 3):74.

by replacing the tenth or the eleventh item of the SHSS:C with a "tailor-made" item.

The above briefly described Stanford scales are mainly used in the laboratory for experimental research, but there are also two scales for clinical use, the Stanford Hypnotic Clinical Adult Scale, SHCS-Adult and The Children's Hypnotic Clinical Scale (SHCS-Child), published by Hilgard and Hilgard in 1975 and Morgan and J. Hilgard in 1979.

The Stanford Hypnotic Clinical Adult Scale (SHCS-Adult)

The original Stanford Hypnotic Susceptibility Scales were developed for research purposes, and they test some aspects of hypnotic responses which are irrelevant in clinical use. They are also very time consuming and, for many patients, impractical to administer due to certain restriction in motor mobility. Therefore the Stanford Hypnotic Clinical Adult Scale was developed. This scale uses five items from the existing Stanford scales, namely: moving hands together, a dream, age regression, a posthypnotic suggestion, and posthypnotic amnesia. The SHCS-Adult Scale takes 20 minutes to administer.

The Stanford Hypnotic Scale for Children

This scale serves to measure hypnotic responsiveness in children between the ages of 3 and 16. The test is derived from the Stanford Hypnotic Susceptibility Scale:A (SHSS:A) but is slightly modified for use in children. It uses a five-item scale and consists of a relaxation/eye closure induction and the following test items: hand lowering, hallucinated TV, dream, age regression, and a posthypnotic suggestion to reenter the hypnotic trance at a hand-clap signal.

The scale has two forms, one especially appropriate for children under the age of 6 years. It had been found that very young children feel anxious and frightened when asked to close their eyes, therefore the test was modified and permits the child to keep the eyes open throughout the test procedure. This form also avoids suggestion of the hand-clap reenter signal. Additionally, the modified form relies on an active fantasy induction. The administration of the test to the very young child cannot be done in a formal manner. In general, the help and participation of an adult, preferably a parent of the child, is necessary to initiate fantasy and sustain it. By age 6, the child has developed enough cognitive skills to initiate and sustain it himself.

Harvard Group Scale of Hypnotic Susceptibility, Form A (HGSHS:A)

This scale is an adaptation of the Stanford Hypnotic Susceptibility Scale:A and is being used for group administration as well as for self-scoring. It is a satisfactorily reliable measure for the initial scoring of subjects and their degree of hypnotic trance capacity. Nine of the 12 test items are the same as on the SHSS:A scale and the other three, although different, test the same hypnotic functions. Because of the time-saving element of this test when given simultaneously to a group of subjects, this scale has been widely used in experimental research.

Barber Suggestibility Scale (BSS)

In 1962, Barber and Glass developed the Barber Suggestibility Scale. It differs from the other scales so far described in that it is designed to test hypnotic behavior without formal trance induction. The BSS includes eight standardized test items which were selected as representative of the types of instructions given to hypnotic test subjects. The scale includes several items that ask subjects to imagine and then to experience certain effects. The eight test items are: arm lowering, arm levitation, hand lock, thirst "hallucination," verbal inhibition, body immobility, "posthypnotic-like" response, and selective amnesia. It takes approximately 10 to 15 minutes to administer and score the BSS.

The Creative Imagination Scale

In 1978 Barber and Wilson constructed the Creative Imagination Scale. They felt that the Barber Suggestibility Scale (BSS) was too authoritarian for clinical use and did not allow the subject to use his own fantasy and imagination sufficiently. The Creative Imagination Scale has 10 test items. These test items encourage subjects to use their own thinking and "creative imagining" in order to experience the suggested effects. The 10 test items are the following: arm heaviness, hand levitation, finger anesthesia, water hallucination, olfactory-gustatory hallucination, music hallucination, temperature hallucination, time distortion, age regression, and mind-body relaxation. The test takes a total of 20 to 25 minutes and can be administered either to a group or an individual subject.

Diagnostic Rating Scales (DRS)

In 1959, Orne, and in 1966, O'Connell, Orne, and Shor introduced the Diagnostic Rating Scale. This scale differs from the above-described scales in that it requires the subject to go through the test procedures several times. This test is based on the concept that a person who is hypnotized for the first time may be anxious or overly compliant with the hypnotherapist. After several trials, the subject would relax and level out at a specific "hypnotic plateau" which would represent the subject's true hypnotic trance capacity.

INDUCTION TECHNIQUES

Once hypnotic trance capacity has been measured, hypnotic induction can be administered in a variety of ways. In a broad sense, any device or procedure that draws a subject's focused attention can lead into a trance state. Therefore, we can define as an induction technique any method where one individual, the hypnotherapist, seeks to elicit hypnotic behavior in another individual, the subject or patient. An induction technique should be appropriate to the clinical setting. For instance, if a patient comes to use hypnosis for pain control, the hypnotherapist should use an induction technique that gently guides the patient into the trance. A coercive or threatening approach would be antitherapeutic and, in most cases, the patient would be uncooperative and unresponsive to the therapeutic strategy. Any induction procedure can be divided into three separate stages: the "aura," the psychophysiological enhancement, and the actual trance entry.

The aura is a set of preconceived expectations of the subject, depending on social, cultural, and educational factors. The aura can enhance or decrease the effect of the hypnotic experience. The patient may be inclined to attribute great power and control to the hypnotherapist due to common misconceptions resulting from the old beliefs that hypnosis was "projected" on to the patient by the therapist. A brief explanation to the patient about the nature of hypnosis is frequently enough to alleviate fears and anxieties.

Psychophysiological enhancement simply means that the hypnotherapist enhances and utilizes naturally occurring physiological phenomena to create an atmosphere which may heighten the subject's receptivity. For example, the subject who is asked to fixate his eyes on a specific target will eventually develop some diplopia and blurred vision. His eyes will tire and at this point the therapist will suggest that his "eyes are getting very heavy and tired, so tired that he may just want to close the eyelids and keep them closed." The well-known postural sway test also utilizes a normal physiological occurrence. In this technique the therapist instructs the subject to stand with heels and toes together and allow his body to sway back and forth. The subject has his eyes closed, therefore not allowing the visual input for balance correction. Within seconds, the subject will start swaying, back and forth. The psychophysiological enhancement gives the therapist an opportunity to alert the subject to become aware to certain changes in sensory and physiological perceptions.

The trance entry is the actual transition from the normal state of awareness to the altered state of awareness, the hypnotic trance state. It represents the subject's shift toward focal attention with a concomitant constriction of peripheral awareness and a certain degree of suspension of critical judgment.

Many induction techniques use eye fixation, accompanied by repetitions and monotonous instructions geared toward muscle relaxation. Other techniques rely more on motor changes such as inducing a sense or heaviness in one arm or hand. Many induction techniques are lengthy, tiring, or boring to the patient and therapist. However, individuals with trance capacity can enter into a trance within seconds if guided appropriately.

Hypnotic Induction Profile (HIP)

The Hypnotic Induction Profile (HIP) is an induction procedure and a rating scale for hypnotic trance capacity. It can be administered in 5 to 10 minutes. Because of its brevity, it is an ideal and most practical test for the clinical setting. It is easy to learn the administration and scoring of the test. Contrary to the previously described rating scales which were primarily developed in the laboratory, the Hypnotic Induction Profile has been developed in the course of clinical psychiatric practice. This test was initially developed in 1970 by Spiegel and Bridger. It differs from the other scales in that it does not test a broad range of hypnotic behaviors but only focuses on a few sensory and motor items. It is structured in such a way that it actually induces the trance state and also measures the experience of entry and exit from the trance in a standardized way. In addition to the sensory and motor test items, the HIP also has a biological measure, the eye-roll sign, which allegedly represents an individual's potential for trance capacity. Although there has been some controversy regarding the validity of the eye-roll sign as an indicator of trance capacity, clinical research done on the profile supports the association of the eye-roll sign and hypnotizability. The Hypnotic Induction Profile is especially useful to the clinician not just because of its brevity, but also because of the several purposes it can fulfill. There are three general hypotheses associated with this test: (1) the HIP measures clinically usable hypnotizability, (2) it can be used as a rough screening device for certain psychopathology, and (3) it helps the hypnotherapist to get a broad understanding of the patient's personality structure because the HIP postulates that there are specific personality traits associated with the different levels of trance capacity.

It was observed in clinical practice that a high eye-roll sign was associated with high hypnotizability, while a low eye-roll sign was associated with low or mid-range trance capacity. The eye-roll sign is elicited by asking the subject to look up and while looking up to close his eyelids slowly. It is measured by looking at the distance or amount of sclera between the lower border of the cornea and the lower eyelid before eye closure (Figure 6-1). The eye-roll

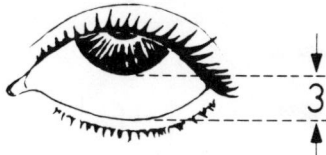

EYE-ROLL MEASUREMENT

Figure 6-1

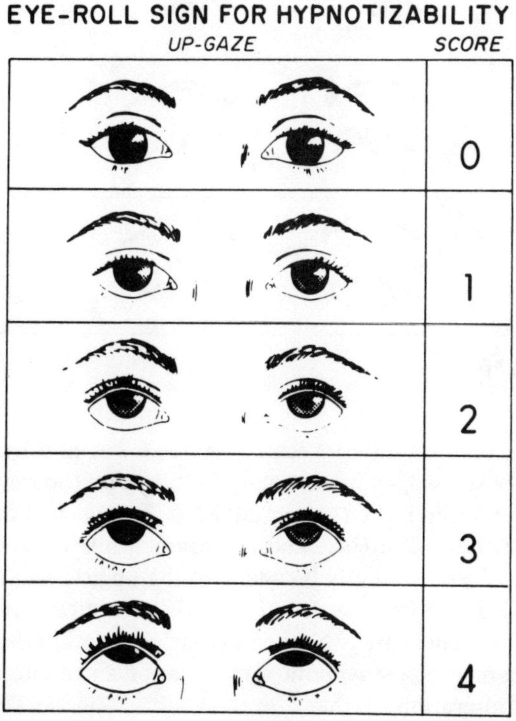

EYE-ROLL SIGN FOR HYPNOTIZABILITY

UP-GAZE	SCORE
	0
	1
	2
	3
	4

Figure 6-2A

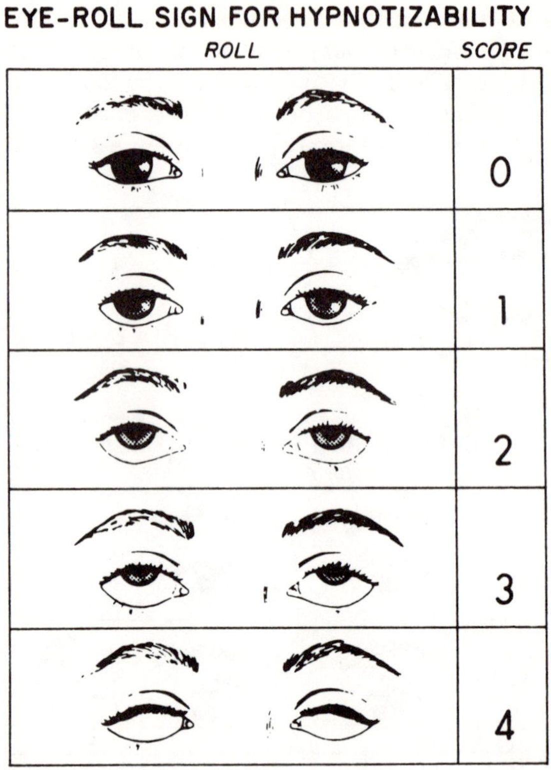

EYE-ROLL SIGN FOR HYPNOTIZABILITY

ROLL	SCORE
	0
	1
	2
	3
	4

Figure 6-2B

sign is scored on a 0 to 4 scale (Figures 6-2 A and B). Some individuals show a squint when asked to roll up their eyes (Figure 6-3). The squint is then simply added to the upgaze. For example, a patient has a 2 upgaze and a 1 squint while closing his eyes, the squint would simply be added to the upgaze and an eye-roll sign of 3 would be recorded. This is the first measuring point of the profile. There are two other measuring points in the final HIP score, namely a posthypnotic arm levitation and an item of motor control alteration.

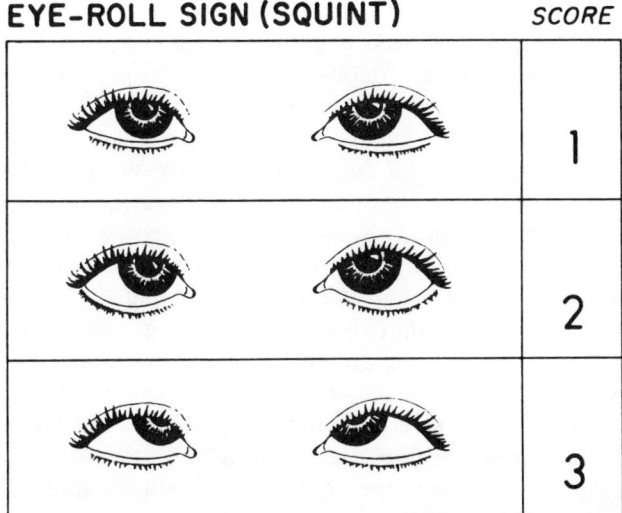

Figure 6-3

There are two methods for scoring the HIP, one of which is based on these three measuring points, giving a final score of 0 to 5, while the other method is composed of five experiential indicators and does not include the eye-roll sign. Both methods of scoring use the same scoring sheet and can be done simultaneously. However, for the purpose of this primer, the 0 to 5 HIP scoring will be predominantly referred to. Note that the final HIP score is on a scale from 0 to 5, although the eye-roll sign is only from 0 to 4. All individuals who achieved an HIP score of 4 are potentially grade 5s. The criteria used to test further trance capacity are the following: (1) the ability to sustain posthypnotic sensory and motor alterations, such as negative or positive hallucinations and/or rigid or flaccid motor paralysis; (2) total spontaneous amnesia to the entire hypnotic experience; and (3) ability to regress to earlier age levels and display age regression in the present tense. This means that the patient shows behavior and verbal communication appropriate for the particular age tested.

If all three test items prove to be positive, we can identify the person as a grade 5, meaning a person who has exceptionally high hypnotic trance capacity. Among the hypnotizable population only 5% fulfill the criteria of the grade 5.

The final HIP score may have three clinically important configurations. A consistent, continuous performance indicates an "intact" profile score, representing an intact capacity to enter into the trance. A "soft" profile score represents "a weakening" of the ribbon of concentration, meaning that the subject showed a positive eye-roll sign, a positive control differential, but no post-induction arm levitation (which had been suggested during the instructions). Inconsistent and discontinuous performance indicates a clear break in the subject's "ribbon of concentration" and this kind of profile is referred to as a "decrement" profile. The soft and decrement profiles usually indicate that the patient is not a candidate or is a poor one for hypnotic treatment approaches. Once the profile score has been determined, the same procedure can be used to induce the trance state for specific treatment strategies (see Figure 6-4 for the different profile configurations).

Before trying to induce a trance in a patient, it is recommended to read and follow the instructions given in the chapter on self-hypnosis. The self-hypnotic method outlined in Chapter 5 is very closely related to the induction used for the Hypnotic Induction Profile, and it will be much easier to administer the profile after having gone through the experience.

The main difference is that when the profile is administered to another person, the hypnotherapist should make an assessment of the eye-roll sign and measure the entire Hypnotic Induction Profile. Once that has been done, the trance induction outlined in the self-hypnotic method can be used to induce the trance. The full administration of the Hypnotic Induction Profile can be found elsewhere and should be learned thoroughly by those who want to use the HIP as a rating scale. However, as outlined here, using the eye-roll sign alone gives the clinician a fairly good understanding of what kind of a hypnotic subject he is dealing with (high, mid, or low range). He misses out on knowing which ones are the "soft" and "decrement" profiles. For this reason, learning to

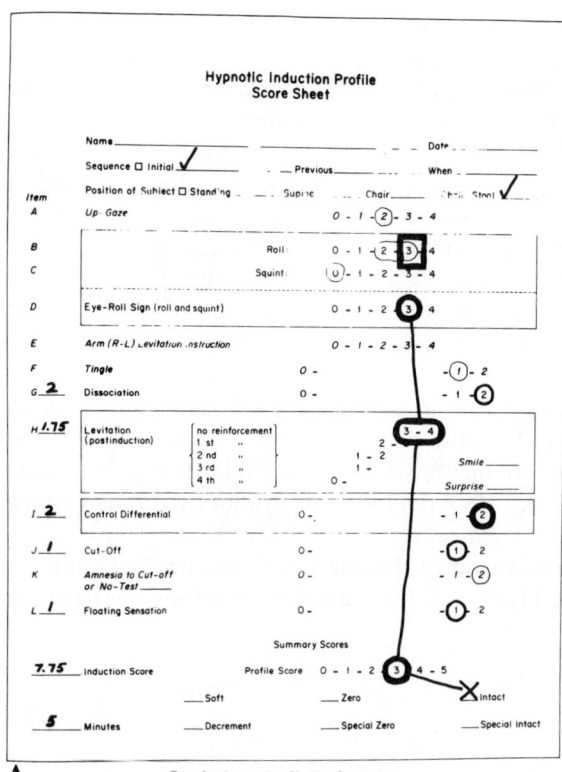

Figure 6-4 The HIP scoring sheet — various configurations. **A** Regular intact profile configuration. **B** Soft profile configuration (see page 82). **C** Decrement profile configuration (see page 83).

administer the entire profile would be of greater value. Using the induction part of the profile, combined with the eye-roll sign gives the clinician an excellent method of trance induction. It is an easily learned technique, as outlined in detail in Chapter 5. And because of its brevity and patient acceptability, it is the most appropriate clinical rating scale and induction technique available at the present time.

Occasionally the clinician has to modify his induction technique according to a patient's specific needs. However, in general it is

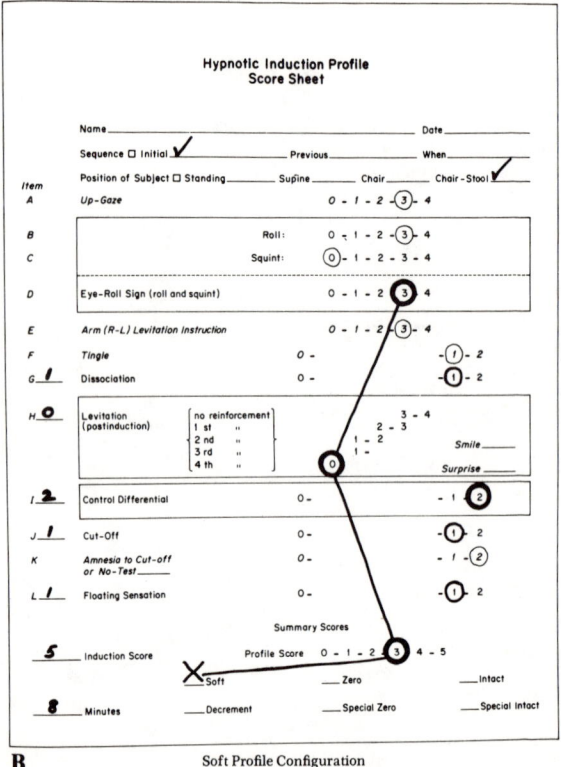

B Soft Profile Configuration

advisable for the clinician to become efficient and comfortable with one specific technique of measuring hypnotic trance capacity and of trance induction.

ACKNOWLEDGMENT

Figures 6-1 through 6-4 are reproduced with permission from Spiegel H, Spiegel D: *Trance and Treatment*. New York, Basic Books, 1978.

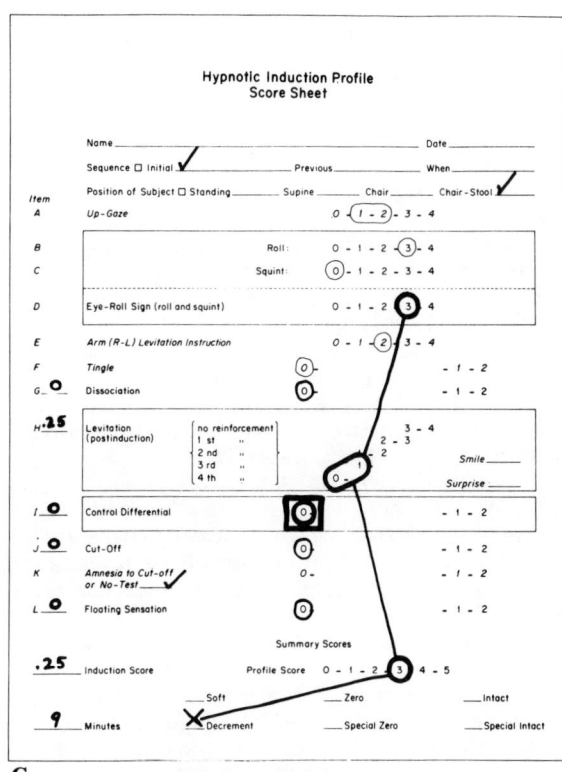

C   Decrement Profile Configuration

SUGGESTED READING AND REFERENCES

Barber TX, Glass LB: Significant factors in hypnotic behavior. *J Abnorm Soc Psychol* 1962;64:222-228.

Barber TX, Spanos NP, Chaves JF: *Hypnotism: Imagination and Human Potentialities.* New York, Pergamon Press, 1974.

DeBetz B, Stern DB: Factor Analysis and score distributions of the HIP — Replication by a Second Examiner. *Am J Clin Hypn* 1979;22(2):95-102.

Frankel FH: Scales measuring hypnotic responsivity: A clinical perspective. *Am J Clin Hypn* 1978/1979;21(273):209-217.

Friedlander JW, Sarbin TR: The depth of hypnosis. *J Abnorm Soc Psychol* 1938;33:453-475.

Hilgard ER: *Hypnotic Susceptibility*. New York, Harcourt, Brace and World, 1965.

Hilgard ER: The Stanford hypnotic susceptibility scales as related to other measures of hypnotic responsiveness. *Am J Clin Hypn* 1978/1979;22(2):68-83.

Morgan AH, Hilgard JR: The Stanford hypnotic clinical scale. Appendix in Hilgard ER, Hilgard JR (eds): *Hypnosis in the Relief of Pain*. Los Altos, Calif, William Kaufman, 1975.

Morgan AH, Hilgard JR: The stanford hypnotic clinical scale: Adult. *Am J Clin Hypn* 1979;21(2&3):134-147.

Morgan AH, Hilgard JR: The stanford hypnotic clinical scale for Children. *Am J Clin Hypn* 1979;21(2&3):148-155.

O'Connell DN, Orne MT, Shor RE: A comparison of hypnotic susceptibility as assessed by diagnostic ratings and initial standardized test scores. *Int J Clin Exper Hypn* 1966;14:324-332.

Orne MT: The nature of hypnosis: Artifact and essence. *J Abnorm Soc Psychol* 1959;58:277-299.

Shor RE, Orne EC: *The Harvard Group Scale of Hypnotic Susceptibility, Form A*. Palo Alto, Calif, Consulting Psychologists Press, 1962.

Spiegel H, Bridger AA: *Manual for Hypnotic Induction Profile*. New York, Soni Medica, 1970.

Spiegel H, Spiegel D: *Trance and Treatment*. New York, Basic Books, 1978, pp 22-78.

Tart TC: Quick and convenient assessment of hypnotic depth: Self-report scales. *Am J Clin Hypn* 1978/1979;21(2 and 3):186-207.

Weitzenhoffer AM, Hilgard ER: *Stanford Hypnotic Susceptibility Scale, Forms A and B*. Palo Alto, Calif, Consulting Psychologists Press, 1959.

Weitzenhoffer AM, Hilgard ER: *Stanford Profile Scales of Hypnotic Susceptibility, Form C*. Palo Alto, Calif, Consulting Psychologists Press, 1962.

Weitzenhoffer AM, Hilgard ER: *Stanford Profile Scales of Hypnotic Susceptibility, Forms I and II*. Palo Alto, Calif, Consulting Psychologists Press, 1963.

Weitzenhoffer AM, Hilgard ER: *Revised Stanford Profile Scales of Hypnotic Susceptibility: Forms I and II*. Palo Alto, Calif, Consulting Psychologists Press, 1967.

Wilson SC, Barber TX: The creative imagination scale as a measure of hypnotic responsiveness: Applications to experimental and clinical hypnosis. *Am J Clin Hypn* 1978;20:235-249.

PART III. THERAPEUTIC APPLICATIONS

7

Anxiety

Gérard Sunnen

Anxiety and anxiety-related conditions are the most common psychological afflictions of man and account for a major percentage of initial complaints to psychiatrists as well as to general practitioners. Although it is estimated that some 5% of the population may suffer from acute or chronic anxiety, with women outnumbering men two to one (Cohen and White, 1950), the numbers are probably significantly higher.

As a symptom, anxiety is a final common pathway for many conditions, physical as well as psychological. As syndromes, anxiety disorders are under intensive study to define more precisely their etiologies and clinical outcomes. Recent studies, showing disturbances of lactate metabolism in certain anxious individuals, point to the possibility that some anxiety states, like some depressive states, have strong biological and genetic determinants.

Hypnosis finds its most common clinical utilization in the treatment of anxiety and its related states, not only because of anxiety's prevalence, but because hypnosis has such a clear role as a potent anti-anxiety agent. In this chapter, we will examine hypnotic behavioral approaches to anxiety, while hypnopsychotherapeutic approaches will be discussed in Chapter 14.

EVALUATION OF ANXIETY

The first task of the hypnotherapist is to evaluate the anxiety condition. At the end of the initial interview, several questions must be asked. Is the anxiety organically determined? Is there a medical, physiological, or otherwise somatic basis for its existence? The list of medical conditions which, as a by-product, contain anxiety is long: hypertension, cardiac arrhythmias, anemia, hypoglycemia, withdrawal from sedative hypnotics (including alcohol), and caffeinism, cocaine, and psychostimulant abuse, among others. Anxiety is also sometimes confused with medical conditions which, in their presentation, share its expressions. Coronary artery disease, with chest pain, respiratory distress, and cardiac symptoms can mimic anxiety states; so can hyperthyroidism, pheochromocytomas and Meniere's disease. The treatment, while not obviating adjunctive psychotherapeutic or hypnotherapeutic intervention, will of course be mainly aimed at treating the primary medical condition.

Is the anxiety an aggravating component of a chronic medical syndrome? Most psychosomatic conditions are intimately connected to anxiety and stress. Flare-ups of such diseases as peptic ulcer, ulcerative colitis, or hypertension produce anxiety. Conversely, difficulties with psychosocial adjustment bring exacerbations in these conditions. Anxiety control is important to ease the interactive play of psyche and soma.

Is the anxiety a part of another psychiatric syndrome? Anxiety weaves into most psychiatric syndromes. Major depression is rarely seen without it, and so is mania. Schizophrenia, especially in the decompensation phase, as the individual experiences ego fragmentation, can be marked by fright — as can organic brain syndromes with their cognitive disruptions. Treatment of anxiety in these conditions is centered on correcting the global psychiatric syndrome.

When medical conditions and major psychiatric syndromes are eliminated as reasons for anxiety, we are left with more functional causes. It is useful, in our therapeutic approach, to see patients' experiences of anxiety as falling into three general categories: (1) individuals reporting chronic, free-floating feelings of fear (generalized anxiety disorder); (2) individuals manifesting discreet episodes of panic, but who, in between attacks, are relatively anxiety free (panic disorders); and (3) mixed syndromes.

There are other syndromes which contain anxiety as a core experiential manifestation.

Phobias are differentiated by the fact that they happen in the context of identifiable situations. They are marked by anxiety and avoidance. Thus agoraphobia is manifested in environments where the individual feels trapped and unable to return to safety, ie, common places include elevators, subways, planes, tunnels and bridges. Social phobias appear in interpersonal situations; and simple phobias are persistent, irrational fears of specific objects or animals. Phobias may be mildly bothersome or severely incapacitating. There are individuals who stay imprisoned in their homes because they fear the anxiety they may experience if they venture outside.

Posttraumatic stress disorders, acute or chronic, have generalized anxiety as a major component of a constellation of somatic and psychological disturbances following an accident, a loss, or any other disaster.

Obsessive compulsive disorders are characterized by tension stemming from the conscious emergence of thoughts, desires, and wishes to perform certain actions, and attempts to deny, ignore, undo, or suppress them. When severe, the anxiety becomes generalized, chronic, and incapacitating.

Adjustment disorders represent maladaptive responses to identifiable psychological stressors. Predominant symptoms in adjustment disorders with anxious mood, are nervousness, worry, and jitteriness.

HYPNOTIC TREATMENT OF SYNDROMES MANIFESTING GENERALIZED ANXIETY

Generalized anxiety disorder (DSM-III,300.02) is characterized by pervasive, persistent anxiety, manifested by motor tension — strained facies, fidgeting, restlessness, fatigueability; autonomic hyperactivity — sweating, palpitations, light-headedness, paresthesias, upset stomach, lump in the throat, high resting pulse and respiratory rate; apprehensive expectation — worry, rumination, anticipation of misfortune to self or others; hyperattentiveness resulting in distractibility, difficulty in concentrating, insomnia, irritability, and impatience. To meet diagnostic criteria, the anxious mood has to have lasted at least a month.

Approaches to chronic generalized anxiety, which may incorporate hypnotic intervention, may be roughly grouped into analytic or behavioral types. Hypnoanalytic methods will be explored in a later chapter. Behavioral techniques do not necessarily exclude the importance of psychodynamic factors but rather, as in the case of anxiety, treat them as incidental to the illness itself, ie, anxiety is not a reflection of an underlying disorder, it is the illness; as a learned maladaptive response it needs to be unlearned. In this model, anxiety, once removed, is not replaced by other symptoms. In clinical practice, however, it is observed that some symptoms occur in a learned maladaptive model, others in a conflict-generated model, and the rest as admixtures of the two. Hypnosis may be woven into most behavioral techniques. In this way, the therapeutic potential of both disciplines may act additively, if not synergistically.

The following methods can be applied to the treatment of the generalized anxiety syndrome.

Hypnotically Induced Relaxation

While neutral hypnosis already assumes generalized relaxation, special hypnotic procedures can allow for its amplification.

The therapist will want to know the anxiety's signature in his particular patient. Where is the anxiety in the body? With what words can it best be described? Does it restrict breathing, speaking clearly, thought, motor performance, or coordination? These notions are important because, during the course of relaxation training, the therapist may choose wording and imagery accordingly. The subject who feels, for example, a burning sensation in the abdomen as an anxiety equivalent, may be asked to imagine sensations of coolness to counteract it; to someone whose anxiety comes out as tightness in the neck muscles, sensations of warmth in these areas may be suggested.

It may be explained to the patient before the induction that relaxation is both a physical and a mental state. It is pointed out that the body, in relaxation, feels slowed down and reluctant to move, the visceral spaces are experienced as comfortably rested, and breathing and heart rate attain natural baseline rhythms. Psychologically, the mind progressively feels detached from concerns, worries, and current stressful emotions.

Asking the subject, "What would you feel like if you were totally and deeply relaxed?" is a useful avenue to explore. In addition to misconceptions in need of modification, the responses may point to useful avenues for tailoring the hypnotic process to powerful preconceived notions.

Knowing that the purpose of hypnotherapy for our patient is relaxation training, the induction is geared to maximizing it. Suggestions are given for feelings which regularly accompany relaxation, ie, restful heaviness of the body. Similarities are drawn to states of mind the subject is already familiar with, which in themselves contain relaxed feelings, ie, daydreaming, reveries, or sleep. At the end of the induction, when the subject has already achieved significant tension reduction, appropriate deepening procedures are used.

The therapist should have at his disposal several procedures for the amplification of relaxation. Some may turn out to be much more effective than others; however, since there is no reliable way to predict beforehand which deepening technique will be most efficient, a trial-and-error approach often has to be attempted. The following techniques are commonly used to dissolve anxiety in the context of the hypnotic trance.

Direct suggestion Direct suggestions for generalized relaxation in the subject who achieves a light to medium trance is often sufficient to attain desired results. Suggestions for total body relaxation, for letting go of tensions, physical and mental, are most effective when rhythmically timed with respiration.

In the same way that anxiety is experienced differently by each individual, so is relaxation. It is important, at the end of the first session, to ask how relaxation manifested itself. If, for example, feelings of floating or drifting were elicited, these same feelings can be directly searched for, brought forth, and expanded in the following sessions for faster induction and further deepening.

Counting method   Some individuals respond best to a counting technique. Many variations of this technique exist. It is explained, for example, that as slow counting progresses from 1 to 20, relaxation will become more and more profound, 20 representing the deepest level of relaxation the subject can attain during the session.

Counting with imagery   Counting may be combined with imagery. For example: "As I count from 1 to 20, you can see yourself walking down 20 steps into the garden of your subconscious mind. In your garden, you will find wonderful feelings of total relaxation flowing throughout your body."

Progressive relaxation   Some subjects are most responsive to a stepwise and methodical method. Individual muscle groups are focused on, starting from the lower extremities or from the head and neck, until all muscle groups are relaxed.

Autogenic training   The production of relaxation in many individuals is facilitated by suggestions or feelings of heaviness and sensations of warmth in the body (see autogenic training, below).

Pure imagery   Imagery techniques for relaxation are the most idiosyncratic of all methods. While, for example, the image of a beach may be attractively soothing for one person, it may leave another indifferent. Preliminary discussions will give the hypnotherapist some idea of what constitutes positive imagery for his patient. During hypnosis, the art of giving imagery suggestions resides in good part on the utilization of multiple sensory modalities—in a beach image, for example, a more engrossing effect can be created by talking about the sights, sounds, smells, and sensations one is likely to experience in such a setting.

Use of touch   Touch, properly used and timed, is a powerful focusing modality for the patient. In the same way that touch may be used to induce analgesia in parts of the body, it may also be applied to suggest deep feelings of relaxation. For example: "As I touch your shoulder, your entire arm becomes deeply relaxed, all the way down to your fingertips. I'll touch your other shoulder and now your forehead; as I do, feelings of deep relaxation begin to drift throughout your body."

Autogenic Training

Autogenic training is a method of psychophysiological self-education containing elements of both hypnosis and meditation. The first of many editions of *Autogenic Training* appeared in 1932. Its author, J.H. Schultz, a German psychiatrist and neurologist, was influenced by research on sleep and hypnosis performed by Oskar Voght at the Berlin Institute some 30 years before. Voght observed that some subjects could produce in themselves states of mind similar or identical to hypnosis by performing certain exercises; and that these self-induced states had therapeutic value — subjects reported improvements in well-being, disappearance of headaches, lowering of anxiety level, and reduction of fatigue and tension. Voght called these exercise "prophylactic rest — autohypnosis."

Schultz streamlined the exercises. He found that most deeply hypnotized subjects invariably experienced sensations of heaviness and warmth in various parts of their bodies and postulated that the creation of these sensations, in a reverse psychophysiological process, could bring about the experience of the trance state.

A series of exercises was designed, in a format of increasing difficulty, and their practice gathered many followers throughout the world. The first of these are physiologically oriented, focusing on the neuromuscular and visceral systems. Subjects are asked, in exercises of introspective creative imagination, to produce sensations of heaviness and pleasant warmth in the limbs — it is easiest initially to produce them in these areas — then in the chest and the abdominal regions. Once mastered, usually after six to 12 months of training, subjects graduate to meditative exercises, which focus on the development of certain higher mental functions.

Preliminary instructions are for the use of a quiet dimly illuminated room, free of disturbances. The subject, in loose clothing, may adopt a fully reclined, semireclined, or a simple sitting posture.

First stage Eyes are gently closed. A gentle bodily introspection eliminates obvious internal muscular tension. The sensations of heaviness of the dominant arm, as it lies on its support, is brought to awareness. Some people find it helpful to repeat silently "my arm feels heavier and heavier." When heaviness is experienced throughout the arm, the same feeling is extended into the other arm through, as Schultz described, a process of generalization; the legs come next, the back, and the regions of the head and neck. When the whole body is experienced as being heavy, the second stage is attempted.

Second stage — warmth For most people, feelings of heaviness are more easily conjured than those of warmth. The same process used to create feelings of heaviness is applied to feelings of warmth, first starting on one extremity, then progressing to the whole body, except for the forehead and temples which are imbued with sensations of coolness. Autosuggestions may help, ie, "my arm feels warmer, pleasantly warm," and imagery may be used, "my body feels like it is resting on the warm sands of the beach."

Third stage — regularization of cardiac rhythm and respiration The object of this stage is not to seek control of cardiac rhythm, as is the aim of some yoga exercises, but to effect a slowdown and regularity of heart function which is congruent with total relaxation. Deep hypnotic and meditative states are accompanied by lowered metabolic work, decreased oxygen consumption, a slow (50 to 60 beats per minute) heart rate, and slower, more abdominal respiration. In the practice of the third stage, awareness is centered on the internal sensations of cardiac pulsations — a hand may be placed over the precordium — and self-instructions are given to help these desired results.

Fourth stage — centering on the upper abdominal region Borrowing from ancient meditative exercises, the subject, having mastered the previous steps, is guided to center a relaxed attentiveness on the upper abdominal regions.

Reported effects of autogenic training Effects of autogenic training are subjective as well as objective. Veteran practitioners talk about a generalized sense of well-being, feelings of energy and stamina, and relative freedom from symptoms commonly associated with stress. Objectively, during autogenically induced states as in meditative states, there is evidence of autonomic and metabolic slowdown.

Jacobson's Method Of Relaxation

While Schultz elaborated his method in Berlin, Germany, Jacobson in the United States worked towards similar goals but through different routes. His method is based on observations that the mere thought of a muscular action brings on electromyographic changes. This, he pointed out, bespeaks of a direct relationship between muscular tonus and psychological tension. For the purpose of achieving relaxation at cortical levels, Jacobson developed a methodical technique involving the progressive relaxation of all muscular groups in the body. Jacobson's method, for proper execution, requires a minimum of six months of training.

Methodology Starting from the tip of one extremity — the right hand, for example — the individual is guided to move his awareness to the wrist, the forearm, in deliberate succession, to cover eventually the totality of the musculature. To help in focusing awareness and to enhance the experience of relaxation, each muscle group is sometimes tensed, then relaxed.

Hypnosis may be used with Jacobson's or modified Jacobson's techniques to stimulate progress. Conversely, and much more frequently practiced, are modified Jacobson techniques used in the context of the hypnotic trance to achieve progressively deeper states of relaxation.

BIOFEEDBACK AND RELAXATION

Through modern biotechnology, many methods of self-monitoring have been developed and applied to the treatment of conditions such as tension headaches, anxiety, neuromuscular rehabilitation, enuresis, hypertension, Raynaud's disease, migraine, asthma, cardiac arrhythmias, bruxism, and epilepsy, among many others.

Applications to anxiety control and to the learning of relaxation states include electromyographic (EMG), galvanic skin response (GSR), thermal, and EEG biofeedback. Due to the fact that anxiety has different manifestations in different individuals, one physiological parameter may be much more useful for anxiety control than another. In some subjects, for example, whose surface expressions of anxiety are translated into muscle activity, EMG training will have greater applicability than, let us say, thermal feedback.

While some individuals do well with biofeedback for anxiety control, others have difficulty generalizing the effects of training to the totality of their experience. Some investigators point out that certain subjects may be able to learn deep muscle relaxation, yet continue to report significant anxiety. Orne and Paskewitz (1974), in studying EEG feedback showed, similarly, that patients could generate high alpha rhythm and still experience debilitating anxiety. These results contradicted the idea that low EMG or high alpha were always incompatible with anxiety.

Some investigators, for purposes of increasing the efficacy of biofeedback treatment, have combined it with hypnosis (hypnobiofeedback). Since hypnosis can facilitate restriction of the field of awareness and promote introspective centering, it is theorized that biofeedback learning can be enhanced and accelerated in the context of a hypnotic state. While this turns out to be true for some subjects, it is not so for all. More sophistication is awaited in this potentially fruitful field, since there is still a paucity of studies using these treatment combinations.

MEDITATIVE TRAINING

In the past three decades, systems of self-training adapted from Eastern cultures, have been practiced on an increasingly large scale in the Western world. The process of meditative training can be seen from different perspectives. From the viewpoint of state theorists, meditation can be understood as a body of methods designed to guide the individual into special conditions of consciousness. Seen from a behavioral perspective, meditation can be conceptualized as a physiological learning process, designed to bring about autonomic slowdown and anxiety control.

In 1935, Dr. Therèse Brosse, a Frenchwoman, traveled to India with a portable ECG machine. She hooked up her machine to a veteran meditator and demonstrated that cardiac rhythm could be influenced by wilfulness. The ECG showed a complete volitional stoppage of the heart for a few seconds. Modern experiments have not only replicated the above effects, but have shown wide-ranging bodily manifestations of meditative training: a toning down of all physiological functions (decrease in heart rate and respiratory rate among others), and of metabolism itself (decrease in oxygen consumption and lactate production) (Wallace 1970).

In spite of considerable interest in meditative training, there remains some confusion in the face of the number of techniques available; there have also been difficulties applying methods meant to be practiced in a sociocultural context so different from our own. In the United States, most of the experimental work has been done with transcendental meditation (TM).

In the technique of transcendental meditation, the subject sits comfortably, eyes closed, for 20 minutes twice a day and maintains persistent awareness of a rhythmically repetitive — usually unspoken — mantra or sound. A universally used sound is "Om," but the word one, which has a similar symbolic meaning, may be substituted.

Studies of TM demonstrate that it stabilizes autonomic functioning and lowers physiological arousal. In addition to its somatic effects, TM is reported to produce ongoing psychological changes such as the positive restructuring of self-concepts, the attainment of feelings of inner peace, and the stabilizing of mood. In addition, veteran meditators describe experiencing poorly definable or describable feelings of mood states, which may be termed states of transcendence.

To be effective, this meditative technique needs to be practiced on a long-term basis. Studies have shown that short-term meditation is no more effective than placebo.

RELATIONSHIP OF HYPNOSIS TO MEDITATION, SELF-HYPNOSIS, AND NEUTRAL HYPNOSIS

In describing the subjective experience of the hypnotic trance, mention was made of alterations in the sense of time flow and of sensations of relative removal from the bonds of the external reality situation. Usually, there is less or no perceived need to move physically, attention is withdrawn from concerns with bodily motion and balance, and there is less or no need to interact socially. Yet, in hypnosis the individual still feels a presence and has awareness of the rapport with another person—that being the hypnotist. In hypnosis, the elements of this relationship are intertwined with the experience of the trance. In hypnosis, part of the patient's psyche is linked to the hypnotist's psyche, in a process of dynamic communication. The hypnotist may communicate with one part of the subject's self, then with another, but there is always a bridge. In the subjective experience of the subject, he or she is not "free." Although the hypnotist may be very permissive, very choice-giving, the confines of the relationship remain.

Self hypnosis brings more autonomy. The link of rapport is broken and a more conscious part of the psyche gives suggestions to another more unconscious part. Usually, self-instructions are fairly specific and invite or reinforce personal change.

Sometimes the individual enters a hypnotic state and does not give himself or herself specific suggestions or directions. This is called neutral hypnosis, a state marked by relaxation, free-floating imagery, and dream fragments or sequences. In neutral hypnosis, the sense of control floats, undirected. The subject may observe and remember or not observe and not remember. It is an unstructured trance state.

If we add one ingredient to this trance state, we have meditation. That ingredient is directed watchfulness.

The meditative trance is similar in quality to the self-hypnotic trance. In meditation, however, the individual starts out with no overt trance-inducing signal, but rather, the resolve to begin, and focuses the observing ego on a part of the body (eg, the solar plexus), a sound (mantra), a symbolic image (mandala), a spiritual feeling, or a universal idea.

Indications for meditative training Although, like most therapies, meditative training has been claimed to relieve many somatic and psychological disorders, its clearest and best documented indication is in the treatment of generalized anxiety.

Demands of meditative training Meditative training takes dedication, motivation, daily practice, patience, and requires a certain soundness of mind from the practitioner. It is not for everyone because it demands an ability to develop a certain mind set of internal relaxed watchfulness, an ability to learn to deal with thought intrusions, and a capacity to accept intermittent progress.

The following case history illustrates the use of clinical meditation.

A 40-year-old businessman came for treatment of anxiety. He mentioned distressing tightness in his chest and an uncomfortable feeling of heat in the upper abdomen. He described a clinical picture typical of a generalized chronic anxiety disorder which he had tried to live with for over a year. He could not recount any significant antecedent changes in his life. A complete medical check had shown no abnormality — even his blood pressure was normal. Surprisingly early during the course of the evaluation, he wanted to talk about treatment options; he had done some thinking and reading on his own and had already come to some decisions about what he did not want. He would refuse medications and was not prepared to spend much time with analytical methods. When hypnotic relaxation training was mentioned, he replied that he did not like the idea of it either. Options were dwindling. He had heard of meditation, and he felt interested and comfortable with this suggestion. The fact that during training he would be "in control" especially appealed to him.

After a preliminary relaxation exercise—a shortened Jacobson technique—he was asked, as he sat calmly, eyes closed, to send his awareness into his upper abdominal region and simply to leave it there for a few minutes. Thought intrusions, he was told, were frequent and were best dealt with by noticing them, letting them pass, and returning to the focus of meditation. He was asked to terminate the experience himself, at his discretion, by simply deciding to do so. Five minutes later, he opened his eyes. The gnawing burning feeling in his abdomen had decreased "by at least half," and his chest cavity felt considerably "lighter." Home practice consisted of two 10-minute sessions a day (this form of meditation is more demanding than TM because more thought intrusions are usually experienced). Six weeks later, he reported a very satisfactory diminution of anxiety symptoms with frequent periods of total clearing.

HYPNOTIC TREATMENT OF PANIC DISORDERS

The most frequently treated phobic disorder is reported to be agoraphobia. The first episode typically occurs in the teens or early 20s. It is so dramatically frightening that all the details of the experience as well as the exact date of occurrence are clearly remembered. A second episode usually occurs several weeks or months thereafter, and increasing anticipatory anxiety, avoidance, and progressive withdrawal develop to the point where, several years later, it is not unusual for the patient to have assumed psychological invalidism. The patient may remain confined, chronically fearful, and depressed. In such patients, there is reported a much higher incidence of alcoholism, hypertension, cardiac illness, and suicide.

Treatment of this disorder has been shown to be most successful if it is multimodal. Pharmacotherapy may include tricyclic antidepressants, monoamine oxidase inhibitors, or alprazolam for the panic attacks; and benzodiazepines for anticipatory anxiety. In addition, beta blockers may be used. Psychotherapy and family therapy address themselves to support, insight and working through. Finally, behavior therapy and hypnosis round out the overall treatment process. Hypnosis is used to decrease anticipatory anxiety, improve self-esteem, raise motivation, and teach the patient that he may regain control over the relaxation process.

SUGGESTED READING AND REFERENCES

Benson H: The Relaxation Response. New York, Avon Books, 1975.
Brosse T: A psychophysiological study of yoga. *Main Currents in Modern Thought* July 1946:77-84.
Cohen ME, White PD: Life situations, emotions, and neurocirculatory asthenia. *Assoc Res Nerv Dis Proc* 1950;29:832.
Deikman A: Experimental meditation, in Tart C(ed): *Altered States of Consciousness.* New York, Doubleday, 1972, pp 203-223.
Diagnostic and Statistical Manual of Mental Disorders, ed 3. American Psychiatric Association, 1980.
Goldfried M, Davidson GE: *Clinical Behavior Therapy.* New York, Holt, Rhinehart & Winston, 1976.
Jacobson E: *Progressive Relaxation.* Chicago, University of Chicago Press, 1938.
Luder M: Behavior and anxiety: Physiologic mechanisms. *J Clin Psychiatry* 1983;44(11, Sec 2):5-10.
Langen D: Autogenic training and psychosomatic medicine, in Burrows G, Dennerstein L (eds): *Handbook of Hypnosis and Psychosomatic Medicine.* Amsterdam, Elsevier/North Holland Biomedical Press, 1980.
Morse DR, Morton S, Furst ML, et al: A physiological and subjective evaluation of meditation, hypnosis, and relaxation. *Psychosomat Med* 1977;39:304-324.
Orne MT, Paskewitz DA: Aversive situational effects on alpha feedback training. *Science* 1974;186:458.
Schultz JH, Luthe W: *Autogenic Training. A Psychophysiologic Approach in Psychotherapy.* New York, Grune and Stratton, 1959.
Seyle H: *The Stress of Life,* ed 2. New York, McGraw-Hill, 1976.
Schuchit M: Anxiety related to medical disease. *J Clin Psychiatry* 1983;44(11, Sec 2):31-36.
Voght O: Zur Kenntnis des Wesens und der pscyhologischen Bedeutung

des Hypnotismus. *Zeitschift fur Hypnotismus* 1894-95:3,227; 1896:4,32,122,229.

Wallace R: Physiological effects of transcendental meditation. *Science* 1970;167:1751-1754.

Walsh R: Meditation practice and research. *J Hum Psychol* 1983;23(1):18-50.

8

Habit Disorders

Barbara DeBetz

The constellation of habits which the individual forms and which constitutes the framework of our daily lives is enormous in its complexity and range. It includes habits of social behavior, habits of bodily functions, such as eating or sleeping habits, work habits, habits of emotional response, and habits of sexual behavior. Once a habit has been formed it is a relatively fixed response. However, we constantly have to readjust or modify our sets of habits to fit the changing demands of our environment.

How do habits develop in the first place? The process of habit formation starts from the first day of life and gives us the basic tools for efficient daily living. Every human being will learn to solve problems and put order into his life by coordinating "actions" and "operations." An operation starts with an action and, if one action is added to another, it becomes an operation. Then, if the operation is repeated again and again, it becomes "automatic" and is, so to speak, a "frozen action" or a habit. Once a particular habit has been formed, that learned process is stored in the memory traces of the brain, making room for new learning. The gradual acquisition of certain sets of habits form our final personality. Small infants, for instance, smile spontaneously until they have reached a certain state of maturation, and then the smile is in response to a specific stimulus like the mother's face or the bottle or anything else that might be anticipated as pleasurable by the infant. If the smile is repeated again and again, eventually the infant will have formed a specific pattern of smiling responses. Or, take a child who learns to button his shirt. The first few times, it needs help from the mother or someone else, and it has to think and put effort into each step involved in the operation of buttoning. After having done it over a period of time, he will have developed a specific habit of buttoning his shirt.

By developing a mosaic of personal habits, we can master our environment with a minimum of thinking energy and maximal output efficiency. These habits become fixed patterns of response even though they require periodic readjustment to the demands of our environment. The set of habits a person has can be compared to a multifaceted, multicolored mosaic where different pieces can be added or deleted without changing the "gestalt" of the whole.

In the same way we develop responses to the world around us, we also develop responses to our own internal world. Our body gives out physiological signals, and we learn to respond to them. We develop eating habits in response to hunger and satiety, sleeping habits in response to physical fatigue, digestive habits in response to the kind of food we eat and the way we eat it, sexual habits in response to our internal sexual urges, just to mention a few. Here again, we tend to develop habits which are appropriate at one time but may be inappropriate at another time. For instance, having stomach cramps in response to having eaten spoiled food is an appropriate response, having stomach cramps in response to frustration in the office or because the teacher gave the student a bad mark is inappropriate. The underlying dynamics are the same. At one point the stomach cramps were meant to get attention that there was something wrong in the system, and it was a call for action; in addition it brought sympathy and concern from the outside world. Thus a pattern might develop to use stomach cramps again when sympathy or attention is wanted and, if effective, the person may develop this kind of maladaptive physiological habit.

In addition to our personal habits, we also develop habits of family and social interaction. Most families have certain habits, typical for their family, such as having dinner together and discussing the events of the day; another family might consider eating unimportant and everyone just grabs something to eat whenever hungry. We will keep some of the habits we developed within our family and will apply them later on when married and having our own families. The same is true for social habits. We develop certain ways of dealing with social situations: how we smile and talk to a person we never met before, how we entertain a group of people invited to our homes, or how we relate to a friend in certain situations. All these are habits we gradually develop. We also develop certain study, work, and leisure habits. By the time a person has reached adulthood, he has become a "collection" of habits, good and bad.

The Czech proverb, "Habits, a shirt made of iron," holds a lot of truth. Many people feel caught and victimized by their habits. This is especially true in interpersonal relationships. When two people meet and are in love with each other, nothing seems to be wrong. But once the "honeymoon" period is over, we start to see and show our "iron shirts," namely our ingrained habits. The more intimate and closer we are to another person, the more we show and see of that tough, fixed pattern. If his or her set of habits overlaps with our own, meaning that there are many similar or complementary habits, then there is no problem. If however, those habits are very much different from our own patterns, it can become a serious problem in the relationship. Once we look at it this way, it becomes easier to separate the habit from the person as a whole, and we can start to "melt" gradually the rigid shirt of iron.

What can be done to change or modify habits that are inappropriate, dangerous, or irritating? Hypnotic treatment strategies have been used with considerable success to help patients overcome or change habits. As mentioned elsewhere, it is not the hypnosis in itself that effects the change, but while in the trance a patient is more responsive to a specific treatment approach. "Restructuring" is one approach to brief symptom-oriented therapy. It involves a mixture of cognitive and emotional components and is meant to give the patient a new perspective in which to view an old problem. Since the trance state is characterized by intense focal concentration, it can be used to maximize the patient's restructuring, relearning, or reorientation towards the habit that needs to be changed. In general, restructuring should be done using a positive perspective rather than fighting the habit, thus putting the emphasis on the individual's ability to change rather than on the habit itself. By restructuring, the patient gains mastery over the symptom and the habit that needed to be changed or overcome. Gradually, through the hypnotic trance and reinforced by self-hypnosis, the individual will learn new responses to situations where at one point the habit had been operating. Eventually the old habit becomes like an old memory but without the intensity and immediacy of the urge which is so characteristic of a habit disorder. In order to clearly help the practitioner to develop treatment strategies to change habits, a few common habits have been chosen to demonstrate the restructuring technique.

TREATMENT STRATEGY FOR SMOKING CONTROL

The cigarette smoking habit and its consequent physical damage constitute a major health problem. Since the surgeon general published his first findings about the ill effects of smoking, numerous people have stopped spontaneously. But there are also a vast number of people who seek help to overcome this habit, especially those people who have had a smoking habit for a long period of time. Considering the fact that many people started smoking without knowledge of the harmful effects of smoking, it is not necessary to spend much time illuminating the reasons for their smoking. The patient comes for treatment because he accepts the premise that smoking is dangerous to his health, and he wants to overcome the urge of smoking.

The clinician should take a brief symptom-oriented history, including questions regarding the length of time the patient has smoked, numbers of cigarettes consumed, and periods of abstinence from smoking. The reasons for wanting to stop should be discussed, as well as fears about stopping. The patient should also be briefly questioned about what aspects of smoking he enjoys the most and at what times, occasions, and situations he anticipates it to be most difficult not to smoke. Questions regarding general physical health should also be asked, with special emphasis on physical symptoms produced by cigarette smoking. After the history has been taken, hypnotic trance capacity should be determined, using one of the previously described tools to measure hypnotic trance capacity, and once that has been established, the trance is induced again, and while in the trance, the specific stop-smoking instructions are given. When the patient emerges from the trance, there will be a posthypnotic discussion (dialogue) elaborating in detail on the points made while the patient was in the trance. Then the patient is instructed in the use of self-hypnosis. For easier understanding here is a short summary of a typical stop-smoking strategy.

While the patient is in the trance the following instructions are given:

"For your body, cigarette smoking is a poison.
You need your body to live.
You owe your body this respect and protection."

Short pause.

"And now think about this: for the last few years you have been polluting your body with the smoke of cigarettes. Every time you inhale the smoke of a cigarette, you actually deprive your body of a basic element of life: oxygen. Your lungs were made to inhale air not smoke. And with every day of not smoking, you will enjoy breathing so much more.

"And now shift your awareness towards your breath and just observe the air go in and out of your body, take a few deep breaths in and out . . . and in and out . . . and just become aware of the pleasant sensation you are getting from breathing.

"And now think about the responsibility you owe your body and the need to protect it from the harm and damage of cigarette smoking. With all this in mind, you have within you the ability to have smoked your very last cigarette.

"And one more time, concentrate on these three commitments you have made today:

"For your body, cigarette smoking is a poison.
You need your body to live.
You owe your body this respect and protection.
Now, think about this and what it means to you."

Pause for a few minutes, then bring the patient out of the trance.

Posthypnotic Discussion

"Notice how this strategy puts the emphasis on what you are for, rather than what you are against. You don't have to fight cigarettes in themselves, all you do is reaffirm your commitment to the health of your body. It is your own free choice not to allow cigarettes to control you and your life. Now you are the one who takes charge and protects your own body from the harm and damage of cigarette smoking."

Smokers, on the whole, tend to be relatively realistic. They are more likely to realize that a habit ingrained over the years cannot be erased magically. One can stop smoking in one treatment session or in a few, but it takes a certain amount of time to adjust to those rituals and activities where smoking has been apart of the routine. At these times, the desire to smoke tends to recur.

This does not mean, however, that the person has to give in and follow through with the behavior of smoking. By admitting the urge — without giving in to the mechanical aspect of smoking — this impulse, which may be strong initially, will become weaker and weaker. Smokers who stop "cold turkey" and never smoke again are usually very determined and highly motivated to keep their commitment for optimum health.

"Furthermore, after you have stopped smoking, if some pressure to light up returns, you know that you have the simple, learned procedure at hand to resist successfully — instead of reaching out for that first cigarette which would trigger the entire 'habit circuit' and in no time you would be back to smoking the same amount as you smoke now. In general, for the person with the smoking habit, it is easier to put it out of his mind completely and focus on the nonsmoking responses, rather than to try and smoke a few cigarettes.

"Now I propose that in the beginning you do the self-hypnotic exercises as often as 10 to 15 times a day. The exercise does not take more than a minute and once you are an expert it will take even less time. And, while in this state of buoyant repose, concentrate on these stages of your treatment program:"

Stage A "Study, learn, and repeat these three incisive sentences which have proved effective in helping many patients to overcome the smoking habit. Say these clear commitments to yourself silently, or aloud if you prefer.

"Reiterate the assertions slowly and meaningfully again and again so that they penetrate deeply and fixedly, imprinted indelibly in your mind. Do this each time that you are in the self-induced trance. Furthermore, instruct yourself to keep reminding yourself of these directives any time that you might think of lighting up after the float:

"For my body, smoking is a poison.
I need my body to live.
I owe my body this respect and protection."

Stage B "While in the trance shift your focused concentration to your inner body . . . and project that 'x-ray picture' on an imaginary TV screen. Now . . . 'look' intensively at your lungs and other inner organs — where you can visualize most clearly the harm being done by the tars, nicotine, the blackening by the cigarette smoke. Then ask yourself:

Do I really want to insult my body with another cigarette? Do I want to kill the life in my body by smoking now? Don't I have the responsibility to respect my body and protect it from the harm and damage of cigarette smoking? Think through the answers to these questions thoroughly and emphatically."

Stage C "Now . . . picture your lungs and other internal organs in close-up, zooming in and scanning those imagined organs (as you personally picture them) on your imaginary inner TV screen. Study in detail how those affected, functioning parts of your living body look to you, as harmed by your smoking . . . see the damaging smoke drifting around, clinging, doing them harm.

"Then, shift your concentration and imagine that your lungs and other smoke-smudged organs gradually improve after you give up cigarettes and stop inflicting this damage on them. And feel the new, pervading sense of mastery and control."

The patient is given an opportunity to ask questions, and then the session is ended. One or two follow-up sessions are recommended. In the follow-up sessions emphasis is placed on the new nonsmoking habits which the patient has developed; questions about situations when it was most difficult not to smoke and alternatives for those occasions are discussed. At the end of the session the three-point stop-smoking strategy is repeated while the patient is in the trance. Long-term follow-up shows an approximate success rate of 28% for hypnotic smoking control treatment approaches.

EATING DISORDERS

Hypnosis can also be a very useful adjunct in the eating disorders discussed below.

Anorexia nervosa The essential features are intense fear of becoming fat, disturbance of body image, significant weight loss, refusal to maintain normal body weight, and amenorrhea (no menstrual periods) in females. It is a serious illness with emotional and physical symptoms. Those afflicted need medical care as well as individual psychotherapy and often additional family therapy. If not treated, the mortality rate is 15% to 21%.

Treatment should be undertaken as soon as possible when the symptoms of drastic and accelerating loss of weight occur below the desired weight. While the use of hypnosis can be a definite aid, medical treatment should be supervised closely.

Bulimia The main features are recurring episodes of binge eating, accompanied by an awareness that the eating pattern is abnormal. The binges are followed by a feeling of not being able to stop eating voluntarily and by a depressed mood and self-disapproval. The binge is usually cut off by abdominal pain, sleep, outside interruption, or self-induced vomiting.

Individuals with bulimia exhibit great concern about their body weight and usually have tried repeatedly to diet in the past. Often they feel that their lives are dominated by conflicts about eating. The disorder usually begins in adolescence or early adult life, with serious medical and psychological problems developing. Psychotherapy and a thorough medical checkup are urgently indicated. With bulimia, the body may not be distorted visually — as with the obvious skeletal appearance characteristic of anorexia. However, there is great danger of serious damage to vital organs within the digestive system.

Simple obesity This eating disorder is not included in the Diagnostic and Statistical Manual of Mental Disorders (DSM-III). It is considered a physical disorder, since it is not generally associated with any distinct psychological or behavioral syndrome. Most patients who come for hypnotic weight control fall into this category, and their range of overweight can be anywhere above their ideal body weight.

Depending on the particular eating disorder the patient presents with, the treatment approach will differ accordingly. All patients who come to use hypnosis to lose weight should have a physical examination to rule out any physical problems that might be present and need medical care. Once this has been established, the program should be developed to suit the individual needs of each particular patient. The bulimic and anorexic patient needs close medical supervision and sessions should be relatively frequent. In the patient with simple obesity, a program should be designed so there is ongoing patient-doctor contact, but it does not have to be on a weekly basis. According to the patient's progress, the sessions can be spaced out every two, three, or even four weeks. When the patient returns to the office, the discussion should include changes the patient has made and difficult situations that have occurred and how he/she coped with them. The patient's weight should be recorded, and then the patient goes into the trance and the therapist reinforces the "eating strategy," emphasizing different areas at different times. The strategy should be based on what was discussed before. Patients should be encouraged to continue therapy until they have reached their ideal body weight. Once there, it is usually beneficial to schedule periodic follow-up visits to ensure weight maintenance.

Below is a generalized eating strategy which should be adjusted according to the particular disorder. Obviously, the anorexic patient would not be told "for your body overeating is a poison," but would be told something like "starving yourself is an insult to your body." To the bulimic patient, the instructions would be "gorging and purging are an insult to your body. . . ."

After the hypnotic trance has been induced, the obese patient is told the following:

"For your body, overeating is a poison.
You need your body to live.
And you owe your body respect and protection."

Short pause.

"Now concentrate on this: Your goal is to slim down to your ideal body weight which you have set at _____ pounds. And while you are slimming down, you want to become a thin eater. A thin eater is a person who looks at food for what it is: Food is nutrition for your body; once you use it for something else, however, then it becomes a poison for your body. Also, the thin eater is a person who is in touch with his body's needs: He eats when he is hungry and stops as soon as he has had enough. You, however, have lost touch with your physical sensations of hunger and satiety. Many times you eat without being hungry and you don't stop when your body has had enough. In order to lose weight and keep it off, you have to learn to be a thin eater at all times.

"One way to become a thin eater is the following: From now on, you want to make every eating experience an exercise in critical analysis of the food in front of you. And, before you put any food into your body, look at that food for 10 or 15 seconds and ask yourself these two simple questions: Am I really hungry? and, Is this food in front of me the right food in amount and quality? If the answer is 'yes,' then go ahead and eat with pleasure. If the answer is 'no,' however, then take this food and put it where it belongs: back into the refrigerator or right into the garbage can, not into your body. Your body is your precious physical plant through which you experience life.

"And one more time concentrate on these three points: *For your body overeating is a poison. You need your body to live. You owe your body respect and protection.* With this in mind, you have within you the ability to reach your goal. Now think about this and what it means to you in your own private way." (Short pause.)

After the patient has been brought out of the trance, a posthypnotic discussion follows about the different aspects of thin eating as compared to fat eating. Towards the end of the session, the patient is encouraged to keep a daily food diary, recording everything that is eaten each day. The patient is also encouraged to engage in daily physical exercise or increase the general level of physical activity. Then the patient is given an opportunity to ask questions and, once all questions have been clarified, the patient is instructed in the use of self-hypnosis which he should do as many times a day as possible, and while in the trance say to himself the three statements: *"For my body overeating is a poison. I need my body to live. I owe my body respect and protection."*

The foregoing examples of a treatment strategy for a smoking habit and eating disorders can also be used for any other habit disorder, such as nail biting, hair pulling, poor sleeping habits, or inappropriate work habits. The basic approach remains the same. After a brief symptom-oriented history has been taken, a treatment strategy should be chosen that helps the patient to restructure his attitudes toward the old maladaptive habit and allows him to gradually develop new responses. In general, any treatment strategy that is chosen should be positive. The emphasis should be on the patient's commitment for change, rather than on fighting the habit. For instance, in the smoking strategy the emphasis is placed on the patient's body and his protective attitude towards it rather than on fighting cigarettes.

With the added leverage effect of the hypnotic trance, the patient can now use the receptive attentiveness of the trance experience to intensify his focus on how to overcome the "bad" habit. Depending on the kind of habit disorder that is being treated, the patient can achieve control and mastery over his habit by putting the problem into a new perspective. By using self-hypnotic exercises as outlined above, the patient will start to feel familiar with the new attitudes and behaviors which initially require a certain amount of effort and motivation but eventually will become again "frozen" actions and, at that point, a new habit has been formed. Depending on each particular patient's trance capacity, motivation, and ability to change, the number of sessions necessary to develop new habits will vary. The average number of sessions ranges from one to five. The endpoint can be determined when the treatment goal has been reached, and the patient feels comfortable with the change.

SUGGESTED READING

Bjorntorp P: *Interrelation Of Physical Activity And Nutrition On Obesity*. Symposium on Diet and Exercise, Synergism in Health Maintenance, American Medical Association, 1982.

Bruch H: *Eating Disorders*. New York, Basic Books, 1973.

Campbell SF: *Piaget Sampler. An Introduction to Jean Piaget Through His Own Words*. New York, John Wiley & Sons, 1976.

Spiegel H, Spiegel D: *Trance And Treatment, Clinical Uses of Hypnosis*. New York, Basic Books, 1978, pp 165-220.

Stunkard AJ (guest editor): Eating disorders: Obesity. *Psychiatric Ann* 1983;13(11).

Stunkard AJ (guest editor): Eating disorders: Anorexia and bulimia. *Psychiatric Ann* 1983;13(12).

9

Pain Control

Barbara DeBetz

Using hypnosis for pain control has been one of the least debated areas in the field. Ever since Esdaile's dramatic descriptions in 1846 of operations performed on his patients, there have been numerous reports of the effectiveness of hypnosis in treating both chronic and acute pain. However, since the introduction of ether (1846) and chloroform (1947), the use of hypnosis in surgery died out rapidly because of the convenience and predictability of chemical anesthesia as compared to hypnotic procedures. In recent years clinicians have renewed their interest in using hypnosis in pain control either as the sole agent or in conjunction with medication.

Pain has an important signal function. It is a message to the brain that something is wrong somewhere in the system, and it is a call for action. There are many unanswered questions about the nature of pain. One question is whether pain should be considered one of the senses, along with touch, vision, smell, and hearing. Melzack and Wall (1965) argued strongly against considering pain to be a sensory modality because there are multiple pathways and several pain centers localized in the brain. Then there is the distinction between pain and distress and between pain and anguish.

Melzack and Wall called this theory the gate theory based on the fact that thresholds for pain could be altered by opening or closing a gate to nerve impulses carrying pain messages. This theory has been diagrammed by Melzack and Casey (1968) as shown in Figure 9-1.

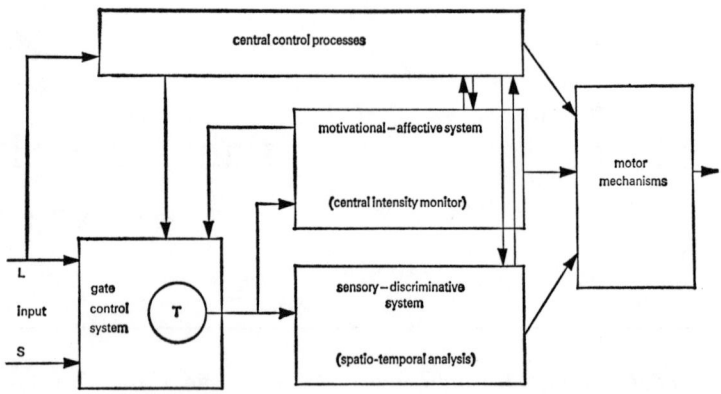

Figure 9-1 Conceptual model of the sensory, motivational and central control determinants of pain. The output of the T cells of the gate-control system projects to the sensory-discriminative system (via neospinothalamic fibers) and the motivational-affective system (via the paramedial ascending system). The central control trigger is represented by a line running from the large fiber system to cetral control processes; these, in turn, project back to the gate-control system, and to the sensory-discriminative and motivational-affective systems. All three systems interact with one another, and project to the motor system. Reproduced with permission from Kenshalo DR: *The Skin Senses.* Springfield, Ill, Charles C. Thomas, 1968.

If we begin at the lower left, we note an input by way of large and small fibers entering the dorsal roots of the spinal cord. The large fibers (A-alpha fibers) transmit impulses rapidly. Note that they divide into two portions, one going directly to higher brain centers, the other going to the gate control system in the dorsal horn of the cord. This system transmits spatiotemporal information about stimulation that is essentially innocuous, that is, without pain. Surgical lesions in this system do not reduce intractable pain (White and Sweet, 1969). Very extensive lesions are necessary to produce any deficits in this system. The large fibers also have collaterals to the gate-control system as shown. Basic to the theory is the idea that these larger collaterals antagonize the excitations produced in the pathways of the smaller fibers.

The smaller fibers enter the cord from the afferent roots. They make synapse with the short fibers of the dorsal horn cells, and these cells from a gray-matter column running the length of the cord. This ascending system has rich connections to the paramedial system in the core of the brain stem subserving aversive motivational and effective functions: the reticular formation, hypothalamus, medial and intralaminal thalamic structures, and (via the thalamic structures) the limbic forebrain system. Ventrolateral spinal tractotomy is a routine neurosurgical procedure performed for intractable pain.

The anatomical details are not shown on the diagram, but the main points for our purposes are that there are the two distinct pain systems: a sensory-discriminative system and a motivational-affective system. This much is well established. The diagram proposes that the balance between these systems is affected by a gate control at the level of the dorsal horn, affected not only by the interactions of impulses from the large and small fibers but by efferent consequences of central processes and feedback from the motivational-affective pain system.

The two afferent systems are now known both neuroanatomically and neurophysiologically, but the details of operation of the gate-control system are still controversial. There can be little doubt, however, that some central controls are operative. For instance, new evidence from animal experimentation shows that electrical stimulation of cells surrounding the cerebral aqueduct in the core of the brain stem abolishes reactions to pain for the duration of the stimulation (Liebeskind and others, 1973). These same cells are sensitive to morphine and are believed to be the biochemical receptors for this pain reducer.

There is now also an increasing body of evidence that the stimulation of the large fibers, bearing innocuous information, can reduce pain. The first report was by Wall and Sweet (1967). They inserted needle electrodes into nerve bundles near the site of pain and found that stimulation of the large fibers reduced the pain for a period of a few minutes to hours after the stimulation. Why the effect should endure was one of their questions, but it may be that once a feedback loop has been interrupted, the felt pain can be reduced for a subsequent period of time.

The relationship of the gate theory to pain reduction in hypnosis is evident. In fact, the possible relationship was first pointed out by Wall (1969), one of the authors of the gate theory. He noted that the suggestions of the hypnotist might affect the modifiable afferent sensory pathways, that this action might suppress not only messages that trigger conscious sensation but also some segmental reflexes. (1) Hypnotic evidence shows that central processes can modify the perception of pain as a consequence of stressful stimulation. (2) The aspect of pain that is found more modifiable, when hypnotic methods are used, is the suffering, hurt or anguish. This is coherent with the modifiable nature of the motivational-affective pain system. (3) The aspect of pain that is least modified is the information regarding the sensory aspects of stimulation. This is again coherent with the uncensored information expected from the sensory–discriminative system.

Pain perception shows a wide range of subjective variation. Some people are more responsive than others. These subjective differences may be due to the fact that the human brain contains systems whose specific function is to modulate or inhibit sensitivity to painful stimuli. This endogenous neural inhibitory system contains both opiate and serotoninergic links, and it appears to be composed of a set of phylogenetically primitive areas of the brain, structures that line the medial and caudal portions of the ventricular system. It has been found that an organism's response to emergency situations is a reduction in sensitivity to pain, involving a pain inhibitory system referred to as the endogenous opioids, the endorphin system. Stress-induced analgesia was an empirical finding, although it has been observed all along. There are numerous examples of soldiers wounded in battle or athletes injured in sports activities who inhibited any kind of pain perception while under the stress of the situation and only became aware of it once the stress had been removed.

The literature also has numerous reports of insensitivity to pain among patients with schizophrenia as well as among patients with affective disorders. The depressed patient seems to be less sensitive to pain than when in a manic or normal state. While previous explanations for these phenomena have been mainly of a psychological nature, recent discovery of opiate-like substances (endorphins) has prompted the suggestion that these phenomena might be mediated by the neural networks integrating pain perception.

In addition to the two pain theories described briefly above, there is also much clinical and experimental evidence that individuals show differences in the way they process pain perception psychologically. This reactive psychological component depends on a variety of factors, including environmental, socioeconomic, cultural, and even religious factors. For example, a martyr who would rather die than betray his religious values might decrease his pain perception to a minimum even if tortured. On the other extreme, a woman being raped will most probably experience the invasion of her body with maximal intensity of pain and anguish.

It is useful to think of pain perception as a complex interaction between the physical stimulus that causes the pain, the neurophysiological reactions, and the psychological reactive component to it. There are certain pain situations where the physical component is so overwhelming that the psychological reactive component is minimal, such as passing a kidney stone, the pain of acute pancreatitis, the sudden pain of a myocardial infarction, or receiving a crushing injury to a limb. This does not mean, however, that hypnosis is only useful in treating pain of psychological origin, so-called functional or psychosomatic pain. On the contrary, pain alleviation is possible with pain of the most obvious organic origin, such as the pain of cancer or burn wounds. Functional and organic pain problems must not be too sharply separated, for functional pain may hurt as much as organic pain. Hypnosis, like any other tool in medicine should be used with sound clinical judgment and only if the circumstances are appropriate. For instance, it would be quite inappropriate to induce total analgesia in a patient having an acute abdomem. Here the pain has a life-saving function of signaling that there is something wrong that needs urgent attention. If hypnotic strategies are designed for acute pain situations, it should always be borne in mind to leave the pain strategy open-ended to allow the natural signal system of change in symptomatology to take place. Pain as a warning of serious physical damage can represent vital information that in normal, even stressful, circumstances ought not to be ignored. Patients who are congenitally insensitive to pain, or those who are addicted to narcotics and/or are on methadone maintenance therapy, very often develop serious, occasionally fatal, medical problems in the absence of an effective pain signal system.

Due to the limited knowledge we have about the phenomenon of hypnosis, we do not fully understand at what level of the pain-perception circuit hypnosis works. It may act at the purely psychological level, the neurophysiological level, or a combination of both. It also may be that it acts at different levels in different kinds of pain situations, and it may depend on the motivation of the patient seeking hypnotic pain control.

In addition to taking a detailed history of the circumstances of the pain condition, it is helpful to distinguish between "rewarding" pain and "nonrewarding" pain. Nonrewarding pain conditions are usually more responsive to hypnotic manipulation. Among the nonrewarding pain conditions are pains of some chronic illnesses, including cancer, burns, and the like. Rewarding pain conditions are those where the patient is getting secondary gain out of being in pain. In such situations, the clinician should first deal with the secondary gain before any attempt at pain control should be made. This is frequently the case in compensation cases. If a patient is being compensated financially and is sent by the insurance company's physician to attempt hypnotic pain control, odds are that this patient will not be very motivated to utilize hypnotic strategies to conquer the pain. The secondary gain is higher than the primary gain of alleviating the painful condition. If, however, you have a patient with a nonrewarding pain condition, such as a burn or cancer patient, in this situation you might have an individual highly motivated to participate and take an active role in the pain management. In nonrewarding pain conditions, the patient feels he is the victim of the pain, therefore he welcomes anything that takes away the feeling of being victimized and allows him, at least to a certain degree, to be an active participant who takes charge and control.

TECHNIQUES FOR TREATMENT OF PAIN

Muscle relaxation and distraction   Before inducing the actual trance for hypnotic pain relief, it is useful to give the patient a brief example on pain perception. The patient is given the following instructions:

"As you may know, the more tense you are, the more severely you are feeling the pain, and the more relaxed you keep your muscles, the less the pain. To make this clearer, make a tight fist, stretching out your arm straight. Now make your fist even harder and harder. Hold it tight like this for a few seconds and concentrate on the pain you feel as a result of this muscle tension. Now, open your fist, relax your hand and notice how the pain from the muscle tension disappears."

This exercise impresses upon the patient the fact that he can control his perception of pain by reducing the muscle tension.

The next example shows the patient his ability to decrease pain by distraction. Here is what the patient is told:

"Now pinch the web of skin between your thumb and forefinger until you feel pain. Hold for a few seconds and register the intensity of the pain. Now stop and let go. Then try again, pinch the web of skin between your thumb and forefinger until you feel the pain. Once you are aware of the pain, shift your awareness to something else. Think of a peaceful stroll through the woods, or just focus your attention on anything around you in the room, a painting, a piece of furniture, whatever catches your interest. Now focus all your attention on your imagery or the object you are looking at. Now stop and tell me if you were equally aware of the pain while pinching the web and concentrating on it as you were when you focused on something else."

Invariably, the patient will have experienced less pain while he distracted himself from the pain of the pinch and allowed his mind to focus on something else. Now, we have the second strategy to change the pain perception, notably that the patient is able to pay attention to something other than the pain. By distracting attention, the patient can reduce the pain considerably or even block it out totally.

The following case history will show how these two above techniques of reducing muscle tension and distraction were used simultaneously.

The patient was a 65-year-old woman who complained of chronic pain radiating from her right temple to the back of her head and neck. Five years ago she had a craniotomy and a meningioma was successfully removed. However, after surgery she was left with a chronic pain condition which her surgeon thought was due to some nerve damage resulting from the operation. She was on codeine which made her feel drowsy and nauseated. At the time of her first visit she was depressed and felt hopeless about herself. She did not like taking medication and felt utterly useless because she could not even take care of her household duties. Her request was to learn hypnosis in an effort to get off the pain medication and control her pain by other means.

The patient's hypnotic trance capacity was tested, and she was found to fall into a mid-range trance level. She was then given the above-described examples to teach patients to become aware of pain perception. Then she was asked to evaluate the intensity of her pain using a scale from 0 to 10, where 0 meant pain free and 10 was the strongest pain level. She put herself at an 8 level. After the trance was induced, she was given instructions to gradually relax all the muscles of her body with special attention paid to her face, head, and neck. Once that was done, she was instructed to imagine that she was looking at a screen (a television or movie screen) or just a blank wall and on this she was to project a scene from her past. We had discussed beforehand what would be relaxing to her. She had chosen rolling green hills from her childhood neighborhood in Ireland. While in the trance she was to focus intensely on this scene and try to capture every detail of it. She remained in this state for approximately five minutes. When she came out, she described the scenes that had come into her mind. She was surprised at some of the details that had emerged, such as seeing herself running down the hill with a childhood friend she had not thought of in 60 years. She recalled names, faces, even the dresses they wore. When asked about her pain intensity, she answered with astonishment: "I was not aware of it at all. Now that you ask me, I can feel it a little bit. But if I had to give it a rating, it can't be more than a 3."

She was then instructed how to use self-hypnosis and was told to do the self-hypnotic exercises including both parts, first the muscle relaxation then the imagery, for as many times a day as possible, preferably every few hours.

There were two follow-up visits in the course of three months. During her last visit she reported 90% improvement, meaning that she was able to reduce the pain by doing her hypnotic exercises daily. She had decreased her pain medication to almost nil. She would take the medication only if the pain would come on suddenly and be at a high level of intensity, but this had become rare. In addition to the major improvement of the pain condition, her depression had lifted as well. She was able to go about her daily activities almost at the same level as she had before surgery.

Pain control through dissociation It is possible to imagine a separation from the painful stimulus. It is similar to what was described above as distraction. Dissociation, however, is more intense and can even go to the point of hallucination.

The following case history will clearly demonstrate the difference between dissociation and distraction.

The patient was a 47-year-old woman who needed reconstructive hand surgery. She had a neuroganglioma in her right thumb causing pain, discomfort, and decreased mobility in that hand. This was especially restricting to this woman because she was a painter and sculptor. When she came to the office first, we used hypnosis to distract her from the pain. She used vivid imagery to take her mind off her hand. She loved to imagine that she was floating on a clear mountain river, the air crisp and clean, and the water refreshingly cool. She became quite efficient in the use of distraction, and she would do it a few times a day when the pain had become excruciating and she had to stop painting. However, the condition got worse, and her surgeon insisted on operating on the hand.

Due to the patient's history of various drug allergies, she wanted to have local anesthesia, instead of general. A few sessions prior to her surgery we "rehearsed" the hypnotic strategy that she wanted to use while undergoing surgery. Due to the fact that she was a painter and sculptor, we used the imagery that her right hand and arm would become heavy, cold, and completely numb, that her arm would not be hers anymore but be part of a beautiful sculpture. The surgeon was the sculptor and her arm and hand was to be a piece of pink marble, completely dissociated from her. The artist (surgeon) would carve the best looking and best functioning hand and arm from the pink marble. The patient was very relaxed prior to surgery, she received minimal sedation, and reported postoperatively how interesting the entire procedure had become. She had "watched with fascination that lump of pink marble being transformed into a beautiful hand and arm . . . " Needless to say, she did well postoperatively and eventually she was able to use her hand with full recovery to normal mobility and no pain.

Transference of glove anesthesia Another method which is used quite commonly and successfully is to induce analgesia first in a hand or one finger which then can easily be transferred to the painful area. It is easier to produce analgesia in the nonpainful area first and later transfer to the painful site. One way of inducing glove anesthesia is the following. After the patient has shifted into the trance, he is told this:

"Imagine yourself sitting in a dentist's chair. Picture the lights in the room, the feeling of the chair, the smells and sounds of a dentist's office. Remember the time when he took out that large needle and injected novocaine into your gum. Try now to recreate that feeling of the pressure in your gum and the gradual numbness spreading throughout your jaw and your cheek. Feel your cheek getting more and more numb, that numbness spreading throughout cheek and mouth; then when you are ready, let your hand float up and touch your cheek and feel how numb it is, and as you feel that numbness, let the numbness spread from your cheek to your fingers, so that your hand begins to feel numb. Then let your hand float over to touch the part of your body in which you feel some discomfort and let that numbness spread. This numbness becomes a filter through which you experience pain, and you learn in this manner to filter the hurt out of the pain."

This kind of pain control can be used either for existing pain conditions, such as cancer pain, but it can also be used prior to expected pain, as for example, numbing of the cheek and jaw in preparation for dentistry, or numbing the abdomen in preparation for childbirth.

Sensory alteration of pain When this kind of pain control is used, it may be helpful to give the patient a few examples to demonstrate how one can alter the perception of one sensation to another. For instance, the patient is told: "When you put your hand into a pot of boiling water, what do you feel? Heat or pain? Or, if you defrost the icebox and keep your hands in there trying to get the ice out, what do you feel? Cold or pain?" Usually the patient is puzzled and realizes that only the temperature or the pain was felt, but not both modalities at the same time. "You see, your brain can only process one modality at one time. Now, we are going to use this knowledge and apply it to you. Let's see if you will be able to transform your pain into a warm glow or a fresh, cold, tingling numbness."

The following case report will clearly demonstrate this technique. A 47-year-old woman was referred by her neurologist for hypnotic pain control. The patient suffered from right-sided trigeminal neuralgia for the last three years. The painful episodes would last from a few days up to several months. At times her pain was so severe that she could not do any activities at all. She was a psychology professor, and her career suffered badly because of her frequent neuralgic attacks. At the time of the visit she was on carbamazepine but it did not help very much. She had also been tried on a variety of other medications, including amitriptyline with only minor improvement.

Her hypnotic trance capacity fell well into the upper mid-range. After giving her the above-described examples about altering pain to temperature sensations, we decided on the following imagery: the patient had once spent a vacation in the Swiss Alps, and she had enjoyed very much swimming in the ice cold crystal clear mountain lake that was there. We used this imagery and, while in the trance, she imagined herself floating in the water, the right side of her face submerged in the water. The cold water would gradually spread over her right cheek, her right temple, her right forehead, and skull, and the cold water would slowly be felt as a cold, tingling numbness, filtering the hurt out of the pain. She would remain in the trance anywhere from three to ten minutes until she had reached a certain degree of relief.

She practiced these self-hypnotic exercises up to ten times per day, and within two months she had achieved total pain control. She was followed over a three-year period with periodic visits. She continued to do the self-hypnosis occasionally but increased it as soon as she had some preliminary symptoms of the neuralgia, such as a sore sensation over her right cheek, increased tearing of her right eye, or sporadic firing of the nerve. She also decreased the carbamazepine and even stayed medication-free for a period of several months.

The same principle is used for the treatment of migraine headaches. It is a well-known fact that during a migraine attack there is vasodilation of the cerebral blood vessels and vasoconstriction in the peripheral circulation, causing cold hands and feet. Based on this knowledge, the strategy that has been used successfully is geared towards pain relief through alteration of temperature perception. The patient in trance is instructed to imagine that a huge cake of ice, or an ice-helmet, is put over his head. (The cake of ice visualization should leave an opening for the mouth and nose to avoid a feeling of claustrophobia or suffocation.) Then the patient is told to imagine the cold ice gradually spreading over the top of the head, face, and neck until there is a cold numbness filtering the hurt out of the pain. Once the patient is able to perceive the cold, tingling numbness, he is instructed to shift his awareness towards his hands and feet and imagine that all the blood that was congested in his head is now floating down into the hands, fingers, and fingertips, as well as into the feet, toes, and tips of the toes. While the patient's head is numb and cold, he is now told to concentrate on his hands and feet getting warm and comfortable. The patient should remain in the trance and concentrate on these different sensations until there is a sense of relief.

There have been reports that hypnosis can alter blood flow, but regardless of the degree of actually occurring changes in the circulation of the head, hands and feet, the majority of migraine patients finds a considerable degree of relief by using this strategy. They can learn to abort the migraine in its earliest stage, and many patients have reported a drastic decrease in the need for analgesic medication.

Patients with chronic arthritis or muscle tension disorders such as the low-back syndrome usually prefer a strategy that uses heat or warmth rather than a cold, tingling numbness. Therefore it is always helpful to ask the patient in advance what kind of modality he considers more soothing and pain relieving for himself.

Individual methods The methods described above for pain control can be used either singly or combined. In addition, there is a wide range of methods which may be tailored to any given patient depending on his hypnotic trance capacity, motivation, interests, capabilities, and the particular circumstances of a given pain condition.

In addition to the physical benefits of hypnotic pain control, it is also an ego-strengthening device to help the patient feel he is a participant who has a certain degree of control over his condition. Hypnosis is a valid tool for the treatment of pain either by itself or in combination with medication or another pain control methods.

SUGGESTED READING AND REFERENCES

Davis CD, Buchsbaum M, Naber D, et al: Altered pain perception and cerebrospinal endorphins in psychiatric illness. *Ann NY Acad Sci* 1982;398:366-373.

Elton D, Burrows GD, Stanley GD, et al: Chronic pain and hypnosis, in Burrows GD, Dennerestein L (eds): *Handbook of Hypnosis and Psychosomatic Medicine*. Elsevier/North Holland Biomedical Press, 1982, pp 269-293.

Esdaile J: *Mesmerism in India and its Application to Surgery and Medicine*. London, 1846. (Reissued as: *Hypnosis in Medicine and Surgery*. New York, Julian Press, 1957).

Hilgard ER: Hypnosis in the treatment of pain, in Dennerstein L, (eds): *Handbook of Hypnosis and Psychosomatic Medicine*. Amsterdam, Elsevier/North-Holland Biomedical Press, 1980, 233-268.

Hilgard ER: Modern gate theory of pain in relation to hypnosis and acupuncture, In Unestahl LE (ed): *Hynosis In The Seventies*. Orebro, Sweden, Veje Verlag, 1975.

Kelly DD: The role of endorphins in stress-induced analgesia. *Ann Acad Sci* 1982;398:260-271.

Liebeskind JC, Guilbaud G, Besson JM, et al: Analgesia from electrical stimulation of the periaqueductal grey matter in the cat: Behavioral observations and inhibitory effects on spinal cord interneurons. *Brain Res* 1973:50:441-446.

Melzack R, Wall PD: Pain mechanisms: A new theory. *Science* 1965;150:971-979.

Melzack R, Casey KI: Sensory, motivational, and central control determinants of pain, in Kenshalo DR (ed): *The Skin Senses*. Springfield, Ill, Charles C Thomas, 1968.

Melzack R: *The Puzzle of Pain*. New York, Basic Books, 1973.

Spiegel H, Spiegel D: *Trance and Treatment*. New York, Basic Books, 1978, pp 251-262.

Wall PD, Sweet WH: Temporary abolition of pain in man. *Science* 1967;155:108-109.

Wall PD: The physiology of controls on sensory pathways with special reference to pain, in Chertok L (ed): *Psychophysiological Mechanisms of Hypnosis*. New York, Springer Verlag, 1969, pp 107-111.

White JC, Sweet WH: *Pain and the neurosurgeon: A forty- year experience*. Springfield, Ill, Charles C Thomas, 1969.

10

Hypnosis in the Hospital Setting

Gérard Sunnen

Hospitalization, even with all available medical technology, remains a trying experience. The same concerns, apprehensions, and fears exist today, as they did centuries ago, in the face of dangers to well-being and to life itself.

In the midst of an alien environment and sophisticated diagnostic and therapeutic procedures, the hospitalized individual's concrete needs are usually well attended to. But beyond the social facade of fortitude, the consultant who is allowed to be privy to deeper feelings will almost always see the strained denial of fear and the relentless tension of anticipatory anxiety. Contemplating unfamiliar procedures or complex operations, uncertain of their medical or even personal destiny, fighting feelings of helplessness, patients are receptive to support and reassurance.

The psychological well-being of hospitalized patients is important not only for humane considerations, but for reasons connected to health and recovery; patients do better when undergoing procedures, recovering from operations, or surmounting the side effects of treatments, if they are relaxed, rested, and feeling hopeful. It is well appreciated that the stress of the milieu can mitigate against the optimal resolution of illness. In cardiac care units, for example, the constant high arousal level can destabilize the delicate process of cardiac healing and increase the likelihood of cardiovascular complications.

The ability of hypnosis to induce deep relaxation, to quell anticipatory anxiety, to increase tolerance to noxious stimuli, and to amplify positive imagery can be adapted to the hospital setting for maximizing the psyche's contributions to healing.

HYPNOSIS IN SPECIAL PROCEDURES

Procedures performed under local anesthesia with or without sedation are often contemplated with the same apprehension as those requiring general anesthesia. The idea of being conscious during a procedure is reassuring in one respect and unsettling in another: the sense of presence and control is maintained; but at the same time, there is uncertainty as to how the experience will be negotiated. Even a simple procedure like a spinal tap can be approached with dramatic imagery: the picture of a needle in the mind is often much larger than it is in reality. The same is true, for example, in cardiac catheterization, in bone marrow biopsy, or even in the benign sigmoidoscopy.

The anticipatory anxiety generated by the patient's fantasies about a procedure should not be neglected. It can turn a routine stay in the hospital into a nightmarish experience and sensitize the patient negatively to future hospitalizations.

The following case history illustrates some of the principles of hospital hypnosis.

A 52-year-old woman who had never been hospitalized was admitted for work-up of a lung shadow. She was to undergo a bronchoscopic examination on the following day. When she became agitated and highly anxious, a consultation was requested. Hurriedly wiping some traces of tears to appear more presentable, she looked distraught and restless in her bed. The procedure, explained to her in a cursory and hurried way, had left her in a state of panic. She imagined a large, cold, straight metallic tube being pushed into her throat, and saw herself in the agonies of choking. Yet, on another level, she spoke amazingly candidly and rationally, "Doctor, I think I know I have cancer and that's what they'll find tomorrow. I've been a smoker for many years. But that, I think, I can come to terms with." The procedure was reexplained to her. The tube was described and even drawn out as flexible and as leaving plenty of space for air to pass. The more relaxed she would be, the more easily air could pass. She heartily agreed to a hypnotic attempt at relaxation. Because of her high level of anxiety, a more directive approach was used, as well as a touch technique (see below).

With her permission, her hand was taken and, gently and slowly as she closed her eyes, brought straight out in front of her. Given suggestions of heaviness, the arm slowly waved itself down, the hand gently releasing itself, until it came to rest on the bed. Her face looked serene and her respiration had slowed down considerably.

After the hypnotic induction, the goal centered on achieving deeper relaxation. Then, freed from the tyranny of her imagination, clear and precise suggestions were presented to her. "You will feel the tube, but your throat and all your air passages will be relaxed; and it will not bother you. You will have plenty of air and with each breath you will feel more and more relaxation sweeping through you. You may, in fact, be so relaxed that you may feel the whole experience as being some distance from you, even far away [dissociation]. Until then, you'll find yourself thinking very little about the procedure, and you may not even think about it at all [repression of anticipatory ideation]."

The next day she had the bronchoscopy. Completed in just a few minutes, the patient had been amazingly calm. The tube had met so little resistance and there were so few secretions that the surgeon called afterwards to get a better understanding of this phenomenon. Asked about her experience, she described how, conscious of the whole procedure and feeling peaceful, she had felt the tube inside her chest, as from a distance, and had mused to herself making a game of it, imagining it was a little train going through some tunnels.

SOME PRINCIPLES OF HOSPITAL HYPNOSIS

While the hospital environment is apt to be busy and noisy, this is no barrier to hypnotic intervention. Even in the most cacophonous ICUs, patients can be efficiently guided into a deep hypnotic state. Patients requiring consultations are usually experiencing discomfort, pain, and fear, and for this reason may need approaches which are not routinely used in a private office. Hypnotic methods need to be more rapid, taking into account a psychological set found more frequently in such settings: an increased sense of dependency and an urgent wish to be relieved quickly of the oppression of discomfort and tension.

The first task of the consultant is to establish rapport with the patient by conveying an understanding of his global emotional experience and by communicating a genuine desire to help. The resultant empathic bridging provides the springboard for the induction. If the patient is in significant pain or is markedly anxious, this first transaction need not take long—just a few words to let the patient know that his state of mind is understood and to explain what the immediate goals of hypnosis are. Formulating these goals, ie, calm, relaxation, freedom from pain, etc, before the induction, mobilizes the patient's interest and cooperation, soothes apprehension about hypnosis, and provides a focus for the treatment.

Due to the unsettled or clearly distraught psychological state of many hospitalized patients needing hypnotic intervention, directive techniques are preferred. The patience and steady attentiveness required of longer, strictly verbal permissive techniques is too demanding and impractical. Too many interruptions, both internal and external, mitigate against this process. The patient needs and wants the therapist to actively point the way towards less painful, more serene states of mind. Suggestions are direct, gentle, insistent, unequivocal. "Please pay attention to my voice, I'd like you to send all of your mind into your arm. Stay with me as I talk to you. As I take your hand, concentrate on the rhythm of your breathing . . . "

USE OF TOUCH

Touching the patient in the context of a doctor-patient relationship, when properly timed and when done in an appropriate way, can have a tremendous positive impact. In psychotherapy, at the end of a difficult and painful session, for example, a handshake initiated by the therapist, communicating empathy and caring, can have a lasting therapeutic effects. The same for the bedridden hospitalized patient or for the patient about to undergo an operation in the last minutes of wakefulness.

There are complex social cultural parameters governing body contact, and judgment in this regard is necessarily very intuitive. Touching the patient during induction in a private office setting is usually not recommended. For many people, this is too anxiety-provoking. In the hospital, however, because it is an "open" environment, in the sense that privacy is limited, therapeutic touching is not only welcome but is highly effective. Used judiciously as part of the hypnotic induction, touching provides an immediate focus towards positive sensations, away from negative ones (ie, pain, discomfort), and rapidly solidifies rapport.

HYPNOSIS IN REHABILITATION MEDICINE

Patients who have suffered catastrophic illnesses usually have long journeys to recovery, requiring global readjustments in life goals, family dynamics, and self-image. Stroke victims, amputees, and those with spinal cord injuries, for example, need multilevel support to help in coping with their shattered world. Rehabilitation is a physical as well as psychological process, aimed at helping severely destabilized patients regain optimal physical competency and psychological integrity. In the face of cataclysmic loss of bodily function, such as in hemiparesis, aphasia, or quadriplegia, the formidable mental adjustments often put into question the will to live. Even minor injuries, such as the loss of a finger, can engender severe depressions, with social withdrawal, suicidal ideation, and destruction of self-esteem. It is clear that adaptations to such tragedies often have even more to do with their symbolic representations than with their objective realities.

The heartening advances of rehabilitation medicine are tied not only to technology but to the realization of the complex psychological needs of patients. Staff know how important their self-generated enthusiasm is in mobilizing their patient's optimism and how loss of motivation can stunt progress or foster regression. The following case history illustrates hypnotic applications to the difficult process of rehabilitation.

A 35-year-old executive returning late from a company meeting was driving on a rainy highway. In his next memory, he was being carried on a stretcher from a ditch, lights of ambulances flashing. He remembered the slow realization that he could not move his arms or legs; even worse, that the feelings in his limbs had been snuffed out. He could only move his head from side to side and sink into his quadriplegic nightmare.

A consultation was called because three weeks into his rehabilitation, he was not progressing satisfactorily. He did poorly on the tilt table and was not eating well. This highly intelligent man talked lucidly about his visions of his future: he would no longer be able to work; his already shaky marriage would crumble; and he would most likely need someone's full-time care to help him live. With all this against him, he asked, how could he find any motivation to live? Such arguments are difficult to counter rationally. Given the premises, he had drawn his own conclusions. To tap into his motivational reservoir, his intellectualizing network would have to be bypassed.

He accepted and readily responded to hypnotic induction. Whereas before the accident his intellectualizing may have posed a defensive barrier to induction, his sense of despair and wish to be helped facilitated the process. Obviously, arm levitation could not be used. Placed in the middle of his forehead, a thumb's pressure provided a focus for his attention. Eyes closed and looking internally at the contact point, a count was started. Suggestions for clearing the mind of all thoughts were followed by inward concentration on the flow of breath in and out of his lungs. He was asked to take three deep consecutive breaths, and was told that at the end of the third breath he would enter hypnosis.

During the course of the ensuing series of ten treatments, hypnotic intervention was aimed at different levels of his psyche. Aside from suggestions of physical comfort, efforts were made to extend the range and intensity of his sensory awareness. The boundaries of his touch sensitivity were determined, and suggestions given to expand them further into his chest and back, as far as he could each time; each time he gained some, albeit little, sensory ground. He was progressively guided to experience a state of mental calm and peace which included a sense of acceptance, mixed with a willingness to try his very best to get better; finally, he was asked to avoid all negative future scenarios created by his imagination. He would have time to get to them later, but for the moment, his rehabilitation's full potential would have to be attempted with all the positive energy he could muster. To this end, he began to apply himself diligently. He graduated from the tilt table, grew stronger, and was eventually sent home with outpatient support services.

For hospitalized patients with catastrophic illnesses, hypnotic intervention does not stop with the first consultation. A series of treatments over time, as in the above case, is most effective, since the goals are approached in small steps in the course of weeks or months. In such cases, it is advantageous to teach patients self-hypnosis for use in relieving periods of private distress.

Hospitalized children can also benefit from hypnotic intervention. The following case history illustrates the judicious use of hypnosis in a hospitalized child.

Gary, a boy of 6, had suffered multiple fractures in an automobile accident. After two weeks in bed with extensive casts and traction, he was becoming sad, cranky, and restless; he cried easily, complained bitterly, and ate and slept poorly. He could not take the prolonged immobility or the itching in his casts, even with the support of a sympathetic staff. Yet he would have to continue treatment for several more weeks.

Rapport was established by talking about his interests, his complaints, his worries, his wishes. Wouldn't it be nice to be able to take all this without being bothered so much; to be able to relax and sleep better and feel more at ease; and even be able to enjoy playing more or watching TV? The nod was wistful. Like most children, he had no trouble using his imagination. He could easily, eyes closed, project himself into a movie house or see himself watch TV, becoming completely engrossed in it. Without difficulty, he could see himself in another time, on vacation, when he was feeling happy and relaxed; once he connected to these feelings, they could expand and fill him, even though he was nearly immobilized in all his casts. Suggestions were given for "healing fast, for feeling good and comfortable; for sleeping and eating well; for keeping a cheerful mood." He went home two weeks sooner than expected.

SOME NOTES ON PEDIATRIC HYPNOSIS

Children are apt to be very good hypnotic responders. The same principles apply as with adults, but some modifications have to be made to account for their greater capacity for imagery, developing cognitive structure, and language proficiency. In very young children hypnotic communication relies more heavily on gestures, mime, and touch. In the beginning, as with adults, rapport must be established. In the hospital especially, children tend to be suspicious of new personnel and have to be "won over." This may take one or, if necessary, several visits, until feelings are comfortably communicated. During that time, the therapist gathers data about his patient's personality, place in the family, cognitive assets, likes and dislikes, style of speech and personal imagery, and intuitively determines when the child can be asked to cooperate in a "relaxation," "sleep," "imagination," or "dream exercise or game." The therapist's demeanor and attitude are important in this regard. Someone who is too aloof, stiff, or using diction out of synchronicity to the child's will not achieve empathic bridging quickly, if at all. Care must be taken not to come across as too authoritative or hurried. Genuineness is quickly picked up by children.

Visualization technique Children starting at age 4 or even sooner have potent visualization potential. Many techniques exist which involve the child in a fantasy process, beckoning him to progressively deeper, more relaxed states of mind. An imagined TV set showing his favorite cartoon, a movie screen, a happy vacation memory, can all be recreated, in which the child is a viewer watching an unfolding scenario, or a participant, as an actor or a star of the show. The scenario is progressively unfolded to bring out positive feelings, sensations, and moods and to absorb therapeutic suggestions.

Mime technique In the context of good rapport with the child, the hypnotherapist can mime the desired effects of hypnosis: relaxation, a sleeplike state, or heaviness and subsequent numbness of the arm extending to other parts of the body, etc. Mime has powerful suggestive impact.

Eye roll, arm levitation This method can be adapted to the age and individual needs of the young patient and is very suitable for hypnosis of the older child (6 and up).

Arm sway and drop (reverse arm levitation) In the context of good rapport, the hypnotherapist, taking the wrist of the young patient, induces a gentle swaying motion or suggests progressive heaviness of the extended arm as a way to lead into therapeutic suggestions.

SUMMARY

Hypnosis is greatly underutilized in hospital settings. Used appropriately, it can, at the very least, make the experience of hospitalization less traumatic and more humane. Its main indications are the following:

1. In hospital anxiety, the patient, in a context of diagnostic or therapeutic uncertainty, forced dependency in a new environment, experiences stress symptoms which interfere with global well-being and decrease resistance. Hypnotic intervention can be aimed

at teaching the patient to relax and to regain a sense of poise and mastery.

2. In anticipatory anxiety, the patient's negative scenarios for the outcome of illness create noxious inner turmoil. Hypnosis can not only be a great dissolver of anticipatory anxiety, but can also cognitively restructure visions of the future to the patient's advantage.

3. Special procedures are best carried out when the patient is physiologically calm. In these conditions, procedures tend to be shorter, smoother, and to result in less physiological antagonism from the patient. On another level, the potential psychological trauma is bypassed, resulting in a better posthospital adjustment.

4. In some hospitalized patients, motivation for recovery is hampered by feelings of futility. Hypnosis can be used to strengthen hopefulness and optimism.

SUGGESTED READING AND REFERENCES

Ambrose G: *Hypnotherapy with Children*, ed 2. London, Staples, 1961.

Burrows G, Dennerstein L (eds): *Handbook of Hypnosis and Psychosomatic Medicine*. New York, Elsevier/North Holland Biomedical Press, 1980.

Cheek DB, LeCron LM: *Clinical Hypnotherapy*. New York, Grune & Stratton, 1968.

Crasilneck, HB, Hall JA: *Clinical Hypnosis: Principles and Applications*. New York, Grune & Stratton, 1975.

Gardner GG, Hinton RM: Hypnosis with children, in Burrows GD, Dennerstein L (eds): *Handbook of Hypnosis and Psychosomatic Medicine*. New York, Elsevier/North-Holland Biomedical Press, 1980.

Gardner G, Olness K: *Hypnosis and Hypnotherapy with Children*. New York, Grune & Stratton, 1981.

Hartland J: *Medical and Dental Hypnosis*. London, Balliere, 1966.

Hilgard ER, Hilgard JR: *Hypnosis in the Relief of Pain*. Los Altos, Calif, William Kaufman, 1975.

Kroger WS: *Clinical and Experimental Hypnosis in Medicine, Dentistry and Psychology*, ed 2. Philadelphia, JB Lippincott, 1977.

Scott, D. *Modern Hospital Hypnosis*. Chicago, Year Book Medical Publishers, 1974.

11

Hypnotic Approaches in the Cancer Patient

Gérard Sunnen

Cancer is a multisystem illness, involving all levels of the organism, from the cellular to the psychological. While the baffling varieties of its manifestations continue to be elucidated, there is a growing awareness of its complex psychological dimensions. Of most humane concern is the intense travail and the varieties of pain cancer patients are likely to experience — pain from the disease itself, from its treatments, and from the deep intrapsychic and social changes it induces. Recently, there has been an expanding appreciation for the varied needs of cancer patients: needs for support, openness of communication, and understanding; and for the sensitivity and professionalism with which issues of death and dying need to be approached.

Hypnosis finds applications at several levels of cancer care. First, it is useful as a means of dealing with the symptoms of the disease itself: pain and symptoms referable to specific organ systems, and nonspecific general symptoms, ie, fatigue, malaise, irritability, and insomnia. Secondly, hypnosis is useful in the management of the side effects of cancer treatments. This is very important because side effects of chemotherapy and radiation are often so uncomfortable that they may cause the patient to drop out of therapy. Thirdly, cancer patients are faced with major psychological adjustments. Many view their diagnosis as a death sentence and are forced to grapple with profound existential issues. Hypnosis has a place in helping with this difficult situation. Lastly and somewhat controversially, hypnosis has been aimed at modifying the course of the disease process itself through the use of imagery. While the first three applications are of proven clinical efficacy, the last has mostly anecdotal support. It will be briefly mentioned, however, because of its current interest and for the fact that it raises interesting issues for research.

HYPNOSIS IN MANAGEMENT OF CANCER SYMPTOMS

Symptoms attributable to cancer are as varied as its subtypes. Pain, the most common symptom aside from fatigue, is highly variable. Some patients with advanced disease report no pain at all, while others suffer from it at the onset. Pain may be dull, constant, diffuse, and related to motion, or it may be sharp, localized, and lancinating. The hypnotherapist will want to know about the history of the pain, its distribution, quality, and evolution, in addition to details about its context in the patient. Is the patient anxious? Depressed? Are there associated symptoms producing concern or worry, ie, difficulty in breathing, swallowing, or walking?

There is a relationship between pain and anxiety. Usually, one will feed into the other, making both worse. If the patient is feeling despair, pain is experienced as more unbearable and hopelessly endless.

Paying attention to the contextual milieu of cancer pain may suggest adjunctive treatment strategies, such as evaluation for a trial of antidepressant therapy or for the addition of antianxiety medications.

In altering or removing pain, care must be taken not to block its warning function. In the early stages of the illness, a new discomfort may herald metastasis and may be important for purposes of changing therapeutic course. In more advanced cases, this is not as relevant. The following case history demonstrates some principles of hypnosis use in symptoms due to cancer.

A 55-year-old man, with a diagnosis of left colon carcinoma made two years previously was referred by his oncologist for hypnotic treatment of pelvic pain. A recent check-up had revealed metastatic liver nodules, and a bone scan showed a solitary lesion in the right pelvic bone. He had started taking aspirin, propoxyphene and, occasionally, codeine. This highly educated man was able to appraise the complexities of his situation with aplomb mixed with open-mindedness. He did not wish to discuss the issues of his death. Those, he said, were clear to him, and many of the feelings he had could not, in his estimation, be communicated adequately. He felt that to do so would be a squandering of his precious time. He stated succinctly, however, that he wanted to be with his family, have time to take care of certain business matters, and be as free as possible of discomfort. His intermittent pelvic pain interfered with walking and with the sexual aspects of his life. Very ambivalent about plans for chemotherapy and radiation, he opted for more time to make a decision about these matters.

He was successful in achieving a medium trance with the arm levitation technique. By gently and repeatedly touching his right hand with a finger and associating suggestions for numbness and coolness (some patients prefer warmth), glove anesthesia was induced. A prick of a thenar skinfold was perceived by him as a faraway flicker of touch. He was told that, by way of the same mechanisms that removed the sensations in his hand, he could induce numbness in any part of his body. His numb hand was brought to rest on his right pelvis. "Imagine the numbness and coolness in your hand, seeping through your skin, extending into your body with each breath, as if you've touched the smooth surface of a pond, and see the concentric rings spreading out in all directions. Please keep your hand there until the numbness is clearly all through your pelvis." His hand, after three minutes, lifted off. "Your ability to repeat this process will stay with you, and you will be able to use it on your own by learning self-hypnosis."

The relief he obtained was variable. Sometimes he could dispel the pain completely and could walk comfortably for up to half an hour. At other times, especially when his mood was low, he could obtain only partial relief. But overall, he felt more relaxed, consequently had more energy, and was more active. He later applied self-hypnosis to help himself cope with chemotherapy.

TECHNIQUES OF PAIN RELIEF IN CANCER

It is well documented that hypnosis has significant potential for alleviating cancer pain, and when used adjunctively with analgesics, serves to reduce their dosage. The following approaches may be used singly or comcomitantly in any patient, depending on hypnotic aptitude.

Direct suggestions for pain removal Some patients respond adequately to direct suggestions that the pain will diminish in intensity to the point of becoming unnoticeable. There is some controversy as to whether the word "pain" should be used during hypnosis or be replaced by a euphemism such as "discomfort." There is no proof that either approach is superior.

Glove anesthesia with extension As in the case above, hypnotic focusing on a part of the body, ie, the hand, is sometimes helpful for the production of sensory alterations. Once the experience is established in the hand, it is only a small psychological step to transfer it to other parts of the body.

Altering the configuration of pain The representation of pain in the mind—the pain "body image"—may be compressed to occupy a "smaller space." Neurophysiologically, this corresponds to a shutting down of association networks. Suggestions are made for the pain to decrease in size as the patient is asked to visualize the pain as a three-dimensional shape in space, shrinking progressively.

Altering the qualitative aspects of pain As pain fibers project from thalamic nuclei through diffuse thalamic radiations to cortical areas, they become associated with the process of experiencing. The feelings within the experiential process are unique to each individual and are malleable by cortical influences. Hypnotic intervention may be able to change the quality of the pain, to associate it with coolness or warmth, or numbness, in order to make it less insistent and less immediate.

Control of anticipatory anxiety Anxiety acts synergistically with pain. Anticipatory anxiety — the anxious sensation that pain may worsen — heightens the dolorous experience. Helping the patient relax, both at the moment and for the future, can provide significant analgesia.

Imagery With some individuals, hypnotic absorption in imagery is the best antidote for pain. The type of imagery to be used with a particular patient will depend on their eidetic style (visual, auditory, somesthetic) and on their personal experience (happy, uplifting, "high" memories). The hypnotherapist obtains an impression of the imagery potential of the patient during the preinduction interview and feeds back appropriate images during the trance.

Dissociation Dissociation is a very important and effective mechanism by which the pain may be experienced as an event moving away from the locus of awareness. "It is there but it doesn't feel like it belongs to me," is a common comment from subjects adept at dissociation.

HYPNOTIC TREATMENT OF CHEMOTHERAPY SIDE EFFECTS

Particularly bothersome for some patients are certain side effects of chemotherapy. Sometimes, in a simple conditioning paradigm, a patient will become so sensitized by the aftereffects of the first treatments that subsequent sessions, or even the thought of them, bring about great autonomic distress. Typically, a nausea-vomiting response occurs one to two hours after the injection of antineoplastic drugs, and it is estimated that at least 25% of chemotherapy patients manifest such respondent conditioning.

Conditioned anticipatory emesis can make chemotherapy excrutiatingly unpleasant and contributes directly to patients dropping out of treatment. Antiemetics are usually marginally effective and have side effects of their own.

Hypnosis has been well documented to have therapeutic potential for conditioned anticipatory emesis. The following case illustrates some of the treatment principles in this condition.

A man of 26 with stage three Hodgkins disease was receiving combination chemotherapy (doxorubicin, bleomycin, vinblastine). Although physically tolerating this regimen well, he became increasingly distressed by nausea following his treatments. Experienced for the first time less than one half hour after the first treatment, it had worsened each time. At the third treatment, he was reporting significant nausea as well as anticipatory anxiety several hours before treatment was started, and described how the mere picturing of the doctor's office had brought him waves of autonomic distress. At the fourth treatment, the feelings had brought on repeated vomiting. Antinausea drugs (prochlorperazine, trimethobenzamide) were unsuccessful, and he was referred for hypnotherapy.

Induction using a standard arm levitation method was followed by medium trance. An ideomotor technique was used to signal degrees of internal discomfort. Every time nausea was experienced, his right index finger moved sideways on the armchair cushion. When it was relieved, he moved it back towards his other fingers. To counter nauseous feelings, sensations of hunger were elicited. A history was obtained of his favorite foods, restaurants, and memorable gastronomical experiences; associated feelings of appetite and hunger were hypnotically rekindled. By small steps, he was asked to imagine the sequence of events characteristic of a typical treatment session, and feelings of hunger were repeatedly reinforced. When nausea appeared during the process, suggestions were given for total relaxation until it disappeared. During the third session, he was able to visualize himself receiving treatment with no comfort. In the actual treatment situation, he experienced only mild nausea but no vomiting, and he was able to finish his entire regimen protocol.

HYPNOTIC APPROACHES TO DRUG-INDUCED NAUSEA

Relaxation   Inducing deep feelings of relaxation is an effective antinausea treatment. Deep relaxation induces a slowing down of peristalsis and a toning down of autonomic hyperactivity. Many patients, by relaxation alone, will significantly decrease the intensity of their experience of nausea. Direct suggestions for the removal of nausea are often of marginal effectiveness. Because nausea stems from massive and extensive autonomic discharge, it tends to be difficult to dispel. Some individuals, however, will easily respond to simple suggestions for its dissolution.

Using hunger as an antidote   Feelings of hunger and the physiological changes that they produce are neutralizing to nausea. Direct suggestions for hunger sensations are made, sometimes using the patient's favorite food, or foods served on special holidays. When the patient is actively nauseous, it is usually best at first to induce a deep state of relaxation, then to introduce hunger imagery.

Imagery   For some subjects, imagery remains the most effective pathway for autonomic control. Images have the property of beckoning the subject's awareness away from negative experiential states to positive ones. Conjured images of significant positive experiences, or of fantasized idealized settings, may lead the patient into experiencing feelings that are incompatible with distress.

Systematic desensitization   This is perhaps the longest method but it is the most consistently successful, especially in refractory cases. The patient needs to be motivated to participate in this, at times, somewhat tedious procedure. Relaxation, or relaxation with suggestions of hunger, gradually paired with a narrative of the treatment situation, from its most neutral to its most adversive conditions, until the latter can be experienced, in the imagination, in a more acceptable context.

Dissociation   Some individuals are very adept at hypnotically pushing nausea away from direct experience. It can then be felt as distant, "barely touching me," or as a tolerable annoyance, thus defusing the gnawing immediacy which may lead to an emetic response.

Sensory alteration Suggestions may be given for the nausea to change in quality to make it less stressful. Having the patient imagine drinking a tall glass of icy water, feeling the sensations of soothing cold seeping through the chest and abdomen, can take the edge off the burning sensation nauseous patients are apt to experience.

HYPNOSIS IN TREATMENT OF PROBLEMS PERTINENT TO CANCER PATIENTS

We have talked about the applications of hypnosis in the care of the outward manifestations of cancer: pain, fatigue, insomnia, and treatment side effects, among others. Beyond these surface symptoms lie deeply personal, intrapsychic issues. The cancer patient is usually experiencing great inner turmoil and is working with massive personal readjustments. While modern treatment procedures have lightened the ominous implications of a cancer diagnosis, many patients are directly thrown into difficult issues of dying and death.

The hypnotherapist needs to develop a personal philosophy of death, especially as it relates to dealing with patients, and needs to elicit, understand, empathize, and respond to the complex manifestations of death anxiety. Before hypnotherapy begins, especially if it is aimed at helping intrapsychic adjustments, illness and patient must be understood in their relationship to each other. Sometime during the first interview, several questions have to be examined. What is the reality of the patient's clinical situation? How does he fit into the social-familial milieu? To what extent has the patient incorporated the diagnosis and its implications? How much denial is being used? What are his strengths and adaptation potentials? What are the patient's philosophies, wishes, aspirations?

Kubler-Ross (1969) delineated five psychological stages of dying: denial, anger, bargaining, depression, and acceptance. It is well recognized that these stages, which may occur as sequelae of any poignant loss, are highly variable in each patient, may not happen in this sequence, and may often manifest themselves concurrently. Some dying individuals use denial until death; others accept, then deny; others spin into a catastrophic depression or mobilize themselves into a frenzied angry rebellion. The dying patient often experiences a multitude of feelings, many of which are poorly describable. The sensitive clinician should be alert to feelings of hope, bitterness, alienation, envy, self-blame, love for life, dependency, and existential despair, among many others. Rare is the individual who accepts death with wisdom.

HYPNOTIC APPROACHES TO PSYCHOLOGICAL ADJUSTMENTS TO CANCER

Cancer patients are commonly prone to certain feelings and coping mechanisms. Besides anxiety, which is universal, there are feelings of helplessness and loss of control; feelings of alienation and aloneness; feelings of guilt—that somehow their forbidden impulses have brought about this great misfortune; and feelings of loss of self-esteem—that somehow they have proven to be supreme failures.

Before proceeding with hypnotherapy, one must have a clear idea of its goals. This will be influenced by the therapist's own approach to death. For some, it is to help the patient look straight on at reality and to map out a rational course of action. Some physicians indeed, in a counterphobic stance, like to "lay it on the line" with a clear breakdown of prognosis, sequence of probable events, and even approximate time of death. Other physicians, as a way of giving in to their own anxieties, are adept at skirting the issues even if confronted directly by their patients.

The goal of hypnotherapy is to maximize the quality of life, to bring comfort, sustenance, freedom from stress and pain, and to work out meaningful family communications. It is important for the therapist to respect denial and work with it, not against it; to acknowledge the legitimacy of the patient's angers; to identify the losses that are faced; to offer ongoing emotional support, yet not give false hopes; to discuss issues relating to personal meaning; to acknowledge the patient's wishes and rights to remain in control by providing choices about treatment; to identify misconceptions the patient may have; and to help set obtainable goals and maintain a hopeful attitude towards achieving them. It is important for the therapist to "be with" the patient at all times and to stay on the lookout for personal reactions which mitigate against the patient's welfare: anxiety, annoyance, withdrawal, or feelings of hopelessness.

Hypnotic approaches to treatment will necessarily be geared to these goals. Very often, hypnotic alleviation of pain and regulation of physiological functions (digestion, insomnia) will bring about marked psychological recovery. The following hypnotic techniques may be used in the context of total patient care.

Inducing relaxation and teaching self-hypnosis The patient's experiences of a state of mind (hypnosis) containing profound feelings of relaxation, peacefulness, tranquility, and freedom from worry in the context of a positively altered state of consciousness can be very uplifting and inspirational. Practicing self-hypnosis to recapture these feelings of relaxation further adds to a sense of inner mastery.

Ego strengthening Feelings of guilt and self-blame, hopelessness, loss of self-esteem, alienation and aloneness, dejection and hurt, and helplessness, which are so commonly experienced by cancer patients, can be directly countered by suggestions reaffirming the integrity of the self-image.

Strengthening repression A 28-year-old man with malignant melanoma complained that the oppressive thoughts of the reality of his cancer were constantly with him. "Doctor, there isn't ten minutes that I'm not thinking about it. I can't enjoy myself, I can't live." Hypnosis was used to expand these "free" periods from ten minutes to hours, and to help him suppress and repress the constant insidious thoughts of finality. He was then much more able to enjoy each day for itself.

Imagery Imagery may be used to strengthen adaptation mechanisms, induce positive feeling states, brighten self-esteem, speed adjustments to stresses, foster acceptance of the illness, focus on realistic goals, decrease anticipatory anxieties, ease hurt, anger, and alienation, and to bolster feelings of self-control and hope. Visualizations of many different types are woven in with appropriate suggestions. Effective images are often created by the patient and the hypnotherapist, working as a dyad. The patient will usually communicate, verbally or nonverbally, his preferences for certain kinds of imagery. Through rapport and intuitive understanding as well as the exploration of different themes, imagery becomes fitted to the patient. Scenes of seashores, mountains, underwater places, or fantasized lands may be as absorbing as the personal memories of peak experiences. Through the medium of hypnotic imagery, the patient can learn to transcend many of the negative cognitions he may have built about his condition.

OTHER USES OF HYPNOSIS IN CANCER CARE

Recently, there has been an interest in imagery not only to guide cancer patients to better frames of mind, but to influence the disease process itself. It is postulated that imagery, through connections with neurohumoral mechanisms, has indirect influences on the immune system. Strengthening the immune system, in this holistic approach to the mind/body problem, could slow down the progress of cancer. Anecdotal case reports tend to support the beneficial influence of imagery. Longitudinal studies, however, have yet to be carefully designed.

The following case history provides an example of this kind of imagery usage in cancer. Although results cannot, of course, be held conclusive, the technique serves to illustrate an important therapeutic function: it can give the patient the sense of playing an active role in the treatment of his cancer and can be instrumental in developing a feeling of being in charge of the situation.

A 30-year-old woman studying the performing arts, noted a small nodule in her left armpit. She preferred not to think much of it. Three months later she woke up in the middle of the night with pain in her axilla radiating to her breast. She received surgery as well as radiation and chemotherapy for carcinoma of the breast. She coped well with some nausea and hair loss and was stabilized. Although there was no evidence of metastasis, she became increasingly worried about this possibility. She came for consultation for the specific reason of learning imagery techniques and with strong motivations to do everything in her power to vanquish her cancer. She had attempted visualization exercises with the help of a therapist, which consisted of imagining white globules, symbolic of her healthy defenses, fighting off black particles, symbolic of cancer cells. She had the conviction, however, that with the help of hypnosis, she could create more effective imagery. This in fact happened. Her eidetic potential was stronger, more "real" in the context of trance.

In medium to deep hypnosis, she repeated the exercise but came to realize that it did not feel right for her—she did not like the idea of fighting, even though it was only globules. Because of this philosophical penchant, it was suggested that she create an image of a glow, a light, or sunlike aura, to see and feel it enveloping her, growing in intensity with each breath until she could actually feel warmth throughout her body. The symbolism was clear but it was nevertheless discussed to make it more meaningful: light, she said, for her symbolized life, and had the property to outshine everything, including cancer. She felt comfortable with this imagery and has continued to use it daily in self-hypnotic practice. It gives her a feeling of self-control and inner peace because she is actively participating in her own health care.

SUMMARY

The adjunctive hypnotic treatment of cancer may be directed to any level in the spectrum of its manifestations. Physical symptoms of cancer, the most common of which is pain, and the physical effects of its treatment (weakness, nausea, and vomiting) may be modified to render daily living more palatable. Hypnosis may also be woven into psychotherapy to assist in the uniquely personal adjustments each patient has to make to his illness.

SUGGESTED READING AND REFERENCES

Ader R (ed): *Psychoneuroimmunology*. New York, Academic Press, 1981.

Bommer K, Newberry BH (eds): *Stress and Cancer*. Toronto, Hogrefe, 1981.

Cangello VW: Hypnosis for the patient with cancer. *Am J Clin Hypn* 1962;4:215-226.

Dash J: Hypnosis with pediatric cancer patients, in Kellerman J (ed): *Psychological Aspects of Childhood Cancer*. Springfield, Ill, Charles C Thomas, 1980.

DiGiusto EL, Bond HW: Imagery and the autonomic nervous system: Some methodological issues. *Perceptual Motor Skills* 1979;48:427-438.

Erickson MH: Hypnosis in painful terminal illness, in Haley J (ed): *Advanced Techniques of Hypnosis and Therapy: Selected Papers of Milton Erickson, MD*. New York, Grune & Stratton, 1967.

Hall H: Hypnosis and the immune system: A review with implications for cancer and the psychology of healing. *Am J Clin Hypn* 1982/1983;25(2-3):92-103.

Hilgard ER, Hilgard JR: *Hypnosis in the Relief of Pain*. Los Altos, Calif, William Kaufman, 1975.

Hoffman E: Hypnosis in general surgery. *Am Surg* 1959;5:163.

Kubler-Ross E: *On Death and Dying*. London, Macmillan, 1969.

Meares A: Meditation: A psychological approach to cancer treatment. *Practitioner* 1979;222:119-122.

Melzack R, Torgerson W: On the language of pain. *Anaesthesiology* 1971;34:50.

Newton B: The use of hypnosis in the treatment of cancer patients. *Am J Clin Hypn* 1982;25(2-3):92-104.

Redd W, Rosenberger P, Hendler C: Controlling chemotherapy side effects. *Am J Clin Hypn* 1982/1983;25(2-3):161-172.

Rogers MP, Dubly D, Reich P: The influence of the psyche and the brain on immunity and disease susceptibility: A critical review. *Psychosomat Med* 1979;41:147-164.

Sacerdote P: Hypnosis and terminal illness, in Burrows G, Dennerstein L (eds): *Handbook of Hypnosis and Psychosomatic Medicine*. Amsterdam, Elsevier/North-Holland Biomedical Press, 1980, pp 421-440.

Sachs LB: Hypnotic self regulation of chronic pain. *Am J Clin Hypn* 1977;20:106.
Simonton OC, Mathews-Simonton S, Sparks TF: Psychological intervention in the treatment of cancer. *Psychosomatics* 1980;21:226-233.
Spiegel H, Spiegel D: *Trance and Treatment: Clinical Uses of Hypnosis.* New York, Basic Books, 1978.
Sternbach R: Clinical aspects of pain, in Sternbach RA (ed): *The Psychology of Pain.* New York, Raven Press, 1978.
Zeltzer L: The adolescent with cancer, in Kellerman J (ed): *Psychological Aspects of Childhood Cancer.* Springfield, Ill, Charles C Thomas, 1980.

12

Hypnosis in Psychosomatic Medicine

Gérard Sunnen

The Group for the Advancement of Psychiatry Report, *Psychopathological Disorders of Childhood: Theoretical Considerations and a Proposed Classification* (1966), refers to these disorders as ones in which there is significant interaction between somatic and psychological components with varying degrees of weighting of each component.

This definition provides a concept of dynamism, of interactional interdependency between body and mind which very correctly identifies a central feature of psychophysiological illnesses.

Certain conditions have long been known to have strong psychogenic influence. This is the case for asthma, whose clinical description was so accurately noted in the time of early Greek physicians. In the 20th century and especially after 1940, a group of illnesses was identified as "psychosomatic" in response to widespread observations that the patient's emotional state had clear repercussions on the manifestations of the disease. In this group were placed conditions such as essential hypertension, asthma, ulcerative colitis, peptic ulcer, atopic dermatitis, and rheumatoid arthritis. Since then, many other conditions have been added to the list (from the APA, DSM-III): acne, allergic reactions, warts, urticaria, tension headaches, skin diseases such as neurodermatitis, angina pectoris, coronary heart disease, diabetes mellitus, painful menstruation, obesity, migraine headaches, hyperthyroidism, and hypoglycemia among others.

With our increasing medical and psychological sophistication, however, we realize that more and more, if not all, diseases have some psychological components. Even the common flu, for example, is well known to be more virulent if the patient is depressed or stressed. The field of psychosomatic medicine is especially fascinating because it directly opens theoretical doors to issues concerning the relationship of the body to the mind.

Heinroth first used the word psychosomatic in 1817, applying it to problems of insomnia. Freud (1900) elucidated mechanisms whereby psychic conflicts expressed themselves in disorders of the voluntary nervous system—the conversion reactions. Ferenczi (1910) expanded the concept of conversion hysteria to apply it to the autonomic nervous system. Cannon (1927) showed how different emotions produced patterns of physiological alterations, emphasizing the importance of the autonomic network. Alexander (1934) stated that psychosomatic illnesses were mediated only through the autonomic nervous system—by definition—and that, in contrast to conversion hysteria, did not have specific symbolic meanings; rather, he felt they derived from chronic psychological states connected to unconscious drives in the context of constitutional predisposing factors. Dunbar (1936) suggested specific personality patterns to fit each psychosomatic disease; her approach, although intuitively attractive, did not bear conclusive results. Deutsh (1939) and Greenacre (1949) searched, equally inconclusively, for early putative traumatic experiences. Seyle (1950) described the stress syndrome, emphasizing the importance of hormonal factors. Wolff (1943) stated that physiological changes, if prolonged, could lead to organ damage. Horney (1939) and others postulated the importance of cultural influences. Grinker (1953) and Lipowski (1970) championed the comprehensive, multifactorial approach to psychosomatic disorders, viewing the patient in a holistic biopsychosocial context.

It is in this biopsychosocial concept of psychosomatic illness that hypnosis finds its niche. To the extent that it can influence the mind-body interaction, hypnosis can be utilized for the purpose of teaching the patient general relaxation, somatic and visceral, for working out conflicts and for modifying certain personality dynamics which may have aggravating influences. Hypnosis has been used in the following psychosomatic conditions with varying degrees of success. It must be appreciated, however, that hypnotic success in this regard has less to do with the types of psychosomatic illnesses present than it does with the particular patient involved.

GASTROINTESTINAL DISORDERS

The activity of the gastrointestinal tract is intimately intertwined with emotional life, past and present. In our language, metaphors abound connecting its functions—ingestion, digestion, indigestion, elimination—with emotional states. "I can't stomach this fellow" or, "he has a lot of guts" are some of the many common expressions which attest to the role of emotions such as anger, sadness, loss, happiness, lust, and courage, among others, in the workings of our digestive systems. In endogenous depressions, there is lack of appetite, decreased salivation, and intestinal peristalsis, constipation, and weight loss. Angry states are sometimes accompanied by aerophagia, and anxious states are often associated with diarrhea. Some individuals under stress show vomiting reactions (psychogenic vomiting).

Alexander (1968) conceptualized upper gastrointestinal disorders as connected, in mental life, to primitive conflicts surrounding the passive incorporative and aggressive biting stages. He also postulated a concomitant constitutional predisposition, as well as neuroendocrine factors, influencing gastric blood flow.

Several clinical conditions have received a lot of attention because of their psychological components. Indeed, when internists treat these disorders, recommendations are often made for adjunctive psychological and/or psychopharmacological treatment.

Peptic ulcer This is manifested by chronic ulceration of the mucosa in the esophagus, stomach, and duodenum. Ulcers in the duodenum are more convincingly linked to psychological factors. It is said that the basic psychodynamic trend in the hypersecreter–duodenal ulcer group has to do with strong needs to be taken care of, to be nurtured, and to have close body contact. These needs may be compensated with a character armor of independence, self-reliance, and aggressiveness.

The hypnotherapist, in the evaluation of the duodenal ulcer patient, will want to gain an understanding of emotional dynamics as they relate to autonomic discharge. What unconscious emotions are experienced and how are they adapted to? What conditions make them flare up to the extent of actually injuring the gastric mucosa? What experiences — early and recent — contribute to the targeting of the stomach? Hypnotherapy is aimed at the experiential clarification of these issues and on visceral relaxation training. The patient is shown how to recognize putative emotions early on and how to process them more constructively, ie, through assertiveness training. Long-term hypnotherapy goals center on the resolution and maturation of needs and impulses — dependency, anger — and on the achievement of higher levels of personality integration.

Wennerstrand, the Swedish hypnotherapist, reported the healing of duodenal ulcers by the technique of prolonged "sleep" through hypnosis. This method is, of course, impractical in modern life, but it shows how hypnotically induced prolonged rest has antistress effects. Techniques such as autogenic training and meditation have also claimed success in treating this common psychosomatic condition.

Common lower intestinal psychologically influenced disorders include ulcerative colitis, regional ileitis, and the irritable bowel syndrome. The lower intestinal tract has rich connections to psychosexual development. Characterological traits, unconscious emotions, and intestinal symptoms may all be interwoven around issues of control versus lack of control, order versus disorder, giving versus withdrawing, infantile anger and fear of abandonment.

Ulcerative colitis This is an inflammatory disease of the mucosa marked by remissions and exacerbations, diarrhea, bleeding, and possible complications in the colon and in other organ systems (hepatic, hematopoietic, renal). Investigations of its causes, which are still unknown, are focused on possible genetic, infectious, immunological, and psychosomatic factors.

Personality characteristics of the ulcerative colitis patient, although far from being universal, often sketch a patient who shows extreme sensitivity, low self-esteem, dependency, and conscientiousness.

Psychosocial stressors are well known to exacerbate the illness. Real or fantasized rejection, intense demands for performance—professionally or in a relationship—disapproval or criticism, especially from important figures, all can set the stage for a complex psychovisceral response which results in the engorgement and sloughing of the colonic mucosa.

Psychotherapy provides a context for hypnotherapy in such patients who, if willing, need longer-term explorative intervention. Hypnotherapy borrows from different strategies, from direct suggestion for symptom attenuation or removal, to the discharge of affect and abreaction, to relaxation, and finally to the long-term goal of personality maturation.

Hypnosis can provide some—usually small but nevertheless significant—positive influence on this complex psychosomatic condition which, for proper treatment, needs the combined attention to medical, psychological, and family-social dimensions of the patient's life.

ANOREXIA NERVOSA

This disorder, first called "nervous atrophy" by Rich Morton in 1689, and given its name by William Gull in 1874, is characterized by weight loss, intense fear of gaining weight, stubborn denial of the illness, peculiar handling of food, disorders of the body image with intense fear of becoming overweight, and often, hyperactivity. Gull recognized the influence of conflicts in anorexia nervosa and recommended that the patient be separated from the family. Theoretical approaches span from the purely psychological

—the rejection of pregnancy wish, oral sadistic impulses, fears of sexuality—to purely genetic or biochemical ones, including hypothalamic disorders.

Treatment of anorexia nervosa is biological, nutritional, behavioral, family-oriented, and psychotherapeutic, and includes hypnotherapy. Only with this multi-modal comprehensive intervention can this potentially lethal disorder show positive response. Psychodynamic psychotherapy has not been shown to be effective (Rollins and Blackwell, 1968; Bruch, 1970). Crasileck and Hall (1975) report that more than half of 70 cases treated with hypnosis showed marked improvement. Initially, suggestions for increased food intake were given and once patients began to eat and to show stabilization of their medical condition, explorative and supportive psychotherapy using hypnosis was applied. In many patients with anorexia nervosa, however, there is no overt acknowledgment of the disease and no cooperation or motivation to work hypnotically.

CARDIOVASCULAR DISORDERS

The cardiovascular system has close, immediate responsivity to the manifestations of many emotions. Fright is accompanied by tachycardia, splanchnic vascular constriction, raised blood pressure, and blood engorgement of voluntary muscles. Anger, excitement, chronic anxiety and stress, elation, even love, have a direct bearing on the psychocardiovascular network. Internally generated imagery also has a direct effect on heart action. In hypnosis, where the experience of imagery is apt to be more intensively perceived, individuals may enhance or decrease cardiovascular responsiveness.

Essential hypertension This is defined as blood pressure levels greater than 160 mm Hg systolic and 95 mm Hg diastolic and accounts for 90% of all hypertensive disorders. It appears at this time that there are likely to be several subtypes of essential hypertension; some hypertensive conditions seem to be more biologically mediated, while others are more dynamically connected to emotional responses.

Personality analyses have not yielded specific congregations of traits or intrapsychic conflicts peculiar to the hypertensive patient. The popular notion that repressed hostility plays a major role has not been experimentally substantiated, but there is ample clinical evidence that anger, guilt and fear, and issues of expressing emotions versus containing them, are operationally important. Hypertensive patients tend to respond with higher and more prolonged blood pressure rises than do normotensives. Stress is also implicated. Cobb and Rose (1973) found a high incidence of hypertension in air-traffic controllers exposed to the pressures of high air-traffic density.

As with other psychosomatic conditions, comprehensive treatment approaches derive from an awareness of the multi-causal nature of essential hypertension. While some cases may simply respond to weight control or salt restriction, others need additional measures such as pharmacotherapy and psychotherapy.

Psychotherapy aims to evaluate and constructively change the environmental impact, family interactions, intrapsychic conflicts, and behaviors which may contribute to this maladaptive response. Since the process of psychotherapy involves the unearthing of affect, care must be taken not to do this too quickly or too intensively before new coping skills are learned. Behavioral methods, including biofeedback, relaxation, meditation, and hypnosis, are increasingly being used for the control of hypertension (Shapiro et al, 1977). When using hypnosis, suggestions may be given for relaxation, calm, a sense of internal peacefulness, and ease of handling such emotions as anger. Imagery exercises may help the patient to visualize aggressive feelings flowing away and out of his system.

RESPIRATORY DISORDERS

The breathing process represents a dynamic interplay between voluntary and involuntary influences, reflecting the involvement of all levels of the neuraxis from the medulla to the cortex. Emotions play directly into the rate, rhythm, and patterns of respiration. Sad or anxious individuals sigh; fear makes breathing shallow; relaxed states are associated with more abdominal breathing.

The most common psychosomatic respiratory illness is asthma. Marked by recurrent bronchial constriction, edema, and excessive secretion, the clinical picture is manifested by recurrent attacks of dyspnea and prolonged expirations with wheezing and coughing. During the attack, the patient usually is tense, anxious, and frightened in the face of experiencing a lack of availability of vital air. Symptoms may be mild and infrequent or severe and life-threatening (status asthmaticus). Several subtypes of bronchial asthma are being investigated. Some tend to be more clearly mediated by specific immunological mechanisms and others by a wide range of irritants.

Psychoanalytic investigations have been enlightening in showing the complexities of psychological factors contributing to asthma. Although no single personality type is singled out, investigators have emphasized the importance of the unconscious fear of the loss of the nurturing mother and have noted the influence of antecedent feeling states of a sexual or hostile nature.

The symptoms in some asthmatic patients are much more responsive to psychological influences than in others. While in some, the exposure to an allergen produces wheezing regardless of mental state, in others, stress or upset is all that is needed to precipitate an attack. The famous case of the glass rose, the sight of which alone brought on asthmatic symptoms, attests to this phenomenon. Although uncontested explanations for the effectiveness of hypnosis in asthma are lacking, clinically and pragmatically, hypnosis has had clear success in this disorder. Many asthmatics suffer from anticipatory fear of the next attack and, while in the throes of an attack, are panic stricken with fears of choking and dying. Hypnosis is helpful in alleviating both anticipatory anxiety and attack panic. It may, at some level, actually increase bronchiolar dilatation and decrease airway resistance

(Edwards, 1960). As with other psychosomatic conditions hypnosis, on a longer-term basis, can be applied to the problems of personality integration and family adjustment.

DERMATOLOGICAL CONDITIONS

The relationship of emotions to skin health and distress is well known. This clear and, in some patients, very direct pathway from the mind to the skin can be illustrated by the production, through suggestion during the hypnotic trance, of erythema, blisters, and urticaria. The literature also contains numerous studies dealing with the hypnotically induced disappearance of warts. Experimental evidence suggests that skin resistance to noxious stimuli — such as heat or irritants — may be intensified through hypnotic suggestion, or decreased, with greater vulnerability. Besides its applications in the treatment of warts and burns, hypnosis has found usefulness in conditions such as ichthyosis, atopic eczema, contact dermatitis, neurodermatitis, psoriasis, and acne rosea (Scott, 1960).

COMMENTARIES ON TREATMENT OF PSYCHOSOMATIC DISORDERS

We have seen how psychosomatic disorders, in their close connections to the mind-body interface, are determined by a multiplicity of factors. Emotions — most commonly anxiety, depression, sadness, hostility, and guilt — have intimate influence on remissions and exacerbations of these illnesses. Characteristically, however, the complaints of psychosomatic patients remain physical rather than psychiatric.

The comprehensive psychomedical treatment of these disorders recognizes the multifactorial nature, the uniqueness of individual expression, and the necessity for a combined approach to therapy. While in the acute stages of psychosomatic illness, medical treatment is a mainstay, psychotherapeutic measures are important to provide emotional ventilation, reassurance, and support.

In this phase, hypnosis can be applied directly to symptom relief. In the chronic phases or during remissions of the illness, psychotherapeutic interventions assume primary importance, with goals centering on the discovery of feelings, conflicts, needs, mood states, and personality dynamics which, if worked through, can disconnect the somatization process.

Difficulties in psychotherapy have to do with patient resistance on several levels. The hardest part of treatment may be obtaining the acknowledgment from the patient that psychological dimensions need to be attended to. Other difficulties include a tendency to "think somatically," a dependency on secondary gains of symptoms, and in some patients, a possible aggravation of symptoms and dropping out of therapy with the uncovering of affects.

Psychological treatment, while rarely curative, may significantly change the pattern of psychosomatic illness. Diabetics, for example, can be more smoothly stabilized with the acceptance of diet and the regulation of exercise; hypnotic treatment has, in some cases, led to decreased insulin requirements. Hypertensives may similarly need lower doses of medications and asthmatics less steroids or bronchodilators.

Hypnotic influence may be applied, in the context of medical and psychosocial treatment, to anyone or all levels of the psychosomatic continuum — from organ dysfunction to higher personality integration. To general visceral relaxation, we may add the hypnotic effect on specific organ systems. There is ample evidence that the psyche, through pathways tapped into by hypnosis, yoga, autogenic training, and biofeedback, among others, can positively modify the physiological functions of specific organs, ie, the heart, skin, etc. On a different level, hypnosis can be applied to the discovery and healthful expression of subconscious affects which directly and symbolically alter — and destroy — specific organs. Finally, in combination with supportive or insight-oriented psychotherapy, hypnosis may help both to accelerate the global maturation process and to transcend the funneling of psychological energies into the soma.

SUGGESTED READING AND REFERENCES

Alexander F, French TM, Pollock GH: *Psychosomatic Specificity: Experimental Study and Results.* Chicago, University of Chicago Press, 1968.

Bruch H: Psychotherapy in primary anorexia nervosa. *J Nerv Ment Dis* 1970;150:51.

Cannon WB: *The Wisdom of the Body.* New York, WW Norton, 1932.

Cobb S, Rose RM: Hypertension, peptic ulcer, and diabetes in air traffic controllers. *JAMA* 1973;224:489.

Crasileck HB, Hall JA: *Clinical Hypnosis: Principles and Practice.* New York, Grune & Stratton, 1975.

Dally P, Gomez J: *Anorexia Nervosa.* London, Heinemann, 1979.

Deutsh F: The Choice of organ in organ neurosis. *Int J Psychoanal* 1939;20:1.

Dunbar F: *Emotions and Bodily Changes.* New York, Columbia University Press, 1954.

Edwards F: Hypnotic treatment of asthma. *Br Med J* 1960;2:492.

Engel G: The clinical application of the biopsychosocial model. *Am J Psychiatry* 1980;137(5):535.

Ferenczi S: *Further Contributions to the Theory and Technique of Psychoanalysis.* London, Hogarth Press, 1926.

Freud S: Fragment of an analysis of a case of hysteria, in *Standard Edition of the Complete Psychological Works of Sigmund Freud,* Vol 7. London, Hogarth Press, 1953, p 40.

Greenacre P: *Trauma, Growth and Personality.* New York, WW Norton, 1953.

Grinker R: *Psychosomatic Research.* New York, WW Norton, 1953.

Group for the Advancement of Psychiatry: *Psychopathological Disorders in Childhood: Theoretical Considerations and a Proposed Classification.* New York, Group for the Advancement of Psychiatry, 1966.

Gull W: Anorexia nervosa (apepsia hysterica, anorexia hysteria). *Trans Clin Soc London* 1874;7:22.

Heinroth JC: Lehrbuch der Storungen des Seelenlebens oder der Seelenstorunger under ihrer, in *Behandlung,* part 2, Leipzig, Vogel, 1818, p 76.

Horney K: *The Neurotic Personality of Our Time.* New York, WW Norton, 1937.

Lipowski ZJ: Psychosomatic perspectives. *Can Psychiatry Assoc J* 1970;15:515.

Morton R: *Phthisiologia—or a Treatise of Consumption,* ed 2. London, Smith, 1720.

Rollins N, Blackwell A: The treatment of anorexia nervosa in children

and adolescents: Stage I. *J Child Psychol Psychiatry* 1968;9:81.
Scott MJ: *Hypnosis in Skin and Allergic Diseases.* Springfield, Ill, Charles C Thomas, 1960.
Seyle H: *The Physiology and Pathology of Exposure to Stress.* Montreal, Acta, 1950.
Shapiro AP, Schwartz GE, Ferguson DCE, et al: Behavioral methods in the treatment of hypertension. *Ann Intern Med* 1977;86:626.
Thakur KS: Treatment of anorexia nervosa with hypnotherapy, in Wain HJ (ed): *Clinical Hypnosis in Medicine.* Miami, Symposia Specialists, 1980, p 147.
Wolff S, Wolff HG: *Human Gastric Function.* New York, Oxford University Press, 1943.

13

Hypnosis and Sex Therapy

Barbara DeBetz

Hypnosis is a useful adjunct in the treatment of sexual dysfunction. Within the last few years, increasing attention has been given to the potential benefits of using hypnosis in the treatment of sexual problems. Unfortunately, most case reports of hypnotic interventions are anecdotal and fail to include significant information regarding patient selection, diagnostic criteria, specific therapeutic intervention, and follow-up data. Controlled studies are needed to evaluate more thoroughly the efficacy of hypnosis in sex therapy. This is obviously a difficult area in which to do well-designed research.

With our new awareness and understanding of sexuality in the last decade, we have come to view sexual activity not simply as a biological function for reproduction but also as a basic human experience bringing pleasure and closeness to a relationship. It can be regarded as a way of communicating interpersonal feelings. Due to the "sexual revolution" involving role changes and new ways to cope and adapt to psychological, social, and physical changes, many people have not been able to adapt to their new situations, environments, and stresses. As a result, a relatively large portion of people demonstrate diminished sexual enjoyment and impaired sexual functioning.

In order to comprehensively evaluate the sexual functioning of an individual who presents with a sexual complaint, the clinician should have knowledge of the basic physiology of human sexuality, as well as have some understanding of the most important milestones of psychosexual development.

Any form of therapeutic intervention, including hypnosis, requires a clear understanding of the underlying primary organic factors as well as the secondary reactive, behavioral, psychological components. Frequently, a mixture of these two types of dysfunction are present in a given patient. In order to develop an effective treatment strategy, it is important to differentiate one from the other because each may require different approaches. The following case history will demonstrate this point.

CASE HISTORY

The patient was a 34-year-old married woman. She was referred by her gynecologist for sexual counseling. Due to an infection after placement of an intrauterine device, she had needed a hysterectomy. Although she recovered well from the surgery, she started to complain about total loss of sexual desire, dyspareunia, and anorgasmia. By history she had an active and satisfying regular sex life with her husband prior to the hysterectomy. They had sex two or three times per week and she had orgasms most of the time. Her gynecologist had treated the dyspareunia with estrogen cream because there was a slight degree of vaginal atrophy due to the hormonal changes after surgery. In spite of the cream, the patient continued to complain about lack of lubrication of the vagina, pain during intercourse, and total lack of desire.

It became clear that her real problem was not physical but her reactive psychological adjustment to the hysterectomy. She had become very insecure as a woman, gradually had lost her self-esteem, and she saw herself as "less" of a woman. She felt unattractive, unfeminine and "sexually mutilated." It took several therapy sessions to get at her feelings of loss and the impact of the surgery on her sense of self and her body image.

It took several months of psychotherapy and eventual hypnotherapy to help her restore her sense of self-esteem and accept herself as a worthwhile human being and woman.

The treatment consisted of three different approaches. The initial approach was done by the gynecologist, treating the physical (organic) primary aspect of this patient's sexual dysfunction. The second part was the supportive and insight-oriented psychotherapy, and the third was the hypnosis used to help her overcome her resistance to getting involved sexually with her husband and help restore her sexual desire. This was achieved by giving her self-hypnotic relaxation exercises just prior to having sexual intercourse, so that her body would be fully relaxed and her mind cleared from interfering mental blocks. In addition, she was taught the use of self-hypnosis to revive imagery of sexual events from the past when she fully enjoyed sex with her husband. It took several months to correct her sexual malfunctioning. An important aspect of her treatment was the recognition that there was a mixture of organic and psychological symptoms which needed different approaches.

Hypnosis can be used in sex therapy in several different ways. It can be used as a diagnostic tool to uncover etiological factors as well as factors responsible for maintaining a specific sexual problem. It is also used to give nonspecific suggestions to relieve tension and anxiety, a prime contributor to many sexual dysfunctions, as an adjunct to behavior therapy and cognitive restructuring, and to give directive instructions aimed at the direct removal of the symptom. Finally, hypnosis is helpful in increasing a patient's sexual awareness through using imagery and fantasies, restoring self-esteem, and improving communication between sexual partners.

Before deciding on the treatment approach, a thorough sexual history should be obtained. Specific emphasis should be placed on getting information of the exact nature and duration of the sexual complaint; assessment of previous sexual functioning, and general sexual attitudes. Determination of physical versus psychological difficulties should be done. It is also of importance to ascertain a patient's sociological background and sexual development and activities during childhood, adolescence, and adulthood. Attention should be paid to alcohol and drug use, medications taken, and physical conditions present at the time of assessment.

Questions should be asked regarding the patient's relationships, marital or otherwise, patterns of communication, and interaction between the two partners. If appropriate, the patient's partner should also be interviewed. It is also helpful to find out the patient's insight into the problem and the treatment goals and expectations. If any physical cause for the sexual dysfunction is suspected, the patient should be either examined or referred for evaluation to the appropriate specialist.

After the sexual assessment has been completed, the patient's hypnotic trance capacity should be determined in order to decide if hypnosis would be an appropriate treatment modality.

Below is an outline of the two major sexual dysfunctions and the way hypnosis can be used to help implement the specific treatment strategy.

ANORGASMIA

Anorgasmia is the most common female psychosexual dysfunction. Ten percent of all women never reach orgasm, 10% are not able to climax with a partner but are able to climax through masturbation. Fifty percent of women reach orgasm with intercourse plus clitoral stimulation. Thirty percent have orgasm during intercourse without any clitoral stimulation.

In the past, sexologists differentiated between vaginal and clitoral orgasm, but nowadays it is pretty well understood that the final physiological response is the same regardless of the beginning point, vagina or clitoris.

Women vary in how easily they reach orgasm. If we keep in mind that only 30% of all women reach orgasm through intercourse without additional stimulation, we are left with 70% of women who have some degree of dysfunction. According to Helen Singer Kaplan, anorgasmia is the easiest sexual dysfunction to treat and cure.

What is the cause of anorgasmia? The cause (or causes) for anorgasmia is not fully known, but it most likely involves intrapsychic, interpersonal, cultural, and experimental-behavioral factors (see list of most common causes below). When treating the anorgasmic woman, one has to establish what kind of anorgasmia she suffers from. Has she always been anorgasmic, occasionally, or only with a certain partner? Has she had episodes of orgasm, followed by episodes of anorgasmia? Have there been changes in the relationship, changes in her health, changes in her job or home situation? The woman who is afflicted with this problem usually has a normal sexual desire; she enjoys sex, lubricates normally when aroused, but has difficulties reaching orgasm. She achieves a certain level of sexual arousal, but when it comes to "letting go," there is the problem of climaxing. Women vary as to how much stimulation they need to reach orgasm. Some women can only climax when they are alone masturbating, but the presence of a partner, an "audience," makes them too tense to reach orgasm. Often these women feel they are taking too long or that their partner will reject them if he has "to work" at getting her to climax.

For many women who climax easily while masturbating, it takes additional clitoral stimulation when together with a partner. Some women who take a long time or who are anorgasmic pretend to have an orgasm because they are embarrassed to communicate their difficulty to their partner. Most of these women could actually climax if they gave themselves a chance, but they are frequently oversensitive to rejection and criticism, or overanxious to please their partner. Faking orgasm interferes with developing a good sexual relationship, and it tends to just make the problem worse. Many women feel pressured into having orgasm at the same time as their partner, or feel that in order to enjoy sex fully, one must have multiple orgasms, or that orgasm must always be an ecstatic experience.

All of these are misconceptions and have little to do with full sexual enjoyment. For most people, it is not the quantity but the quality of sex and the relationship between the two partners. It is true that orgasm has become more important to women over the last 20 years or so, but it has largely been overemphasized. The final phase of sexual intercourse, the orgasm, is important, but it should be put in proper perspective of the human experience of having sex.

Most common causes of anorgasmia:

1. Primary (never experienced orgasm)
   - Cultural
   - Educational
   - Learned behavior
   - Moral
   - Religious
   - Gender confusion
   - Homosexual orientation (anorgasmic with person of other sex but possibly orgasmic with partner of same sex)
   - Traumatic past events such as incest, rape, homosexual experience, physical trauma due to illness or surgery
2. Secondary
   - Same as above
   - Abortion
   - Fear of intimacy
   - Fear of sexuality in general
   - Fear of pregnancy
   - Infidelity
   - Infertility
   - Menopause
   - Physical illness
   - Medication causing loss of sexual desire
   - Drug use, including alcohol abuse
   - Venereal disease
   - Stress
   - Fatigue
   - Depression
   - Obesity or other eating disorders
   - Low self-esteem
   - Anxiety states

- Miscellaneous other physical or emotional factors

Treatment

The treatment proposed here consists of two different phases: phase one is to be done by the anorgasmic woman without involving a partner and phase two will involve the partner.

Phase one (patient alone, without the partner) After the patient has been taught the use of self-hypnosis, the following instructions are given:

"Once you feel confident in reaching the self-hypnotic trance state, do the following: Choose a time of day or evening when you have some privacy and while in the trance ask yourself the following questions:

1. Are you having any problems with your interest in having sex?
2. Has there been a change in your level of interest?
3. Have any recent or past events influenced your interest in sex?
4. Do fantasies play part in your sexual enjoyment?
5. Are there any specific situations, feelings, or attitudes which cause you to enjoy sex less or not at all?
6. How often do you have sex and what part do you enjoy/not enjoy?
7. Do you feel guilty about enjoying sex?
8. Do you lubricate well when you get aroused?
9. Do you communicate your sexual desires to your partner?
10. Do you feel comfortable asking your partner to stimulate you?
11. Under what circumstances can you achieve orgasm (intercourse, manual stimulation, oral sex, vibrator, anal sex, masturbation, other)?

12. Is there anything about your orgasmic response that troubles you?
13. What, if, anything, interferes with your ability to reach orgasm?
14. Are you afraid that having an orgasm means losing control?

"While in the trance, you are more in touch with your feelings and your thoughts can surface more clearly to you. If any of the above questions, or any other questions floated into your mind, repeat that question to yourself. By doing this you already have narrowed down the problem area. The next step will be to find the answer for yourself, either by yourself or in therapy." (Note: Part A can be done either together with the therapist or the patient can do it by herself.)

Use of fantasy "Use sexual fantasy to increase your desire and explore what can arouse you most. Go into the trance, imagine that you are looking at a screen, a TV screen or a movie screen, and on this screen project your favorite fantasy. Sexual fantasies are used commonly by many people. They can be used while having sex or at any other time when it is appropriate. The most common fantasies involve images such as being held by the person you love, being caressed by the person you love, making love to the person you love. Other people find it more exciting to fantasize about making love to a stranger, making love to someone of the same sex, participating in an orgy, having anal intercourse, oral sex, being tied up, or whatever else comes to your mind. Allow that fantasy to be projected on the screen. It is perfectly safe and private, no one will hurt you, criticize you, or punish you."

Body trip "Another exercise to do in your mind is the following: Again, go into the trance, and now go on a 'body trip.' In the buoyantly relaxed hypnotic state try to explore your body. Just think about the different parts of your body and try to visualize them or feel them. Think about the external parts of your genitals, the clitoris, the entrance to the vagina, the inside of your vagina, and try to get in touch with the different sensations you get from all these different areas. While you do this, think about your body in a 'friendly' way, rather than being angry at your 'anorgasmic' body. It is not your body, it is your mind that blocks the full physiological response. Your body is perfectly well equipped to experience orgasm, you have to learn to get back in touch with it."

Use of masturbation "Before trying to have an orgasm with a partner, it might be easier to first experiment through masturbation the reflex response of orgasm. Most people explore themselves in childhood and adolesence and, before engaging in heterosexual intercourse, they have learned the orgasmic response through masturbation. Again, masturbation is highly individual and masturbatory practices differ from one person to another. However, the technique described below is probably the most common one and can serve you as a guideline. Go into the trance and shift your attention to your genitals. Gently rub your clitoris and breasts and become acutely aware of the pleasurable sensations it gives you. Just allow yourself to explore your body and play with yourself until your body is so excited that orgasm will occur naturally. Once you have reached a critical level of physical arousal, orgasm is just a reflex reaction of the involved muscles. When you climax, fully enjoy each moment of it and register it in your brain. Do not pull back, physically or emotionally, or feel embarrassed or guilty. This is a learning experience for you, and you want to fully assimilate and process it in your brain. The brain is an important part to the sexual experience and most probably the part that has been holding you back from reaching orgasm. Once your 'braincomputer' has registered the orgasmic reflex, it will eventually respond in the same way when you are with a partner. After you have reached orgasm, come out of the trance and do it again if you wish to."

Phase two (with partner if available) "Most probably you are already comfortable by now with the sensation of orgasm by yourself and now you only have to respond the same way with a partner. If you are in an on-going relationship, open communication is recommended. Discuss with your partner that you have a problem with reaching orgasm and discuss how to overcome it together.

By now you already have a pretty good idea how to be stimulated to reach orgasm. Don't be embarrassed to discuss things such as foreplay, clitoral stimulation, or other arousal factors with your partner. If it is difficult for you to put these things into direct words, another way would be to guide him with your hand to the areas where you would like to be stimulated. Do not assume that he should 'know.' Also, encourage him to stimulate you manually or orally if he has come before you. There is nothing wrong with climaxing after him. Faking orgasm is not a solution, it will just compound the dysfunction.

"How do you use the self-hypnosis in this specific event? The first few times of trial, I would recommend doing the hypnotic exercise shortly before engaging in sex, not while having sex. By doing it before, you body will be physically relaxed and your mind will be set to enjoy it. While you do it, just think about your partner and what you enjoy about him, and then shift your awareness towards your genitals and just think about them, getting ready, starting to lubricate, getting engorged, etc.

"If you are faced with a situation with a new partner, there are two ways to go: (1) plunge in and just trust that you have 'taught' your body how to respond; (2) tell your partner that you are a bit apprehensive about sex and that in the past you had found it difficult to climax but that you really want to be with him and that he should not see it as a reflection on him."

ERECTILE DYSFUNCTION (IMPOTENCE)

The definition of impotence is impairment of the erectile reflex due to physical or psychological factors resulting in erectile dysfunction. The vascular reflex mechanism fails to pump enough blood into the cavernous sinuses of the penis to render it firm and erect. The erectile and ejaculatory reflexes can be dissociated, and some impotent men are able to ejaculate despite a flaccid penis.

Erectile difficulties may occur in men at any age. Approximately half the male population has experienced occasional transient episodes of impotence. This is called secondary impotence. Primary impotence occurs in men who have never been able to be potent with a woman, although they may have erections while masturbating or have spontaneous erections in other situations. Secondary impotence has a very favorable therapeutic outcome, while primary impotence is frequently associated with serious underlying psychopathology which needs to be treated with conventional psychotherapy.

Causes:

1. Physical
   - Fatigue
   - Diabetes mellitus
   - Chronic illness due to spinal cord injury or other injury in that region
   - Low hormone level
   - Excessive use of drugs, including alcohol
   - Medications, such as tranquilizers, sleeping pills, blood pressure medications
   - Neurological illnesses such as multiple sclerosis
   - Prostatic conditions
   - Peyronie's disease of the penis

Every patient presenting with erectile dysfunction should have a thorough medical check-up to rule out any physical causes for the impotence.

2. Psychological
   - Performance anxiety—most common cause
   - Castration anxiety
   - Fear, shame, and guilt about sexuality
   - Destructive interactions between a couple
   - Anger and resentment between a couple
   - Control and power conflicts between a couple

Treatment

Open discussion between the dysfunctional partner and his wife/partner is important, as is an agreement on a "no-pressure" sexual ambiance to overcome the problem. The basic premise on which therapy rests is that anxiety occurring at the moment of sexual intercourse disrupts the patient's erectile reflex. The main objective of therapy, therefore, is to eliminate this anxiety or prevent its appearance. Restoration of sexual confidence is critical.

The initial treatment strategy is to enhance the arousal and stimulation factors and decrease those factors which create anxiety in the patient (vaginal intercourse).

Patient is instructed as follows:

Week 1, Part A: "Every day I want you to do the self-hypnotic exercises approximately three times by yourself. While in the trance imagine that you are looking at an imaginary screen, like a TV screen. On this screen I want you to project your sexual fears: in your mind imagine one of your typical sexual episodes where you have had erectile problems. When you look at them on the screen, allow your feelings to surface inside of you and try to become fully aware of what causes your fears and anxieties. By doing it repeatedly you will see that eventually you will have a pretty good understanding of what it is. Once you have understood, you can either discuss it with your partner if it is related to her, or you may put it into the right perspective yourself."

Week 1, Part B: "During the first four to seven days of work together with your partner, you should abstain from intercourse and ejaculation. However, this time of genital abstinance is used to explore each other: sexual arousal by playing, kissing, caressing, and gently stimulating each other.

"Each night or morning, depending on when you usually have sex, you do the following:

1. "You go into the trance state, and while you are in the trance have your partner caress you all over your body, excluding the

genital area. She should caress you for 5 to 10 minutes. Then you bring yourself out of the trance and tell her how her caresses felt on your body and what you enjoyed the most.

2. "Now you take turns. Now you caress your partner with your hands and mouth all over her body, excluding her genital area. Register how her skin feels in the different places of her body. When you are through, ask her to tell you how it felt and what she enjoyed most.

"The mutual pleasuring should be done two to three nights or mornings until both partners feel fully satisfied and fully anxiety-free while doing it.

"You probably had spontaneous erections while you were pleasing each other, but pay no attention to them. They are not important right now."

3. "This time you pleasure each other simultaneously in the way you have done it taking turns before. Do this simultaneous phase two to three nights or mornings until fully satisfied and completely anxiety free."

4. "Same as step 1 but add touching of genitals. You may get erections, partially or fully. If so, just allow your mind to register the pleasant sensation of your penis. If it goes flaccid, do not be concerned. Under no circumstances are you to ejaculate.

5. "Same as step 2, now you pleasure your partner including manual and oral touching of the genitals. You are not allowed to ejaculate when she touches you. If she, however, gets very excited, let her climax, but do not insert your penis into her even if you have an erection. You should first feel 100% confident with steps 4 and 5. This should be done a couple of nights or mornings until each detail is fully satisfying and totally anxiety-free.

"At this point you are both experts at giving pleasure to each other without having sexual intercourse. It takes an average of four to ten days to be ready to go to the next phases of treatment."

After erectile confidence has been established, intercourse is resumed between the couple, initially in the following way.

Part C Step 1: "You lie on your back and go into the trance and have your partner stimulate you until you have an erection. When your erection is firm have your partner sit on top of you, lowering herself onto your penis which will slide into her vagina. Then have her move up and down slowly. Do not move your penis, just focus on the pleasurable sensations you are getting from your partner's movements. Do not let her stimulate to orgasm, separate before. It is important to do this in order to erase your feeling of 'performing'."

Step 2: "Begin the same as in the step before but this time thrust your penis in and out of your partner's vagina in rhythm with her. Let your penis be stimulated fully to orgasm."

Steps 1 and 2 are not to be seen as permanent and sole coital positions. They are merely the transition to the final goal which is secure and confident sexual activities but in a nondemanding, anxiety-free atmosphere.

The two steps above should take two to four nights or mornings until there is enough confidence built up. Once regular sexual activities are resumed, the couple should make an effort to keep the newly learned channels of communication open and not fall back into their old anxiety-producing patterns. If there is a relapse of impotence, the couple should go back either to the entire sequence of exercises or at least the last two steps outlined above. The dysfunctional partner may continue or use the self-hypnotic exercise prior to intercourse as long as necessary. This will differ greatly from one person to another.

The use of hypnosis and self-hypnosis for the treatment of sexual dysfunctions can be viewed mainly as a facilitator. As outlined above for anorgasmia and impotence, conventional treatment strategies were chosen and implemented while the patient was in the trance or while doing self-hypnosis by himself at home. Again, the patient with hypnotic trance capacity seems to be more intensely responsive to a specific treatment approach. In addition to using the hypnosis to implement specific strategies, it should also be kept in mind that most sexual dysfunctional patients have a high degree of anxiety associated with their sexual problem. The use of self-hypnosis is an excellent way to alleviate that anxiety, thus clearing the way for improved sexual functioning.

SUGGESTED READING

Araoz DL: *Hypnosis and Sex Therapy.* New York, Brunner/Mazel, 1982.
Brown JM, Chaves JT: Hypnosis in the treatment of sexual dysfunction. *J Sex Marital Ther* 1980;6(1):63-74.
Crasilneck HB: A follow-up study in the use of hypnotherapy in the treatment of psychogenic impotency. *Am J Clin Hypn* 1982;25(1):52-61.
DeBetz B, Baker SS: *Erotic Focus, The New Way to Enhance Your Sexual Pleasure.* New York, New American Library, 1985.
Kaplan HS: *The New Sex Therapy.* New York, Brunner/Mazel, 1974.
Masters WH, Johnson VE: *Human Sexual Inadequacy.* Boston, Little Brown, 1966.
Meyer JK (ed): *Clinical Management of Sexual Disorders.* Baltimore, The Williams and Wilkins Company, 1976.

14

Hypnosis in Psychotherapy

Gérard Sunnen

The essence of psychotherapy is personal change. As a science dedicated to alleviate emotional distress and devoted to personality growth and individual development, modern psychotherapy brings together the findings of many disciplines. To psychoanalysis, which has been the guiding light of this interpersonal process for the first part of the 20th century, several new approaches have been developed in response to society's needs and inspired from contributions from related fields — from sociology to behavioral medicine.

The modern trend in psychotherapy, as in most fields, is increasing efficiency. How, in the best and most streamlined way, without compromising quality of care, can this individual's dilemmas and distresses be alleviated in the shortest possible time? This question is as important to the patient as it is to the therapist. Times have changed since the days when the only quality option was the couch, five times a week, in strict analytic style. Today, combination treatments are likely to be considered, with the idea that one treatment need not displace another. It is not uncommon, for example, to see a patient engaged in psychoanalytically oriented psychotherapy also be concomitantly treated, when indicated, by psychotropic medication or behavioral adjuncts.

It is in this context that hypnotherapy finds its most sophisticated applications. Hypnosis, in its therapeutic infancy, was used to remove symptoms by a direct head-on approach. Symptoms were ordered out, cajoled into disappearing, and threatened lest they came back — which they often did. In the early days of hypnosis, symptoms were seen as thorns and hypnosis as tweezers. In this model, the patient had the subjective sensation that a magical cure had been performed, that the resolution of symptoms had been done by forces beyond his control without participation of personal resources, and that ego strength had not been enhanced. Direct symptom removal is, however, not a useless technique. In the right patient, at the right time and for the right reasons, symptoms may be hypnotically banished without symptoms substitution — especially if new experiences or adaptive behaviors are learned concomitantly.

Today, with much greater, but undoubtedly still rudimentary, understanding of mental mechanisms, we see symptoms and resistances in the context of what has been called the ecology of the mind — as compromises in a dynamic structure of forces.

Hypnosis, responding to the increased sophistication of psychological concepts, is used as much to explore psychodynamics as it is to foster the experience of conflict resolution, all in the interest of increasing ego integrity.

Analytic hypnotherapy refers to a set of techniques which integrate hypnosis with analytically oriented psychotherapy. Using the patient's trance capacity and some of the phenomena inherent in hypnosis, from relaxation to dream formation, hypnotherapy holds the promise of making personal change more efficient and more rapid.

This is not to say that hypnotherapy seeks to compress in time all phases of psychotherapy. Indeed, certain phases, especially those dealing with the creation and solidification of human contact and rapport, need and must have ample time. Other phases, however, can be condensed or otherwise accelerated, without compromising clinical effectiveness. In fact, speedier discovery of conflicts and shortened resolution time, by the impact of the reality of positive change, often have a galvanizing effect, inspiring patients to the possibility of further change.

The practice of hypnotherapy has no set formula. Hypnosis may be used in the early (investigative), middle (working through), or final (termination) stages of psychotherapy. Some clinicians use it consistently, dividing each session into a hypnotic and nonhypnotic part; others apply it on an as-needed basis.

Regardless of theoretical perspectives, there are certain practical issues which must be attended to in any psychotherapeutic interchange. The patient presents with an awareness of emotional difficulties which may be stated explicitly or may remain couched in the most general terms. At times, the stated complaints are not the real ones — the conscious explanation being only a mirror of the unconscious distress, ie, the patient presenting with tension headaches who, despite initial denial, turns out to have a depressive condition.

The initial task of the therapist is to clarify issues at hand. Why is this individual seeking therapy at this time? Very often, the patient does not know. Anxiety, fears, feelings of guilt, depression, and aggressive ideation are final common pathways to conflicts which, resurfacing now, may have long roots in the patient's past. Clarification may happen during all phases of treatment, from exploration of current issues in the initial sessions, to the elucidation of more historical conflicts further on.

Sometimes, presenting conflicts are directly related to experiences repressed for years. Clarification in such cases entails not only an exploration of current symptoms but necessarily demands the bringing to light of these important experiences which directly feed them. The following case illustrates clarification by the use of a technique called the affect bridge (Watkins, 1971), whereby the current emotion is linked to its epigenetic center. In psychotherapy, the same technique is used when we ask: When did you first experience this emotion? Hypnotherapy can make for shorter transit time from current emotion to its antecedent repressed counterpart. A bomber copilot sought help for inner turmoil, tension, and generalized anxiety which had built up appreciably in the past 24 hours. He had just flown a mission and was very apprehensive about leaving on another one soon. Very distressed, he admitted having had frightening, destructive fantasies while last flying the airplane: an impulse to punch out the control panels had left him shaken and doubtful of himself.

This high level of anxiety prevented him from being insightful about his situation. Searching for clues to these recent feelings, he mentioned a personality conflict with the pilot, but could not make it account for the degree of turmoil he experienced. His apprehension about the next mission was all the more fueled by his need to save face—he had to fly; he could not accept the idea of being taken off flying status and possibly being looked down upon.

He accepted the suggestion of using hypnosis for relaxation and, perhaps, clarification of his feelings. His anxiety level dropped off considerably during the latter part of the induction, and deepening of the trance left him sitting without any sign of the tremulous anxiety he manifested when first stepping through the door. In searching for the emotions accompanying, and hidden by, his anxiety, he was asked to go back, in mental image, to his seat in the cockpit of the airplane. Invited to talk, he described an insidiously escalating conflict between himself and the pilot. He was angry, sullen, and felt violent. In hypnosis, he showed mildly strained, reddened facies. 'When was it, back in time, that you felt similar feelings?" After fleeting moments, he started talking slowly. He was back with his older brother 15 years previously, playing around his family home. He was taunted by him and a group of his friends, belittled, infantilized. Overwrought with rage, he had gone back home, where, in privacy, he had kicked his brother's belongings. This incident stood out as one among several similar ones.

"It is clear to you and to me, as you sit here, that the pilot, although he reminded you of your brother by some of his actions toward you, is not your brother. This will be very clear to you from now on, and you will, as a consequence, act toward your colleague only as the present situation warrants; you will not bring anything into it back from your past."

He was also given ego-strengthening suggestions, ie, enhancement of the ability to handle emotions, development of his ability to relax and master situations, etc. Future missions were completely uneventful and three follow-up sessions centering on his relationship with his brother served to free up old angers and liberate some self-esteem.

In this example, several processes were called into play during the hypnotic intervention. The patient was led to the elucidation of current affects. Then, through a bridging technique, he was able to age regress and to reexperience the pictorial and emotional imagery which tied into his conflicts. He was provided with cognitive restructuring, ie, "the pilot is not your brother," and finally, in the context of ego-supportive measures, was able to integrate previously unconscious material into his field of consciousness.

Clarification of conflicts basically entails the discovery of all the feelings that enter into them. The following case example illustrates this process, used hypnotically, in a conflict involving the superego in its relationship to a constellation of sexual feelings, guilt, anxiety, and anger.

An attractive young woman was brought to the emergency room by the police. She had been wandering around the street, early in the morning, with few clothes, no papers, and no money. She was alert, suffered no trauma, and was clear medically. Her eyes were lucid and her demeanor appropriate; she was tense, polite, and concerned about her situation. Especially disturbing to her was the fact that the very last memory she had about herself dated back an entire week when she was attending to her job as a secretary in a neighboring city. She could talk about her life, her family in Europe, her strict religious schooling, her immigration to the United States, in detail, but she could not, however hard she tried, recall any of the events for an entire week that culminated in her dramatic admission to a major city hospital.

An amobarbitol sodium (Amytal) interview could have been done at this point. The amnesic hiatus—a week of this woman's life subtracted from the reach of her conscious mind—could be retrieved; but as the drug leaves the body, the amnesia returns. Using hypnosis, if feasible, is preferable because not only can memories and their emotional connections be brought out of the unconscious, but they can be worked with to encourage resolution.

She spoke and related well. The fact that she was in a helping environment was clear to her. She consented to hypnosis, with assurances that utmost care would be taken to make the experience as gentle as possible. Her somewhat agitated state gave way to a certain torpor, as a counting method was underway: "10, 11, 12, as we get to 20 we are more and more able to communicate with your subconscious mind. As you may know, your subconscious is a powerful part of your mind that contains dreams and all memories, from childhood on. And if your subconscious mind is willing, maybe it can let us in on some things it knows, at its own pace, for the purpose of making you feel better, more complete and whole . . . 13, 14 . . ." Hand levitation followed. "As you sit here in deep hypnosis, and we are here with you, maybe you can begin to think back to the time, some weeks ago, when you were working as a secretary . . ."

She began to speak. During her narrative, she was questioned, open endedly, about the sequence of events in her recent past. At times she became anxious and had to be guided back into relaxation before returning to her story. She described how, in the last few weeks, she had felt alone and with few friends. She had received an invitation to spend a day with a "family friend," a man she had known peripherally for a number of years. To her surprise, when she came to his home, he had prepared dinner, and to quell her feelings of shyness and social anxiety, she readily accepted the many drinks he offered her.

In the first hypnotic session, she could not recall the events that transpired from dinner time to the next few hours when, in the very early light of the morning, she found herself, half dressed, stumbling out of the apartment into the street. An amnesic core stayed on, which, in subsequent sessions, was clarified and eventually integrated. The forces of her superego, fueled by her intensive education and family tradition had pushed this first sexual experience beyond the doors of awareness, and at the same time, for the sake of ensuring completeness, had taken a whole week of her life along with it.

Hypnotherapy was mixed with short-term psychotherapy to modify some of the strong superego forces (by tempering their severity), to help with the ventilation and attenuation of affect, and to restore and even enhance self-esteem. She left the hospital two days later with all memories at her conscious disposal.

Psychogenic amnesia is a defense and a resistance protecting the equilibrium of the psyche from sudden overwhelming affect. Resistance, the sum of forces resisting therapeutic change, is a hallmark of any psychotherapeutic process, hypnotic or not, and although only few affects are involved—anxiety being the main one — its manifestation has many faces, from coming late or missing sessions to avoiding certain topics, from developing other symptoms to acting out. Hypnotherapy must treat defenses as forces with a purpose and not as static barriers in need of being broken.

In most hypnoanalytic interventions, supportive as well as insight methods are used. Supportive measures, in this context, do not imply blanket reassurances for the patient. Rather, they convey, first, an understanding of dynamic forces, then a strategy of encouraging or reinforcing healthy constructive ones and repressing or weakening those which are not. In the above example, punitive superego forces are dampened, with a view toward expanding the self-concept to accept the healthiness of having sexual desires.

Another facet of the therapy involves the ventilation and catharsis of repressed affect, which although not integrative in itself, provides for attenuation of emotion and for subsequent easier handling. Several techniques exist for hypnotic catharsis including open, expressive catharsis; implosive desensitization; or silent abreaction, ie, the use of projective imagery to "see oneself" emote.

Hypnotherapy may similarly be used to treat phobic disorders, when the phobia has a focal beginning in the patient's life. In such cases, "depth hypnotherapy"—hypnosis to retrieve painful experiences and historical conflicts—may be combined with more "surface hypnotherapy"—hypnosis to teach relaxation and to control the manifestations of anxiety.

The following case demonstrates how the capacity to create

dream imagery in hypnosis may be tapped to arrive at traumatic memories. Dream induction is often preferable to other techniques for phobia exploration because the subject is able to protect himself from intense anxiety through a number of different mechanisms including dissociation (the dreamer as observer witnesses the scene) and symbolization. At the same time, dreams provide dues which, like guideposts in a forest, weave through the barriers of defense to lead to better understanding.

A church organist came for consultation because of increasing anxiety, sometimes bordering on panic, during his performances. At 38, he was an accomplished musician whose services were very much sought after. Two months before, during a well-attended service, he remembers looking up at the high vaults and the rose windows and feeling twinges of apprehension; his fingers developed mild numbness, and he began to sweat. He was puzzled, and even more so when the same feelings, more pronounced, returned during his next performance a few days later. By now, he was clearly apprehensive. He could not understand this novel and distressing reaction which only occurred in this setting. His syndrome worsened and, when his anticipatory anxiety began consistently to darken his daily activities, he sought help.

He brought up the possibility of using hypnosis himself. Clinical experience shows that when patients do so, they are more likely to respond and benefit from the treatment.

The induction led to deep relaxation and to a good working trance level. Some time was spent making him aware of how deep relaxation felt within his body. "As you sit here deeply relaxed in a soothing hypnotic trance, I am going to ask the part of your mind that creates dreams to help us today. We have talked about the distressing feelings you have had recently, and it would be very helpful to know more about how they came to be. Your subconscious mind knows about that, I am almost certain. So I'll ask that part of your mind, if it would be kind enough to, to put together a dream that will tell us about your feelings, using any images it wants, for whatever length of time. Please let it do so after I count to three, and I will remain quiet until you signal me with your right index finger (ideomotor response) that you have stopped."

Four minutes later he raised his index finger. He was guided out of the trance and recounted the following dream. "I was real small, maybe 7 or 8 years old and I visited our neighbor, an older woman who used to give me candies. She gave me some, and then started singing a song, a religious song. I found it strange because I had never heard her sing. It was getting very noisy; I looked up and I saw the chandelier shaking, then the ceiling. I got scared, so I cupped my hands over my ears and hid under the table."

Using this dream and free association to elucidate symbolism, we arrived in time at the following memory: as a child of five, his mother (the neighbor in the dream) took him to church. It was a special occasion; maybe, he thinks, a mass for someone's death. The church was packed with people standing all around him. He held his mother's hand as the coats, dresses, and knees of people pressed against him. The music was loud, sonorous. It was a hot day (loud in the dream) and even hotter inside. He felt pushed, pressed, constricted—and frightened. He wanted to leave, to get some fresh air, some light. He looked up to see his mother but could not, because of obstructing faces, and instead fixed his eyes on a rose window high above. The church felt like it was spinning; then he fainted.

Subsequent exploration revealed that he had had his first anxiety episode, two months before, on the first anniversary of his mother's death. When all these memories and connections fell into place, he experienced a sense of release and relief. Given, in addition, posthypnotic suggestions for relaxation and self-mastery, he continued in his work symptom-free and with unhampered creativity.

The dream techniques carry a prominent position in hypnotherapy because they can be applied to a wide range of clinical problems—from exploration of complaints and resolution of symptoms to the task of finding creative solutions. The hypnotized subject may be asked to create a dream during the trance or, more open endedly, may be given a posthypnotic suggestion to have and remember any number of dreams until the next session. Depending on the patient, and current therapeutic demands, instructions for the elaboration of dreams may center on the distant past, on present reality-based problems, or on the future, ie, "as you see yourself in this future situation, how do you imagine yourself feeling? How would you like to see yourself experiencing and handling this event? What do you envision would be best for you?"

Symbolism, condensation, displacement, and other primary process mechanisms in hypnotic dreams are the same as those found in sleep dreams. In hypnotic dreams, however, some degree of volitional control and guidance may be applied in the context of hypnotic rapport so that, if need be, the patient may be asked to redream about the same conflict, to use different, perhaps more understandable symbols, to remember the dream clearly, and to be insightful about its meanings.

Clarification of the presenting dilemma sometimes is the only treatment needed as is exemplified in the following case.

A highly successful 50-year-old marketing specialist came to be treated for an ill-defined sense of unhappiness. Although happily married with two children doing exceedingly well, productive and financially rewarded in his work, he had had, for several months, a sense of following a path in life "that is not quite right." He made the following analogy "I feel I am on a fast moving train but that maybe I should be on another." Sifting the details of his life failed to bring up solid reasons for his sense of disquietude; in addition, he showed no evidence of any psychiatric or medical disorder. He mentioned that recently he had published his third article in a fiction magazine, and he had remarked, with some wonderment, on finding himself more interested in European history than at any time in his life.

A man with a flair for new experiences, he readily accepted a trial of hypnosis for purposes of clarification of these vague feelings of unhappiness. "I would ask you, as you sit here in hypnosis, to bring up some of the feelings we have been talking about, and for you to approach them and experience them even more than you have so far (affect enhancement), so that you can describe them better. Maybe this feeling of unhappiness contains other feelings. If it does, look at them with an eye on identifying them more and more clearly. If at any time you want to say something, please do; otherwise, I'll just stay here quietly while you search . . ."

He said nothing. Minutes later, a smile came across his face, which some seconds later left an imperceptible glow of contentment. After exiting from hypnosis, he was asked about the meaning of his smile. He described that moment of smiling as one of discovery; his dilemma was understood — not resolved, but understood. He clearly saw how he was trapped by success. He was living his life much too much as he "should be," "should" referring to the expectations of all those around him, reinforced by the tangible evidence of his proficiencies. He always had strong leanings to devote energies to writing, only to be stifled (well meaningly so he admitted) by his parents who pushed his business career. He was afraid to rearrange his priorities. Would he lose the interest, respect, and support of those around him if he tried to be even a part time writer? Could he possibly make a transition to what was closer to his heart, writing, yet be equally successful?

He had had, as is not uncommon, an "ah ha" experience during hypnosis. Although he may have had this realization by himself in his own time at some point in the future, in psychotherapy or not, hypnosis provided the context for several disconcruent dimensions of his life to be suddenly perceived as a "whole." In this case, one hypnotic session provided him with what he wanted. He eventually reached a solution of compromise, cutting down his job responsibilities progressively, and at the same time, writing and getting published.

This case illustrates the growing attention to what may be called problems of personal meaning or existential worth. It is increasingly realized clinically that a wide range of human problems are generated by frustrations to the creative expression of the drive for individual meta-significance.

Hypnotherapy may be called upon to deal with more complex patterns of mentation and behavior which, unlike delineated symptoms, have diffuse ramifications for the personality, permeating, often destructively, the patient's life pattern.

Ego state therapy (Watkins, 1979), based on the contributions of Federn (1952), sees patterns of behavior and experience as manifestations of ego subsystems which have a certain autonomy and internal consistency. Unlike multiple personality disorders, which have relatively rigid boundaries, ego states are more loosely integrated into the total personality. Yet, as structures of drives, fears, wishes, cognitions, and experiences rooted in their own developmental stages, they have the power to influence the final common pathways to behavior.

When a patient is to be treated with ego state therapy, it is helpful to begin with an exploration of these concepts in the waking state, with mention that the hypnotherapist, during hypnosis, may ask to communicate with some subparts of the personality. Often, concerns about having multiple personalities are raised by the patient; but differences should then be brought out, including the fact that many of the expressions of ego states are already known to the patient.

A computer-science student sought therapy for reasons that she could not clearly define in the first sessions. Especially bothersome to her, yet somehow comforting, was her lifestyle. At 28, she found herself alone most of the time, experiencing intense feelings of separateness. She worked out her schedule so that she was up most of the night and attended some classes in the late afternoon. The idea that she was sabotaging relationships was not new to her. At times, she would have a series of several dates; but when a male relationship became important to her, she started "behaving erratically," leading predictably, to its dissolution.

Explorative psychotherapy led to discussion about her family life. Having lived alone for over 10 years, she recalled with anxious sadness the turmoil between her parents. Her much older sister had already left the household. She brought back images of her parents fighting constantly, her father and her mother threatening to leave each other, and her comforting her mother who, often crying in her room by herself, would tell her what a crucifixion marriage was. She also tried to placate her father so that he would calm down enough to stay in the family.

In her daily routine, she felt alone and painfully awake in the early hours of the morning, dealing with gnawing sensations of internal void and of bitterness mixed, all too rarely, with fleeting hope. There was maybe, she would tell herself, a reason for all this, a way out, and a promise of a more normal life. This is how she sought therapy.

Agreement was made for exploration with hypnotherapy. She reached medium to deep hypnotic trance levels. 'Could you let us know [notice the use of "us" to reinforce the idea of a therapeutic alliance] if some of the feelings we have talked about in your daily life have connections with the experiences you had in your family as you were growing up?" It didn't take much time for her to nod yes. "I know it may be a little uncomfortable for you to do so, but let us, if you would, go back to that time, so we can retrieve some experiences, some feelings that can help our understanding of you, some memories that will help you eventually to feel better and happier."

Within a few moments she started talking. She placed herself in the middle of a heated argument between her parents. Each threatened the other with instantaneous departure. Frantically, yet unable to do much, she tried to ease their threats. What if my mother left, or father, or both? I would be all alone (like I am now, living out what I dreaded most).

She was asked to give this part of her, the one caught in this triangular family scenario, a name. First she said "the mediator." Later, she changed it to "the savior" (of the family), and later, in subsequent sessions, she called it "the frightened little girl."

The "frightened little girl" carried with her a vision of relationships wrought with tragedy. In hypnosis, she was able to answer questions, almost as a separate entity, about her own likes, dislikes, fears, and fantasies. In adult life, when a relationship became intimate, the "frightened little girl," through subconscious mechanisms, was able to alter total behavior, making the patient "erratic" — emotionally labile, irritable and angry, suddenly sullen.

In hypnosis she said "If it goes any farther, I will be faced with the same situation like with mom and dad."

In ego state therapy, these subparts of the patient are not told to go away or to stop their bothersome activities. From their perspective, these semiautonomous ego states are looking out for their welfare and existence, presumably in the interest of the whole person. Instead, efforts are made for their fears and wishes to be expressed and understood, and in turn, for them to understand, albeit in their own primitive ways, how certain changes could benefit all parties involved.

The cases and the commentaries above give the reader an idea of the tremendous range of applicability hypnosis has in the psychotherapeutic context. One should not remain, however, with the impression that hypnotherapy is a magical royal road to mental health. Like any other therapeutic intervention, it has to deal with the fabric of the patient's character structure and the various defensive forces along the way. There are also failures of hypnotherapy, stemming from misperceptions or misconceptions of patients' problems. Even Erickson writes of a seemingly innocuous hypnotic suggestion which set back therapeutic progress for three weeks. He asked a young woman "to see the loveliest thing you ever saw in your life," and she recreated her mother's lovely face in the aftermath of a fatal automobile accident.

Hypnotic phenomena, however, much like snow tires on an icy road, can be applied to therapeutic traction, helping many phases of psychotherapeutic work, from the exploration of the past and resolution of the present to the shaping of one's future directions.

ERICKSONIAN APPROACHES TO HYPNOTHERAPY

There are many ways to integrate hypnosis into psychotherapy, and many more are undoubtedly awaiting discovery. One integrative approach which has received a lot of attention derives from the work of Milton Erickson whose teachings of clinical hypnosis have been noted for their creativity and their attention to complex human psychological dynamics.

Erickson's style and methods of dealing with the hypnotic situation were unique and innovative enough so that the title "Ericksonian approaches to hypnotherapy" is clearly warranted. His beliefs were opposed to all strictly formulated theories for psychotherapy, with or without hypnosis (Moore, 1982). For him, theoretical constructs of human mentation and behavior were unduly restrictive and inhibited the therapist's awareness of the unique individual to individual interactions between himself and his patient. No one psychotherapeutic encounter is identical to the next; indeed, each moment of psychotherapy is unique in its own right.

Erickson did not have a personality theory into which the patient could fit. Rather, it was the other way around; he developed a personality theory for each patient, taking account of the patient's private way of processing life. Even his use of the terms "conscious" and "unconscious" were personalized to the patient. Rather than adhering to a Freudian topographic model, he preferred to think of the conscious in the dynamic context of the unconscious, with both dimensions being accessible to the many levels of interpersonal communication.

In view of the fact that these techniques require integration into the personal style of the therapist, a high degree of skill and intuitive understanding, they are not for the beginner. They are, first and foremost, strategies of psychotherapy to which hypnosis may be judiciously applied, and for this reason, a "how-to" explanation could not do them justice. Although the art of his craft poses challenges to the observer, in view of the complexities of the hypnotic interaction, the lack of controls, and the uniqueness of each individual patient treated, certain concepts may nevertheless be extracted from his work which, when integrated, become the essence of his therapeutic illuminations.

Erickson used formal induction in less than 10% of his cases. Instead, he infused the important elements of induction into the stream of interpersonal communication. In the trance, the individual's locus of self moves from external to internal realities.

The therapist observes and experiences the patient's mode of communication on as many different levels as possible — verbal, nonverbal, emotional, styles of imagery, cognitive functioning, and "enters" the patient's frame of reference, ie, his interpretation of reality, internal, and external. The therapist gradually modifies the patient's cognitions and behaviors so that the resulting change will be experienced by the patient as self-benefiting and ego syntonic.

To move with and around the critical observing and defensive ego, various techniques may be used, usually unobtrusively, and integrated into the casual conversation. Confusing the logical mind, much in the same way as the "koan" — the insoluble riddles of Zen — opens the way for new perceptions outside the patient's ordinary frame of reference. Surprise statements, paradoxes, and double binds jolt ordinary perspectives and call for novel ways to consider solutions. Indirect approaches sidestep ego vigilance, and focusing awareness on different sense modalities opens doors to the use of other mental areas (the right hemisphere for example).

Symptoms and their connected defensive forces are approached with respect and with the understanding that they represent purposeful, albeit maladaptive, compromises. The aim of hypnotherapy, or of all psychotherapy for that matter, is for the patient to incorporate symptoms into his field of control, in ways that will benefit growth, maturation, and happiness. Symptoms are then "mastered" and may be recreated or let go at will. To this end, different techniques may be called upon. Symptom prescription allows the patient to approach dreaded or distasteful symptoms with less fear or repulsion and to establish some jurisdiction over when, where, and how strongly or weakly they appear. The patient may then be asked to practice experiencing a mood, a feeling, or performing certain behaviors that already exist, or even to encourage the continuation of a symptom that appears to be waning. Prescribing the symptom to its worst extreme or to the absurd carries the process even further.

Defenses and resistances, as parts of the symptom complex, are similarly handled, sometimes encouraging them, sometimes challenging them, always in a style that is nonrigid, fluid, and adaptive. One is reminded of the Japanese method of psychological and physical training, Aikido, where force is not met with counterforce but is allowed to spend itself or to be diverted to new directions.

Many of Erickson's therapeutic results have yet to be adequately explained, their mechanisms comprehensively systematized, and their outcomes replicated. This is an example of how the clinical practice of hypnosis differs from laboratory analysis, how techniques relate to their craft, and how theory has yet to account for the uncharted areas of the human mind.

SUGGESTED READING AND REFERENCES

Arieti S: *Creativity, the Magic Synthesis.* New York, Basic Books, 1976.

Beahrs J: *Unity and Multiplicity: Multilevel Consciousness of Self in Hypnosis, Psychiatric Disorder and Mental Health.* New York, Brunner/Mazel, 1982.

Bowers K, Bowers P: Hypnosis and creativity: A theoretical and empirical rapproachement, in Fromm E, Shor R (eds): *Hypnosis: Research Developments and Perspectives.* Chicago, Aldine-Atherton, 1972.

Breuer J, Freud S: (1895) *Studies in Hysteria.* New York, Nervous and Mental Diseases Publishing Co, 1937.

Cousins N: Anatomy of an illness (as perceived by the patient). *N Engl J Med* 1976;295:1458.

Dengrove E: *Hypnosis and Behavior Therapy.* Springfield, Ill, Charles C Thomas, 1976.

Edelstein G: *Trauma, Trance, and Transformation. A Clinical Guide to Hypnotherapy.* New York, Brunner/Mazel, 1981.

Ellenberger H: *The Discovery of the Unconscious.* New York, Basic Books, 1970.

Erickson M: The confusion technique in hypnosis. *Am J Clin Hypn* 1964;6:183.

Esdaille J: *Hypnosis in Medicine and Surgery*(1846). New York, Julian Press, 1957.

Federn P: in Weiss E (ed): *Ego Psychology and the Psychoses.* New York, Basic Books, 1952.

Frankel FH: *Hypnosis: Trance as a Coping Mechanism.* New York, Plenum Medical Book, 1976.

Kampman R: Hypnotically induced multiple personality: An experimental study. *Int J Clin Exp Hypn* 1976;24:215-227.

Lazarus AA: *Behavior Therapy and Beyond.* New York, McGraw-Hill, 1971.

Marmor J: Recent trends in psychotherapy. *Am J Psychiatry* 1980;137:4.

Moore M: Ericksonian theories of hypnosis. *Am J Clin Hypn* 1982;24(3):183.

Raikov V: The possibility of creativity in the active stage of hypnosis. *Int J Clin Exp Hypn* 1976;24(3):258.

Sanders S: Creative problem solving and psychotherapy. *Int J Clin Exp Hypn* 1978;26:15-21.

Shader R, Greenblatt D: Some current treatment options for symptoms of anxiety. *J Clin Psychiatry* 1983;44(11, Sec 2):21-29.

Tokei JK: *Aikido in Daily Life.* Tokyo, Rikugei, 1966.

Wain H: Hypnosis in the control of pain. *Am J Clin Hypn* 1980;23:41.

Watkins J: The affect bridge: A hypnoanalytic technique. *Int J Clin Exp Hypn* 1971;19(1):21-27.

Watkins J, Watkins H: The theory and practice of ego state therapy, in Grayson H (ed): *Short-term Approaches To Psychotherapy.* New York, National Institute for the Psychotherapies and Human Science Press, 1979.

Wolberg L: Hypnosis in psychoanalytic psychotherapy, in Gordon J (ed): *Clinical and Experimental Hypnosis.* New York, Macmillan, 1967.

Wolpe JB: *Psychotherapy by Reciprocal Inhibition.* Stanford, Calif, Stanford University Press, 1958.

Zeig J: Symptoms prescription techniques: Clinical applications using elements of communication. *Am J Clin Hypn* 1980;23:23.

15

Psychotherapy of the Highly Hypnotizable Individual

Barbara DeBetz

Hypnosis in itself does not alleviate psychiatric symptoms, illness, or neurotic behavior. At best it can be regarded as a facilitator of a given treatment approach and, in general, a time-saving device to reach a therapeutic goal. The hypnotic state is a state of attentive, receptive focal concentration in which a patient is able to respond to appropriate instructions given by the hypnotherapist. The hypnotic state may result from a specific formal induction but may also occur spontaneously or may not be present even after a formal induction has been attempted.

If one examines any form of psychotherapy, a similar basic structure or pattern can be observed. The patient comes for help, admitting that there is a problem. In general, the patient believes that the therapist can help him. The therapist and patient then work together to understand the problem and bring about the desired change. Finally, the patient looks for and notices changes when they occur. Hypnosis is particularly effective in those who are hypnotizable and motivated to change. Everything done in hypnosis can also be done without it, but the hypnotic state adds a special leverage effect for implementing a specific treatment strategy. Although most clinicians who use hypnosis in the context of psychotherapy employ specific induction techniques, there is also a school of thought—the Ericksonian approach—which does not employ formal trance induction.

Milton Erickson's therapeutic interventions with hypnosis have become almost legendary and have been studied and dissected minutely by his followers. He has pioneered in a variety of indirect trance inductions. For example, he would induce trance behavior in a patient by just having what appeared to be a casual conversation. Or, there would be a long monologue which the patient would find tedious and boring. However, woven into the conversation or monologue, Erickson would implant specific "key sentences" or "key metaphors" which set the stage for the treatment goal. He explored the possibilities and limits of the hypnotic experience and investigated the nature of the relationship between hypnotherapist and patient. He had a unique approach to psychotherapy by combining it with an unstructured trance state. Not only was he an expert in the use of hypnosis, he was a superb clinician with acute perception and understanding of human behavior and psychodynamics. Erickson himself did not pay much attention to measurements and systematic recording and left it to his followers, such as Jay Haley, Ernest and Sheila Rossi, and others, to systematize and record his important works.

Some workers in the field feel that the person in the trance state is completely passive. However, Erika Fromm postulates that this is not the case. She states that the roles of ego activity, ego passivity, and ego receptivity are altered in the trance state and that hypnosis is characterized by increased ego receptivity in which critical judgment, reality orientation, and active goal-oriented thinking are constricted and kept to a minimum. At the same time, the individual allows unconscious and preconscious material come to the surface. The receptive mode of functioning in the hypnotic state may be related to the activity of the right cerebral hemisphere. Reyher (1977) described this receptive state as being a function of the right hemisphere as contrasted to the expressive mode of functioning of the left hemisphere with its typical analytic and critical functions.

Due to the accelerating effects of hypnosis, it is particularly useful as an adjunct in the short-term, symptom-oriented therapies, such as "cognitive restructuring" and behavior therapy. In short-term therapy, the major emphasis is on rapid and effective assessment of the problem. This kind of approach demands an atmosphere of urgency rather than the leisurely exploration with unlimited time as in the conventional psychotherapies. There seems to be an increasing trend in psychiatry towards these short-term intensive treatment modalities because of patients' time and, often, financial limitations to getting involved in long-term treatment approaches.

Obviously, not every patient is a candidate for short-term therapy, and obviously not every problem can be solved effectively this way. But if it works and the symptom is alleviated, the patient may be fully satisfied and go on to apply the newly learned formula to other problems as well. If the initial short-term intervention fails and the patient cannot master his symptom, a shift in treatment approach would be indicated. Also, as frequently happens, after symptom mastery has occurred, the patient's curiosity is aroused, and he may seek in-depth understanding of what the symptom had meant to him. The following case history will clearly demonstrate this point.

The patient was a 35-year-old woman. She was married but had no children. Both she and her husband were lawyers and were quite committed to their careers. The patient came for therapy because of a lifelong habit of pulling her hair. She had been in conventional psychotherapy on and off, but it never had any positive effect on her trichotillomania. As a last resort she wanted to try hypnosis.

At the time of her visit, her hair had been pulled so badly that she had to wear a wig in order to hide the huge bald spots on her head.

She proved to be of mid-range hypnotic trance capacity. The instructions given to the patient while in the trance were the following: "Hair-pulling is an insult to your body. You need your body to live. You owe your body respect and protection."

Following the formal trance, there was a posthypnotic discussion based on the above three instructions, amplifying those points, and "restructuring" her attitude towards her hair and body. Then she was instructed in the use of self-hypnosis to be done 10 to 15 times daily, repeating to herself the three points.

The patient gained mastery over her hair-pulling within three sessions. At the last follow-up session, the patient expressed her desire to continue in therapy in order to fully understand what her symptom had meant to her all these years. She continued in insight-oriented psychotherapy and came twice each week for the next two and a half years. During that time hypnosis was not used except on two occasions when she had a brief relapse of trichotillomania.

Without going into a detailed description of all the psychodynamics involved, the hair-pulling, which had started around the age of 8, had strong guilt connotations relating to masturbatory practices which also started around that age. In addition, she felt partially responsible for the divorce of her parents and the ensuing conflict about which parent to be loyal to. Both parents remarried and she had serious difficulties relating to either stepparent. Her stepmother disliked her very openly and suffocated any femininity in her. She was especially envious of the patient's beautiful hair and, during one summer vacation, she took her to the beauty parlor and had all the hair cut off. The patient was enraged at the stepmother but found no sympathy from her father or anybody else. She had intense feelings of wanting to kill her stepmother but obviously controlled her impulses and turned them inward. Shortly after the traumatic event, she started pulling her hair. She grew up to be an extremely perfectionistic person with severe self-doubts and conflicts about her femininity. Pulling her hair had become her tool for self-punishment.

What was very interesting in this patient was the fact that she had been in insight-oriented therapy before but did not come to full understanding of her symptom and therapy had had no positive effect on the symptom. However, once she had learned mastery over the symptom, she was able to come to a clear understanding of the symptom. Mastery through hypnotic restructuring and insight through continued therapy helped this patient to stop pulling her hair.

This is contrary to old beliefs, especially in analytically oriented thinking, that symptom removal gives rise to a new symptom unless the symptom has been clearly "worked through." In the above case, it was the other way around: the patient could only work through the problem after symptom mastery had taken place. There is ever more growing evidence that individuals with a certain amount of ego strength and strong motivation can mobilize their resources in a relatively short period of time and respond effectively to short-term treatment interventions.

If the therapist wants to provide an optimal therapeutic strategy in a minimal amount of time, the therapist has to know how to assess the patient's presenting problem and be able to formulate a treatment strategy which is geared to restructuring the patient's complaint in a dialectically meaningful manner. The therapist has to be able to sift through a variety of problems and symptoms which are at times clearly described by the patient and at other times vaguely and evasively described. The therapist has to "zoom" into focus the major theme of the patient's complaints and select the most relevant problem to be dealt with at that time.

The Hypnotic Induction Profile (HIP), which has been described earlier in this text, can provide a rough starting point in the organization of the patient's data. It provides information about the patient's hypnotic trance capacity on a continuum from not being hypnotizable at all to low-range, mid-range, and high-range hypnotizability. In addition, it provides a certain amount of information about an individual's relative state of mental health as outlined in Figure 15-1, page 202. It should be noted here that the correlation of the HIP and psychopathology are hypothetical and further research needs to be done to validate this hypothesis. However, for the purpose of short-term therapy it is helpful to use the information derived from the HIP as a rough indicator for psychopathology. In addition to the psychopathology hypothesis, the HIP postulates that, depending on a patient's level of hypnotizability, three distinct personality styles can be identified.

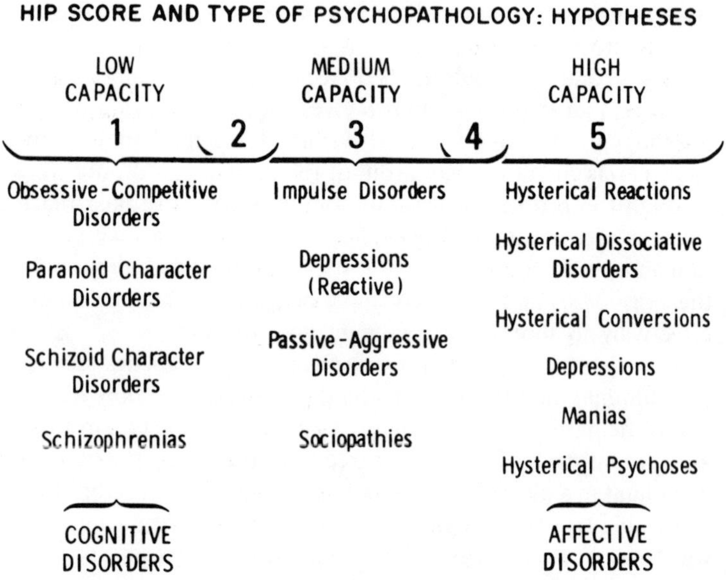

HIP SCORE AND TYPE OF PSYCHOPATHOLOGY: HYPOTHESES

LOW CAPACITY	MEDIUM CAPACITY	HIGH CAPACITY
1 2	3 4	5
Obsessive-Competitive Disorders	Impulse Disorders	Hysterical Reactions
Paranoid Character Disorders	Depressions (Reactive)	Hysterical Dissociative Disorders
Schizoid Character Disorders	Passive-Aggressive Disorders	Hysterical Conversions
		Depressions
Schizophrenias	Sociopathies	Manias
		Hysterical Psychoses
COGNITIVE DISORDERS		AFFECTIVE DISORDERS

Figure 15-1

Spiegel calls these three personality types Apollonian, Odysean, and Dionysian. There is ample literature on the relationship between hypnotizability and personality traits. None so far have come up with consistent data. But certain trends have been confirmed. Individuals with high hypnotizability have been found to generally have an optimistic disposition and a "bright" mood. They have a somewhat naive and trusting approach to people. Low hypnotic trance capacity has been associated with being less outgoing and being more critical and suspicious. Certain attributes, such as stability and extroversion, along with low anxiety levels, have been related to hypnotizability, as have the capacity for imaginative creativity and an ability to experience total absorption with constricted peripheral awareness.

Despite the controversy regarding the validity of correlating hypnotizability with specific personality traits, it can be helpful to the short-term therapist to get a broad understanding of the kind of personality he is dealing with. Using the Spiegel classification of personality types as related to hypnotizability, the following traits have been found in a large sample of patients seen in clinical practice.

The Apollonians are those who fall into the low range of hypnotizability. They tend to be rational and logical. Even with intense concentration, they do not get totally absorbed in an activity they are doing, always keeping their spatial awareness. Their time perception is primarily past or future, often to the extent of missing out in the present. They have a strong need to be in control all the time. They are usually critical and do not trust easily. They are more interested in implementing their ideas rather than being overly imaginative and creative in new ideas. They tend to take their responsibilities very seriously, are very organized, and tend to keep their commitments. If they have a choice to experience something new by either seeing it or touching it, they usually prefer the visual experience to a tactile one.

The Dionysians are those who fall into the high range of hypnotizability. They tend to be capable of getting totally absorbed in something they are doing to the extent of losing awareness of their spatial orientation. Their time sense is primarily the present, not being overly concerned with past or future. They tend to give preference to their feelings rather than logic reasoning. They tend to feel comfortable with relinquishing control to others and they are prone to trust easily to the extreme of being gullible. They tend to suspend their critical judgment as they assimilate new information. Frequently they lack a sense of responsibility, are less organized but have a rich fantasy and creative imagination. They enjoy experiencing the world around them in a tactile, rather than visual, way.

The Odysseans are those who fall into the mid-range of hypnotizability, and they have personality features that represent a mixture of the traits found in the two extreme groups, the Apollonians and the Dionysians. Their spatial sense, time perception, and affective cognitive balance, issues related to control and trust,

STRUCTURAL THEMES AND HYPNOTIZABILITY

GRADE:	Hypnotic Induction Profile	0	1	2	3	4	5
	CHARACTER TYPES		APOLLONIAN		ODYSSEAN		DIONYSIAN
STRUCTURES	A) Space Awareness (Absorption)		PERIPHERAL / Focal		FOCAL-PERIPHERAL		FOCAL \ Peripheral
	B) Time Perception		PAST-FUTURE		PAST-PRESENT-FUTURE		PRESENT
	C) Myth-Belief Constellation (Premises)		COGNITIVE / Affective		AFFECTIVE-COGNITIVE		AFFECTIVE \ Cognitive
	1) Locus of Interpersonal Control		INTERNAL		INTERNAL-EXTERNAL		EXTERNAL
	2) Trust Proneness		LOW		VARIED		HIGH
	3) Critical Appraisal		IMMEDIATE		VARIED		SUSPENDED
	4) Learning Style		ASSIMILATION		ACCOMMODATION		AFFILIATION
	5) Responsibility		HIGH		VARIED		LOW
	6) Preferred Contact Mode		VISUAL		VISUAL-TACTILE		TACTILE
	D) Processing		Premise / IMPLEMENT		MIXED		PREMISE \ Implement
	1) Writing Value		HIGH		VARIED		LOW

Figure 15-2

are all more in the mid-range rather than extreme as in the other two groups. The Odyssean constellation of personality traits represents the majority of individuals due to the fact that the majority of the hypnotizable population falls into a mid-range trance capacity. For schematic representation of the different personality traits as correlated to the HIP, see Figure 15-2.

GRADE 5 SYNDROME

The highly hypnotizable individual who has emotional problems presents a special challenge to the psychotherapist. When these patients decompensate, are under stress or tension, they tend to present with hysterical symptoms, conversion reactions, or dissociative states. Spiegel called this the grade 5 syndrome. Patients falling into that category usually have a high eye roll sign and score a 4 to 5 on the HIP. All patients who have a HIP of 4 are potential 5s. As outlined before, the grade 5 can be tested by additional tests given after the HIP has been determined. These extra test items are: age regression in the present tense, sustained posthypnotic motor alterations, negative hallucinations, and global amnesia for the entire hypnotic event. If the individual tests positively on all these test items, he is considered a grade 5; if only one or two items are present, he is considered a 4 to 5 and, if none, a grade 4.

These are the typical traits found in those who are considered grade 5s: high propensity for trust, suspension of critical judgment, an ease in assimilating new events, and a relatively telescoped sense of time. There is also the ability to feel at ease with logical incongruitites, a phenomenon identified by Orne as "trance logic." They have an excellent memory, learn uncritically, and absorb new information easily. They have an intense capacity for concentrating and dissociating. Although the grade 5s are very responsive and suggestible, there seems to be a fixed personality core under the malleable overlay. This paradoxical relationship between fixed personality core and chameleon-like malleability can lead in these individuals to role confusion and a reactive sense of inferiority. For example, even when the grade 5 individual performs well or receives good grades in school because of the ease with which the grade 5 can learn, he may feel as if it was not really his accomplishment. The grade 5 is also a person who is very responsive to external cues and frequently complies with those external cues at the expense of not asserting his own wishes and desires. They try to live up to other people's expectations. The grade 5s frequently possess an acute sense of perceiving other people's feelings which may range from sincere empathy to pathological fusion with another person. They tend to form dependent interpersonal relationships. They often seek situations in which another person provides structure and control which they cannot provide for themselves. The grade 5s also tend to have difficulties communicating in clearly understandable ways, especially if there are conflicts in a relationship. Frequently these individuals will choose somatic metaphors to express their difficulties, leaving it up to the outside world to decipher the metaphorical message. These individuals have special treatment requirements. They usually do not do very well in insight-oriented psychotherapy because of their need to comply with the therapist and be a good patient. They also feel anxious and confused if left to free unguided associations. The treatment of the grade 5 syndrome patient involves guidance in perceiving alternatives and exercising their right to assert themselves. They do better if short-term goals as well as long-term goals are clearly spelled out from the beginning of treatment. They need to recognize negative field forces. Because they are so urgently in need of guidance and direction, they fail to criticallly assess the outside world and can become easy victims for exploitation. The most effective approach to the grade 5 syndrome patient is supportive guidance with emphasis on guidelines to help the patient perceive clearly the metaphors operating in his life. There needs to be clarifications of goals and values and the ways to reach them. Under duress and stress, the grade 5 individual may present with symptoms of hysteria, conversion reaction, hysterical psychosis and, occasionally, multiple personality.

What is the role of hypnosis in the grade 5 syndrome patient? Because of these individuals' high trance capacity, they need to be aware of their proneness to shift into spontaneous trance states and learn to recognize their personality traits. The hypnotic trance is used to identify these individuals but later, during the course of therapy, hypnosis is only used occasionally either for anxiety control, abreaction, age regression, or personality integration in the multiple personality. The following case history* will clearly demonstrate the different aspects of treating the grade 5 syndrome patient.

---

* Reprinted with permission from Spiegel H, Spiegel D: *Trance and Treatment.* New York, Basic Books, 1978.

K.N. was a 24-year-old New York-born female who was diagnosed as having multiple sclerosis two and a half years prior to coming to the author's attention. Her initial symptoms included weakness, pain, and tingling in her left leg. Over the next several months she complained of blurred vision, diplopia, urinary frequency, increasing weakness in her lower extremities, ataxia, slurred speech, and other transitory symptoms.

The patient was first seen in Madrid, where she lived. Later she came to New York for further neurological testing. The objective findings were: slight ataxia in the lower extremity, slight hyperreflexia of the left biceps and left patella, and questionable minimal temporal pallor of the left optic disc. After the New York work-up she went to a southern medical center for further treatment. She had skull x-rays, electroencephalograms, a brain scan, echoencephalogram, and cerebrospinal fluid studies, all of which were within normal limits. She also had a myelogram with foramen magnum studies which were normal, but she developed a pulmonary embolus postmyelogram.

She received coumadin, intrathecal steroids, intravenous ACTH, and a course of immunosuppressive drugs (Imuran). While on Imuran, she got pregnant and obtained a therapeutic abortion because of the medication. Approximately one year after the onset of the illness, she was again admitted to a New York hospital and received another course of intrathecal steroids, with a resulting chemical meningitis. She also developed an allergy to ACTH. She got progressively worse and was finally confined to a wheelchair.

The patient's past medical history was essentially negative, except for seven episodes of thrombophlebitis when in nursing school. She was a middle child in a family of seven siblings. One brother had an episode of blindness at the age of 18 which had lasted for one month. Although he was diagnosed as having multiple sclerosis, he had since been well for over 10 years. One first-degree female cousin had a diagnosis of multiple sclerosis was nursed by the patient for a while. The patient's father had chronic disc disease and had multiple operations for it. Her mother had had several episodes of thrombophlebitis.

The patient came from a middle-class family and described her childhood as relatively happy and uneventful. At the age of 8, a few days after her mother returned from the hospital with a new baby, she developed "brain fever" and was hospitalized. She remembered thinking at that time how nice it would be to receive attention while being in the hospital. During high school she had dysmenorrhea which was conveniently used to avoid taking tests. She had frequent colds and episodes of thrombophlebitis while going to nursing school. After graduation, her phlebitic episodes stopped completely. She worked as a psychiatric nurse, felt very competent, and had no physical complaints.

As a nurse, she met her husband, a Spanish lawyer getting graduate training in the United States. After he finished his training, they got married and moved to Madrid. The patient was faced with adjusting to a rather different way of living. His family did not readily accept an American as their son's wife; also, they constantly criticized her for not having a maid, for being too independent, and for not becoming pregnant right away. Her husband started his law practice and had less and less time for her. At about that time her first symptom appeared. Two and half years later, she returned to new York for further hospitalization. One of the neurologists started to have doubts about the diagnosis because of the lack of objective findings throughout the illness. Psychiatric consultation was done, and the patient was found to be a grade 5. Psychological testing showed no organicity, but evidence of the dynamics of a hysterical conversion reaction with depressive features. She was discharged from the hospital and referred to the author for appropriate psychotherapy.

The patient was seen for a total of 11 therapy sessions over a period of two months. The treatment strategy consisted of the following steps. First, several basic questions had to be clarified, such as "What got her into the situation of using a conversion mechanism to express her conflict? What cues did she get from her environment to act in this specific way? Why did she use somatic metaphors as means of communication? What was the secondary gain element?"

In summary, the clarification of these questions follows: K.N. had married into a family which did not really want her and which had a different language, culture and value system. When in New York, she was in charge and on top of the situation; in Spain, her husband was. His family put pressure on her to be something she could not be, a Spanish wife. Initially, she rebelled against them, but the pressure increased and the message she received was: "You better be a helpless, submissive dependent woman if you want to make it with us." She got the message and became progressively more debilitated, needed a maid, could not ride her bicycle anymore, and needed an escort even to leave the house. Now she was helpless and dependent. She had fulfilled and caricatured their expectations.

The patient used a body metaphor because it had worked for her before, ie, when she was 8 years old and had that strange brain fever to get more attention than the newly arrived baby. In high school dysmenorrhea had been convenient and in nursing school thrombophlebitis had been useful. Her family had always responded to illness. The secondary gain factor was that when she was totally disabled, her husband and his entire family got very involved with her. After all, who would be rejecting towards someone who has such a tragic disease as multiple schlerosis? Not only did she receive attention at home, but also as a patient. In any hospital she rapidly became the favorite and most interesting patient. One of the many doctors consulted during her illness was so fascinated by her as a patient that he wanted her to leave her husband and stay with him.

After these issues were clarified with her, therapy consisted of a restructuring of her metaphors. She progressed rapidly and learned to recognize her vulnerabilities and how to master them. Therapy did not include gaining analytic insight in a longitudinal way, but was rather present- and future-oriented. The transference between patient and therapist was left completely untouched. Since treatment two and one-half years ago the patient has been symptom-free, has delivered her first child, and has maintained a full schedule of physical and intellectual activities.

MULTIPLE PERSONALITY

Multiple personality has been considered, until recently, a clinical rarity, and it has probably received far more public than professional attention. Despite the growing interest and research that has been done, the multiple personality disorder remains a controversial condition. It used to be grouped diagnostically with the hysterias. Currently it has been reclassified as a dissociative disorder.

According to the Diagnostic and Statistical Manual of Mental Disorders (DSM-III),* the essential feature of the multiple personality is the existence of two or more distinct personalities within the individual. Each of these personalities is dominant at a particular time. Each personality is a fully integrated and complex unit with unique memories, behavior patterns, and social relationships that determine the nature of the individual's acts when that personality is dominant. Transition from one personality to another is sudden and often associated with psychosocial stress.

Usually the original personality has no knowledge or awareness of the existence of any of the other personalities (subpersonalities). When there are more than two subpersonalities in one individual, each is aware of the others to varying degrees. The subpersonalities may not know each other or be constant companions. At any given moment one personality will interact verbally with the external environment, but none or any number of the other personalities may actively perceive (ie, "listen in on") all that is going on.

The original personality and all of the subpersonalities are aware of lost periods of time. "They" will usually admit to this if asked, but will seldom volunteer this information.

The individual personalities are nearly always quite discrepant and frequently seem to be opposites. For example, a quiet, retiring spinster may alternate with a flamboyant, promiscuous bar

---

* Reprinted with permission from American Psychiatric Association: *Diagnostic and Statistical Manual of Mental Disorders,* ed 3. Washington, DC, APA, 1980.

habitue on certain nights. Over the course of the disorder, usually one of the personalities is dominant.

Associated features One or more of the personalties may function with a reasonable degree of adaption (eg, be gainfully employed) while alternating with another personality that is clearly maladapted or has a specific, separate, mental disorder. Studies have demonstrated that various subpersonalities in the same individual may have different responses to physiological and psychological measurements.

One or more of the subpersonalities may report being of the opposite sex, of a different race or age, or from a different family than the original personality. Each subpersonality, however, displays behaviors characteristic of its stated age, which is usually younger than the actual age.

One or more of the personalities may be aware of hearing or having heard the voice(s) of one or more of the other personalities or may report having talked with or engaged in activities with one or more of the other personalities. These internal conversations and the belief that one has engaged in activities with another personality when the latter is actually a dissociated aspect of the original personality must be differentiated from other forms of hallucinatory and delusional experiences.

The subpersonalities often exist in groups of two or three, all of whom represent the same period of life (eg, adolescence). When this occurs, one or more of these subpersonalities tends to have the role of protector of another member(s) of the group.

Psychosocial stress most often precipitates the transition from one personality to another; hypnosis may also effect this change. Usually transitions occur in a dramatic manner.

Most often, the subpersonalities have proper names, usually different from the first name, and sometimes from both the first and last names, of the original personality. Occasionally one or more subpersonalities are unnamed.

Somatoform disorders and psychological factors affecting physical condition apparently are common in individuals with multiple personality. Differential diagnosis, psychogenic fugue, and psychogenic amnesia may be confused with multiple personality, but do not present its characteristic repeated shifts of identity and usually are limited to a single, brief episode. Also, in both psychogenic amnesia and psychogenic fuge, awareness of the original personality is absent. Complex social activities, memories, behavior patterns, and friendships are not present in psychogenic amnesia and are uncommon in psychogenic fuge.

Psychotic disorders such as schizophrenic disorders may be confused with multiple personality because the individual reports hearing or talking with the voices of other personalities. Malingering can present a difficult diagnostic dilemma. The presence of secondary gain suggests malingering.

In summary, the diagnostic criteria for multiple personality are: (1) the existence within the individual of two or more distinct personalities, each of which is dominant at a particular time; (2) the personality that is dominant at any particular time determines the individual's behavior; and (3) each individual personality is complex and integrated with its own unique behavior patterns and social relationships.

Hypnotic treatment approaches Patients with multiple personality disorder are generally highly hypnotizable individuals. There has been controversy regarding the creation of new personalites in individuals with this disorder through hypnosis. However, no clear clinical evidence to this effect has been established. Hypnosis is a useful tool when used in patients suffering from this disorder, but it should be used cautiously, especially by the clinician who is not thoroughly familiar with hypnosis. If hypnosis is employed, it usually accelerates diagnostic clarification as well as treatment. Timing of the hypnotic intervention is important. If the patient is confronted too early with the diagnosis and a solid, trusting, therapeutic relationship has not been developed yet, the patient might get frightened and drop out of therapy. If the practitioner waits too long, the patient will become impatient and feel that the therapist is not in touch with his problems. Hypnosis can be used to confirm a suspected diagnosis, and once the patient has accepted the existence of multiple personalities, specific treatment can begin.

The first step in the treatment strategy consists of establishing the fact that the therapist cannot control the patient through hypnosis. Issues of control are very delicate matters in these individuals. Therefore, early on in the treatment, it is helpful to teach the patient the use of self-hypnosis in addition to the therapist-guided hypnosis.

Hypnosis can be used to gather historical information about the alternate personalities. It can also be used to call upon another personality and allow that personality to be treated and express feelings about existing problems. The various personalities have to be contacted in order to establish treatment alliances, agreements not to form new personalities, not to be violent, suicidal, destructive, promiscuous, or whatever else the problem may be. Frequently, some personalites exist without being revealed to the therapist. This may lead to resistance during induction procedures. There also may be anxiety on the part of the dominant personality, being afraid of the influence of another personality. This is relatively easy to overcome by reassuring the dominant personality that it will be brought back regardless of the wishes of any of the other personalities.

Hypnosis is helpful to abreact childhood traumata or other traumatic experiences and to express repressed affects. It generally requires several sessions to allow sufficient abreaction and relief. Sometimes several personalites show different reactions to the same event or affect.

After sufficient information has been gathered, the psychodynamic issues of each personality must be worked through so that integration will yield a functional entity, not a fragmented one. This phase of therapy can be done with or without hypnosis.

The next step towards integration, or fusion, is the establishment of clear communication among the different personalities. This can be done by using the image of a "switchboard," where the therapist is the switchboard operator. Each personality has to go through the operator who gives the messages to the appropriate personality. Later on, communication is done through an internalized switchboard operator. At this point integration may occur either spontaneously or through the final ceremony of a hypnotic session.

Most fusions occur with one personality at a time, but fusions of several or all personalites have been seen. Various fusion techniques, or rituals, have been described. The most common ones are images of union, merger or rebirth, in which all personalites are preserved and just fuse into one strong individual, unified forever. Once integration has occurred, therapy should be geared towards teaching the individual new coping skills, such as relaxation, behavior rehearsal, imagery, and assertiveness training.

In summary, it appears clear that hypnosis plays an important role in the treatment strategy of the multiple personality disorder. Due to the complexity of this syndrome, the therapist should carefully plan and develop the treatment schedule. The major limitations of the use of hypnosis for these patients are the skill and experience of the therapist. The inexperienced hypnotherapist can cause more harm than help and would do well to seek the assistance of an experienced clinician before proceeding with hypnosis.

AGE REGRESSION

Hypnotic age regression is a state in which the individual regresses to a previous episode or period in his life. It is generally accepted that only the highly hypnotizable individual can experience age regression in the present tense. Those falling into the midrange or low range of hypnotizability may also experience age regression, but it is only partial and not felt and experienced in the same way as when the highly hypnotizable patient is regressed.

There are different views regarding the phenomenon of age regression. Orne as well as Sarbin define age regression as a form of role-playing. This coincides with Weitzenhoffer's view of his type I age regression. In type I the adult acts out or role-plays an earlier time. In type II regression there is a true psychophysiological return to an earlier period, an actual revivification. Weitzenhoffer also stated that most regressions show a mixture of types I and II. Reiff and Scheerer (1959) described regression in terms of early memory traces being reactivated and thus becoming more easily accessible to conscious awareness. Although there have been various physiological and psychological studies of individuals who were age regressed, no clear cut evidence has been found. Therefore, it may be helpful to adopt the concept that age regression in a morphological sense is not possible and that there is no true return to infancy or childhood. The perceptual–cognitive systems of the adult are organized differently from those of the child. When adults regress, they reactivate infantile conflicts, wishes, and fears, but at the same time they keep their adult coping and defense mechanisms. Since a true biological regression is not possible, it is meaningless to ask whether the age-regressed individual is really behaving like a 7-year-old or only acting like one. Rather, the question should be, does the regressed patient behave as he imagines a child to function, feel, or behave and does this lead to coming into contact with early memory traces or cognitive structures.

What use is age regression in therapy? In addition to being a diagnostic tool, it can be used for certain treatment situations. However, age regression should be only done by an experienced and knowledgable hypnotherapist. It should be avoided in situations such as lecture or classroom demonstrations because of the possible traumatic events that may come up. There should also be enough time allowed so that the patient can adjust comfortably after he has come out of the age regression.

It is helpful to first explore with the patient, in a face-to-face interview, which areas will be covered while regressed. This way the therapist will have some guidelines on how to proceed and how far to regress the patient. Before regressing the patient towards the conflict areas, it is always a good idea to run through a trial regression. This means that the therapist induces a trance and just regresses the patient to a specific age, such as a 16th, 10th, or 6th birthday. Birthdays are usually neutral landmarks for age regression. Once regressed to age 6 for example, the tester should ask questions such as: "What's your name?" "How old are you today?" "Anything special today?" "Do you know who the president of the United States is?" etc. The responses of the age-regressed individual should be appropriate to the age tested. The highly hypnotizable person will respond appropriately to the age he regressed to, including vocabulary, tone of voice, and motor behavior. Some individuals become even nonverbal when regressed below the age of one year and may develop a grasping, sucking, or even Babinski reflex. These reflexes are characteristic of infants but disappear later on. These primitive reflexes and infantile emotional responses remain stored in the unconscious, and in some highly hypnotizable individuals they may be tapped and uncovered through the use of hypnosis.

The following two case histories represent the therapeutic use of age regression.

Abused Child—Age Regression and Abreaction

The patient was a 38-year-old woman of German descent. She was married, had one child, age 5, and worked as a nurse in a home for abused children. She had been in therapy for several years already and was referred by her therapist specifically to try age regression. The therapist and the patient both felt that getting some knowledge about her early childhood was important. According to the patient, her parents had left Nazi Germany because they both had some Jewish ancestry and were afraid to remain in Europe. They emmigrated to Puerto Rico where the father became a successful businessman. Two years after they had settled down in Puerto Rico, Helen D., the patient, was born. Helen's mother died of pneumonia shortly after Helen's birth. The patient did not remember the exact circumstances. According to Helen's father, she was taken care of by a variety of nurses, babysitters, and housekeepers. The father spent very little time with her. At age 7, the father remarried, and the family moved to New York. The patient had no recollection whatsoever of any events that occurred in Puerto Rico where she spent the first 7 years of her life.

She went into therapy because she had problems relating to her 5-year-old daughter, and there had been some incidents where she lost control and hit her daughter harder than she intended to. The patient and her therapist both felt that there might have been events in her first 7 years of life that would be important for Helen to know. An interesting fact was that she neither spoke nor understood Spanish, although she had lived in Puerto Rico and had had mainly Spanish-speaking caretakers. She spoke some German because her father would speak to her in that language.

She was grade 4 to 5 on the Hypnotic Induction Profile. She regressed in the present tense and had vivid recollection of her 10th birthday which had been a very happy occasion with two of her cousins having come to visit from Europe. When she was regressed to age 6, she did not respond to English instructions, and the author (therapist) switched to speaking in German. Helen responded and her face gradually turned sad. "Daddy is never home. I don't want Olga anymore," she said in German. "Who is Olga?" "Olga, you know Olga . . . ," tears started to come to Helen's eyes. The trance was terminated at that point and Helen was brought back to the present time. When she came out of the hypnotic trance, she did not remember what we had talked about.

The next few sessions were spent going back in time recalling the years in Puerto Rico. Helen produced vivid recall; some of it was rather painful. What gradually developed was a picture of a variety of caretakers, some of whom had been very cruel and unloving towards her. There was, for instance, one woman who had tied Helen's hands and feet when she was 5 years old and had force-fed her. Helen abreacted this event with intense anxiety and affect. Several of her caretakers had been German and some had been Spanish. Over the time of regression, Helen also started to recollect some knowledge of Spanish. However, most of the age regression was done in German because this was the language she spoke best at that age. The picture evolved that she had been an abused child during those years and obviously, as a defense mechanism, she had repressed this entire period of her life.

During the initial sessions of age regression, Helen had amnesia for most of the memories, but gradually she started to remember. It was also suggested to her that she could get in touch with these memories gradually, or even through her dreams. We had a total of six sessions, then she returned to her regular therapist.

Having gone through age regression and abreaction of some of the painful past events helped her to understand why she had repressed those seven years of her life totally. It also helped her to understand the paradox of working and loving her work as a nurse in the child abuse clinic and at the same time having strong impulses of abusing her own child. Having relived her own abused childhood allowed her to gradually incorporate these memories and work them through in therapy.

Memory Retrieval of Hiding Place

The following case is a demonstration of partial age regression. The patient was a 25-year-old man who wanted to use hypnosis for the purpose of retracing a place in his attic where he had hidden some incriminating sexual pictures of himself and another man. His parents were in the process of selling the family house and when John K., the patient, found out, he was panic stricken because he had hidden those pictures in the attic approximately four years prior to the impending sale. He had gone up to the attic several times but just could not remember the hiding place.

His Hypnotic Induction Profile was a mid-range profile that of a 2 to 3. The patient was guided into the trance, and he was regressed back in time to the day when he had been hiding those pictures. While in the trance, he was instructed to describe in great detail every detail of that day: the clothes he was wearing, the time of the year, the weather, and finally the attic. He was instructed to trace back each step that he took while deciding on the hiding place.

During hypnosis, he had some vague recollections of the attic and where he had moved around up there, but he did not come to any clear picture. He was instructed to use self-hypnosis at home, several times each day. He was told to imagine that he was looking at a screen (a television or movie screen) or just a blank wall, and once he had the screen in clear focus to project the events of that hiding day onto the screen, going over the attic again and again. In between trials, he was supposed to come out of the trance, go about his usual business and then go into the trance again. By the third day, he had enough recollection of the hiding place to again attempt to go up to the attic. And, sure enough, he did find the pictures which he had safely put under the wood floor in one specific corner. In this case, the patient used self-hypnosis to get a clearer understanding and image of what he was searching for.

Material gathered during age regression is not always exact and real. Frequently, especially in those individuals who do not fall into the upper range of hypnotic trance capacity, patients may add fantasy material or confabulation. Material that has been gathered in the trance should be gradually incorporated into therapy, especially if there is posthypnotic amnesia. The mechanism of regression is often a defense mechanism to bar painful material from consciousness. The therapist should keep this in mind and not force a patient to accept material for which he may not be ready. Therefore, it is good clinical practice to give a suggestion that the patient may or may not remember what had happened, or the recollection will gradually come over a period of days or weeks, or there may be a dream related to the material uncovered during the hypnotic age regression.

SUGGESTED READING AND REFERENCES

Diagnostic and Statistical Manual of Mental Disorders, ed 3. DSM-III, The American Psychiatric Association, 1980;257-259.
Erickson MH, Rossi EL, Rossi SI: *Hypnotic Realities.* New York, Irvington Publishers, 1978.
Foenander G, Burrows GD: Phenoma of Hypnosis, Age Regression, in

Burrows GD, Dennerstein L (eds): *Handbook of Hypnosis and Psychosomatic Medicine*. Amsterdam, Elsevier/North-Holland Biomedical Press, 1980, pp 68-81.

Fromm E: An ego-psychological theory of altered states of consciousness. *Int J Clin Exp Hypn* 1977;25:372-387.

Haley J: *Strategies of Psychotherapy*. New York, Grune & Stratton, 1963.

Kluft RP: Varieties of hypnotic interventions in the treatment of multiple personality. *Am J Clin Hypn* 1982;24(4):230-240.

Kluft RP (guest editor): Multiple personality disorder. *Psychiatric Ann* 1984;14(1):19-24, 27-31, 34-40.

Marmor J: Recent trends in psychotherapy. *Am J Psychiatry* 1980;137(4):409-416.

Mott T: The role of hypnosis in psychotherapy. *Am J Clin Hypn* 1982;24(4):241-248.

Orne MT: The mechanisms of hypnotic age regression: An experimental study. *J Abnorm Soc Psychol* 1951;46:213-225.

Reiff R, Scheerer M: Memory and hypnotic age regression. New York, International University Press. 1959.

Reyher J: Clinical and experimental hypnosis: Implications for theory and methodology. *Ann New York Acad Sci* 1977;296:69-85.

Sarbin TR: Mental age changes in experimental regression. *J Personality* 1950;19:221-228.

Spiegel H, Spiegel D: *Trance and Treatment*. New York, Basic Books, 1978, pp 32-33, 296-297.

Weitzenhoffer AM: *Hypnotism: An Objective Study in Suggestibility*. New York, Wiley, 1953.

16

Miscellaneous Medical Applications of Hypnosis

Gérard Sunnen

While hypnosis, in the medical setting, has traditionally been used for anxiety and pain control—its most popular applications—it has also been used for some of the individual needs of medicine's specialties. Each specialty, dealing with different facets of human problems and treatment, has found ways to apply hypnosis successfully to the problem of improving patient care.

HYPNOSIS IN OBSTETRICS

The practice of hypnotically assisted deliveries has a history of over a century. Falling into disfavor due to competition from chemical anesthesia, hypnosis has seen a revival in the last two decades. One important reason for this comeback is the realization that hypnosis may find usefulness not only in obstetric analgesia or anesthesia, but in all phases of giving birth from pregnancy to postpartum recovery.

Russian medicine has had extensive experience with obstetric hypnosis. Platanov, in the 1920s, became well known for his hypnoobstetric successes. Impressed by this approach, Stalin later set up a nationwide program headed by Velvoski, who originally combined hypnosis with Pavlovian techniques but eventually used the later almost exclusively. Ferdinand Lamaze, having visited Russia, brought back to France "childbirth without pain through the psychological method," which in turn showed more reflexologic than hypnotic inspiration.

In the Western hemisphere, Roig-Garcia used suggestion, given in the hypnotic trance during predelivery training, to decondition, mostly by verbal means, the patient's culturally determined associations to childbirth. Seeking to counter the deeply ingrained but nevertheless learned concepts that equate uterine contraction with pain and fear, Roig-Garcia, in his hypnoreflexogenic method, worked to manage delivery in a state of "vigil," where the patient, fully awake, aware, and conscious of uterine contractions, is free of a "pain complex or component." In hypnotically assisted deliveries, it is found that the well-relaxed patient makes smoother transitions from one stage of labor to the next. Relaxed deliveries are not noted for their rapidity—nor should they be. Deliveries that are unhurried and made within the context of global physiological and psychological comfort allow all tissues—the mother's as well as the child's—to adapt gently to changing conditions.

In the United States there has been an increased interest in these methods since the 1960s. The reasons are undoubtedly complex. Often cited is a trend towards respect for natural physiological processes, and dissatisfaction with chemical, mechanical, or operative interventions. There is, indeed, always some risk to the mother and to the infant when chemical anesthetics are used. Hypnosis, on the other hand, has never been shown to be injurious to either.

Werner, in the United States, delivered over 3000 babies since 1959 with hypnotic adjunctive techniques (before that time he delivered 6000 babies with chemical anesthesia). Ten percent of women did not respond to trance induction; 30% required some and always less, chemical anesthesia; the remaining 60% used no chemical anesthesia at all.

Advantages of using hypnosis in obstetrics The advantages of using hypnosis in the delivery process are summarized below.

1. Hypnosis as a physiological and psychological relaxant can make the delivery process more humane. By giving the patient

a sense of handling this natural function by her own mental resources, self-esteem is increased.

2. If adjunctive chemical anesthetics are needed, they can be administered promptly and easily. The interesting feature, however, is that if they need to be used, lesser amounts are clinically effective, with benefits to mother and child (August, 1960; Oystragh 1970).

3. Hypnosis does not inhibit normal emotional responses to the birth process and the immediate bonding to the child, as does chemical anesthesia. If properly negotiated in a natural fashion, giving birth in the state of vigil is a profound, deeply constructive human experience.

4. Hypnosis helps in the preparation for delivery and in the recovery process. Anticipatory anxiety can be lessened and the return to normal functioning can be optimized. Often, chemical anesthetics cause a hangover which can last up to two days. Using hypnotic techniques, there is smoother transition back to normalcy.

Objections to using hypnosis in obstetrics In 1961, the American Psychiatric Association issued an official statement which contained the following: "Hypnosis is a specialized psychiatric procedure and, as such, is an aspect of the doctor-patient relationship. Hypnosis provides an adjunct to research, to diagnosis, and to treatment in psychiatric practice. It is also of some value in other areas of medical practice and research"; and "whoever makes use of hypnotic techniques, therefore, should have sufficient knowledge of psychiatry, and particularly psychiatric dynamics, to avoid its use in clinical situations where it is is contraindicated or even dangerous." This ruling has dampened the general use of hypnosis in obstetrics, and there are still controversies deriving from it. By all evidence, a rational stance may be embodied in the opinion that obstetric hypnosis is safe in the hands of adequately trained medical personnel. In cases where the patient has shown psychopathology, by history or mental status, it may be argued that special consultation be made with a psychiatrically oriented hypnotherapist.

Is hypnosis too time-consuming? The same question is often posed concerning dental hypnosis. Perhaps, at face value, the patient hours spent for hypnotic training do not appear to be cost-efficient. However, if we look at other factors, such as ease of delivery, increased speed of recovery, and the global benefits to the mother as well as the child, the question may be quickly settled.

Practical considerations Women may receive hypnotic training individually or in groups. While individual sessions suit the needs of many patients, the group experience offers the opportunity to share important feelings.

In training sessions, the patient is taught how to produce a trance, first through the doctor-patient relationship (heterohypnosis), then by herself (autohypnosis). An important part of the program is education: the anatomy, physiology, chronobiology, and physiology of the birth process including an exploration of the feelings commonly encountered and how to experience them in natural perspective, ie, tension as tension, not as pain. Training progresses to the learning of deep relaxation and to the technique of dissociation, ie, "if you begin to feel the uterus contracting strongly, and if you want to take a rest while it does so by itself, simply let yourself drift further into deep trance . . . "

Hypnotic training may begin, ideally, as early as the first trimester of pregnancy. Many patients, however, who have not had the benefit of advance preparation, may be helped by trance induction even when labor has already begun.

Utilized during pregnancy, hypnosis may help patients cope with some of its physiological effects. Nausea and vomiting, a frequent manifestation (up to 50%) of pregnancies, usually starting in the fourth or fifth week and lasting for an indefinite period, can be debilitating and even dangerous. Drugs, of course, should be avoided because of possible teratogenic effects. Hypnotic treatment of nausea and vomiting has been talked about in Chapter 11. Although resulting from different mechanisms than those responsible for anti-neoplastic drug effects, nausea and vomiting during pregnancy can be successfully approached through these same techniques. Since many women complain of unpleasant metallic tastes in the mouth, suggestions are given for fresh minty breath, as well as for easy transit of foods. Ptyalism (the overproduction of saliva), pruritus, and heartburn are all antenatal conditions which may respond to hypnotic treatment.

Hypnosis and related natural childbirth methods Several methods of preparation for childbirth have been developed in the last few decades, and the number of participants attest to the interest and need of women for a holistic approach to giving birth. The natural childbirth method of Read (1953), the psychoprophylactic method of Velvoski, and the painless childbirth method of Lamaze (1958) all use suggestion to various degrees, emphasize relaxation, and give the patient reassurance and a sense of control over the entire process. Although no formal induction exists in these methods, the degree of similitude to hypnosis is striking.

HYPNOSIS AND SURGERY

The hypnotic phenomenon which perhaps inspires the most awe and drama involves the unanesthetized patient who undergoes major surgery. According to Moll, the first surgical operations on magnetized subjects were those performed by Recamier in 1821. Cloquet followed him in 1829, Elliotson in England, Dr. Albert Wheeler in the United States, and the well-known Dr. Esdaille in India (1840).

In suitable subjects, it is recognized that through hypnotic mechanisms, a sufficient level of anesthesia may be produced to block all subjective perceptions of pain. However, many authors point out that pain is a sensation intimately intertwined with fear and that surgical procedures performed with hypnotic anesthesia owe their success to the abolition of anxiety as much as to the abolition of pain. Furthermore, a careful analysis of historical cases, as well as modern ones, points to the fact that major operations may not have been as pain free as originally supposed.

Since 1950, interest in hypnoanesthesia has rekindled. Suppressed by the discovery of chloroform, ether, and nitrous oxide for over a century, this new interest has been fueled not only by the growing sophistication in understanding hypnosis, but by new philosophies of patient care: patients should have access to any treatment modality capable of easing the stress of disease and its treatments.

If hypnosis is able to achieve pain block in only a small minority of patients, it is pointed out that as a partial anesthetic and a tranquilizer, it may reduce the dosage of premedication and of anesthetics. Seeing that many patients have compromised pulmonary, cardiac and renal status, and that anesthetic deaths account for one per ten thousand cases, hypnotic intervention could have appreciable benefits.

Several modern accounts of surgery using hypnoanesthesia — usually used because of the patient's poor previous response to anesthetics, and for such procedures as prostatectomy, breast tumor or thyroid nodule excision, and temporal lobectomy among others — indicate that hypnosis has a wide range of effectiveness for anxiety and pain reduction. In a small proportion of cases where hypnoanesthesia was unaccompanied by any medications, some patients appeared to experience pain sensations, as evidenced by increased blood pressure, increased cardiac and respiratory rate, wincing, and frowning, while others did not. In those who seemed to feel pain, recollection was variable, and in cases where adjunctive medications were used, ie, opiates, local anesthetics, sedatives, and anxiolytics, doses were usually smaller than in the average case.

It is estimated by some investigators that 10% of the population could undergo major procedures with hypnoanesthesia (Lederman et al, 1958); others estimate the figure to be far lower (Wallace and Coppolino, 1960).

Patient selection appears to be very important. Adequate studies are lacking, but we would expect good candidates for hypnoanesthesia to be highly hypnotizable. However, high hypnotizability is not necessarily correlated with heightened ability to achieve anesthesia. The importance of other factors, including motivation and rapport, has not been measured.

Few people today seriously suggest that hypnoanesthesia should be used as the sole anesthetic in major surgery. The percentage of suitable candidates is too few and the variables and unpredictability of responses are too great. The combination of chemical and hypno-anesthesia, however, is stimulating serious interest. Besides the already mentioned effects of reducing doses of sedatives and analgesics, hypnosis may address itself to subconscious mechanisms which may positively influence operative outcome and recovery.

Preoperative preparations The preoperative hypnotic preparation of the patient can be handled in a variety of ways. Some authors recommend that that there be a rehearsal of the operation under hypnosis, with recreated conditions made to be as real as possible, to familiarize the patient with the procedures, the sensations commonly encountered, ie, the wet sponge to prep the skin for incision, the sound of clamps, hemostats, etc (Crasilneck and Hall, 1975).

Less time-consuming, but possibly not as effective, is a preoperative hypnotic induction during which a general description of the procedure is drawn and appropriate suggestions are given. Mention may be made before the operation that the patient will be calm, will rest soundly, and eat or not eat as required, with comfort; that, as anesthesia is given, it is to be accepted willingly and that pain sensations will be blocked; that during the operation, breathing will be restfully slowed and healing dreams are likely to be encountered. For the postoperative period, the patient is told that recovery will be rapid, discomfort minimal, and healing accelerated.

Such hypnotic procedures may be applied to any phase of the operative process. Preoperatively, it allays anticipatory anxiety and allows for more restful adaptation. If the hypnotherapist is to be present during the operation, this should be mentioned to the patient because it will set the stage for future hypnotic rapport.

Commentaries on "anesthesia awareness" It has been assumed for decades that a patient in the deeper or even moderate levels of chemical anesthesia was in a state of other worldliness and had given up all semblance of consciousness. Crile (1947) reported the case of a patient receiving nitrous oxide (as well as his own case in his autobiography) where some awareness of the environment was preserved. While insufficient levels of anesthesia were first invoked, reports of more cases of preservation of partial awareness in documented deep levels of anesthesia prompted studies to investigate this phenomenon.

Wilson and Turner (1969), in a study involving questioning of 150 postcesarean patients, found three who accurately recalled factual events and 46 who maintained some dreamlike experiences of the operation. More recent studies have focused on the hypnotic recollection of the operative experience. While consciously, patients may have little or no recall, some — especially highly hypnotizable ones — are able in the context of trance, to reexperience important events within the operative procedure. It has been reasonably established that such patients are attuned, in such situations, to meaningful communications by the treating personnel, especially the perceived significant personnel, ie, the surgeon and anesthesiologist. This has prompted hypnotherapists in their preoperative hypnotic induction to add suggestions to protect their patients against inadvertently negative communications which may be reacted to, physiologically and psychologically, with stress reactions. If, for example, one of the surgeons mentions "there's a lot of blood loss here," the patient may respond with a rise in blood pressure and increased heart rate, making cardiac instability more likely.

Uses of hypnosis during the operation The clinical implications of the maintenance of some awareness during anesthesia, as far as the hypnotherapist is concerned, is that some degree of hypnotic contact may be established during the course of the operation for purposes of helping the patient adjust to its vicissitudes. It is well known, for example, that given some tightness of the abdominal muscles, surgeons often ask for more anesthesia. This may not be necessary, if the hypnotherapist gently whispers suggestions to that effect to his deeply anesthetized patient.

Hypnosis in the postoperative period If the patient has been adequately prepared in the preoperative hypnotic session, very little time need be spent in the postoperative induction. The patient, readily entering the trance, can be given suggestions for dealing with all phases of the recovery process: rest, comfort, biological functions, control of bleeding, etc.

HYPNOSIS IN BURN PATIENTS

Patients who are severely burned characteristically show a variety of major problems. In addition to severe constant pain and the trauma engendered by the need for repeated treatments such as debridement, there are loss of appetite, contractures, poor mobility, and often severe psychological symptoms: despair, hopelessness, helplessness, regression, and a psychological set of "giving up." Nausea and anorexia compound the problem by causing weight loss.

The treatment of the burned patient may start as early as a few minutes to several hours after the time of the burn. Some clinicians report that post-burn hypnotic anesthesia can decrease the inflammatory response and lead to lessened destructiveness of the injury. Suggestions may be given for coolness of all burned areas by using imagery of ice and snow (Ewin, 1978).

The burned patient has a long, arduous road to recovery, and hypnosis may be of help in reestablishing adequate physiological functions and in maintaining hope and the will to live.

HYPNOSIS AND DENTISTRY

The use of hypnosis in dentistry has a long history. In 1837, Oudet, a French dentist, used hypnoanesthesia for a dental extraction—the first reported case. Ribaud and Kiaro, in Poitiers, France, similarly excised a tumor of the jaw in 1847. Since then, many reports dealing with hypnodontia—the use of hypnosis in dentistry—have attested to the increasing sophistication of hypnotic procedures to deal with the special problems of the dental patient. Besides smoothing out dental procedures by way of its generalized antianxiety effects, it can increase overall patient comfort, make the dental experience acceptable and bearable, decrease resistance to future intervention, and through posthypnotic suggestions, encourage more rapid recovery.

The orofacial region holds special importance for its connections to vital functions and for its place in the individual's psychosexual development. This area is inherently connected to major sensory pathways—vision, hearing, sight, smell, and touch—and has intimate jurisdiction over breathing, food intake, and communication of speech and feelings. Freud (1953) labeled the oropharynx as an erotogenic zone and Erickson (1950) described early oral experiences as of central importance to the development of basic trust. Teeth, in reality and symbolically, have priceless value.

Indications for using hypnosis in dentistry It is understandable, in view of these considerations, that many individuals have anxieties about dental procedures. Some, in fact, are so phobic that they prefer to allow serious pathology to develop, rather than to seek help. Apprehensive patients usually have difficulties citing specific fears they may have about dental procedures—fears of pain while constrained in the chair, a variant of claustrophobia is often cited, as is the fear of choking or drowning in secretions, the fear of mutilation, the fear of fainting, of being unable to talk, and the fear of disapproval by the dentist for lack of self care. Some of these fears may tie into other, more primitive ones, such as the fear of castration, helplessness, or oral aggression.

While some anxiety and tension is normal with most dental procedures, higher levels interfere significantly with the treatment. Some investigators place the incidence of dental phobias at 6.9% of the general population, and 16% in school-age children (Gale and Ayer, 1969).

When mild, an anxiety tension response can be managed by

the dentist through the use of reassurance, explanation, and suggestions for relaxation. Of significant benefit is mellifluous music as well as the pleasant chattiness of the dentist.

When phobias are more severe, the patient is commonly found sitting stiffly in the chair or exhibiting strained movements. The facial and nuchal muscles are contracted, the jaw barely open, and attempts at evaluation and treatment are met with stiff unvolitional opposition. Ordinary relaxation procedures are partially and inadequately effective. A sedative hypnotic taken an hour before the visit is also only partially effective and has the drawback of sedating the patient for several hours. Such a patient may benefit from a formal hypnotic induction with the examination and treatment done in the trance state or in a posthypnotic relaxed state. While some dentists may balk at the idea of taking time to tap into the benefits of hypnosis, it is pointed out that once the patient is relaxed, procedures are done much more quickly and subsequent procedures are handled much more smoothly through the use of posthypnotic suggestions.

Sample suggestions may include the following "as you sit relaxed, I'd like you to listen to the music around you, letting yourself flow with it. It takes you automatically into relaxation, your whole body becoming more relaxed with each breath; your jaw and mouth and gums and throat become so relaxed that the muscles get softer. While you're listening to the music, your entire mouth can feel to be further and further away from you — you feel it but it is out there in the distance; and as I open your jaw gently and take a look at your gums, you may feel your whole body becoming more comfortable and relaxed. As I do my work, I'll describe everything that I do beforehand so that you know what is going on."

Some dental phobias may require hypnobehavioral techniques, ie, hypnodesensitization, flooding (anxiety evoking stimuli are presented to the hypnotized patient in stepwise fashion or the hypnotized patient is presented with maximally anxiogenic material). Other approaches include psychotherapy or hypnotic age regression. Stolzenberg (1950) used the latter method to elicit from two patients the fact that they were frightened because of dental stories that they had heard several years previously.

Gagging is connected to anxiety and can present major problems for the dental patient. Some patients find it very difficult to have impressions taken or to wear dentures. Hypnosis has had marked success in the control of this unpleasant reflex.

Hypnosis for dental analgesia   Using hypnosis in dentistry for analgesia presents several benefits over chemical anesthesia. It does not produce chemical numbness, which annoys the patient for several hours after the procedure and is responsible for patients slurring their speech or inadvertently biting their inner cheek; it avoids chemical risk factors; and it avoids the often dreaded needle. As in hypnoanesthesia used in surgery, unfortunately, it can only be satisfactorily and completely effective when used alone in about 10% of the population. However, it is partially and significantly effective in a much larger percentage, and when more extensive dental work is necessary it is able to reduce chemical anesthetic dosages.

Extractions, root canal procedures, deep filling, and periodontal work can all be made to be more pleasant and paradoxically less time-consuming by attempting a simple induction and giving suggestions for numbness and relaxation. In the dental setting, numbness of the index finger can first be produced; the patient's hand is then guided into his mouth to touch the gums and teeth. Seeing the interrelationship of pain and anxiety previously mentioned, suggestions are also provided for calm and for "being here now," to dissipate anticipatory ideation. In an alternative technique, the dentist, while the patient is in a trance, touches the area of the jaw, first externally then internally with paired suggestions for relaxation and numbness, gradually extending numbness to the entire oropharynx, with preservation of essential reflexes such as swallowing and gagging.

Control of bleeding   The purported ability of hypnosis to decrease bleeding has been widely mentioned in the literature (Newman, 1974). Anecdotal reports attest to a phenomenon found in hypnotized patients in which incisions are remarkably free of bleeders. A study comparing clotting before and during the hypnotic trance did not demonstrate significant changes. Hypnosis, however, if indeed it has effects on bleeding, probably does so at the tissue arteriolar level rather than on clotting time.

Because bleeding in dental procedures is not a serious problem, the use of hypnosis to control bleeding has mostly been indicated for hemophiliacs.

Pediatric dental hypnosis Good dental education is best done early. Due to the impressionable and highly suggestible nature of children, it is especially important to provide, from the start, programs of dental care which are as free of discomfort as possible and even possibly somewhat fun. Some dentists, for example, with commendable imagination, mention to their young patients that the dental office can be thought of as a modified spaceship.

In most cases, an unhurried empathic attitude, combined with reassurances will suffice. Hypnosis may be indicated for the child needing more involved work or the child who has had previous negative experiences.

Hypnotic work with children, while similar to adult hypnosis in substance, requires some modifications. The shorter attention span of children requires more absorbing, interesting, and innovative induction procedures. The suggestions and language must correspond to the child's verbal capabilities. The child needs immediate reward and praise for his hypnotic achievements. Successful techniques are more apt to use fantasy or imagery, concrete suggestions using specific images, and ego-strengthening methods to enhance the child's self-image for mastering the problems at hand.

HYPNOSIS IN OTHER MEDICAL CONDITIONS AND SPECIALTIES

The hypnotherapist, to be maximally effective and innovative, needs to develop knowledge of the wide ranges of possible applications of hypnotic techniques in different medical settings and for different medical problems. The literature contains many examples of how hypnosis has been applied, often creatively, to aid in the overall management of patients with specialized problems.

Neurological applications have included using hypnosis in Parkinsonism since psychological factors tend to aggravate the expression of disease. Along with chemotherapy, hypnosis can be applied to relaxation, to the improvement of ambulation and speech, and to the diminution or abolition of negative scenarios the patient may have built up about his illness.

The symptoms of multiple sclerosis, whose remissions and exacerbations can be accompanied — and contributed to — by anxiety, depression, and stress, can be better managed by the adjunctive use of hypnosis. Although the pathophysiology of the lesions is not altered by hypnosis, the subjectively ominous or catastrophic reactions to exacerbations can be softened.

In orthopedics, hypnosis can be used for helping the patient adjust to different positions required for longer-term healing. In the emergency situation, hypnosis can assist the frightened and tense patient who needs a reduction procedure.

In plastic surgery, similarly, when it may be necessary for the patient to maintain an uncomfortable position for successful skin or pedicle grafting, hypnosis can minimize bodily irritations and the desire to move.

In gynecology, clinicians have used hypnosis for functional dysmenorrhea, premenstrual and menopausal syndromes, and special procedures.

The ophthalmological and otolaryngeal specialties have found hypnosis to have positive effects on glaucoma (Berger and Zamet, 1960) and suppression of amblyopia; it has also been used in cataract removal and for the adjustment to contact lenses. Globus hystericus, hysterical aphonia, gagging, and tinnitus are other conditions with strong psychogenic overlays which are especially responsive to hypnotherapy.

In urology, hypnosis has found applications in cystoscopy and vasectomy, not only to make the procedures more comfortable, but to help ensure smooth psychological adjustment.

All symptoms and all diseases have or are repercussions on some aspect of mental functioning. Keeping this fact in mind, the clinician may, when applicable and appropriate, think about using hypnosis to enhance total patient care.

SUGGESTED READING AND REFERENCES

Abramson M, Freenfield I, Heron WT: Response to or perception of auditory stimuli under deep surgical anesthesia. *Am J Obstet Gynecol* 1966;96:584.

American Psychiatric Association: Training in Medical Hypnosis: A Statement of Position by the APA. Document available from the Central Office, Washington, D.C. Feb. 15, 1961, p 3.

August R: *Hypnosis in Obstetrics.* New York, McGraw-Hill, 1961.

Berger AJ, Zamet CH: Emotional factors in primary glaucoma. *Psychosomat Med* 1960;22:391.

Bernstein HR: Observations on the use of hypnosis with burned patients on a pediatric ward. *Int J Clin Exp Hypn* 1965;13:1.

Bowers KS: Hypnosis and Healing. *Aust J Clin Exp Hypn* 1979;7:261.

Brunn JT: The capacity to hear, understand, and to remember experiences during chemoanesthesia: A personal experience. *Am J Clin Hypn* 1963;6:27.

Cheek DB: Use of preoperative hypnosis to protect patients from careless conversation. *Am J Clin Hypn* 1960;3:101.

Chertok LS: *Psychosomatic Methods in Painless Childbirth: History, Theory and Practice.* New York, Pergamon Press, 1959.

Coulton D: Prenatal and postpartum uses of hypnosis. *Am J Clin Hypn* 1966;8:192.

Crasilneck HB, Hall JA: *Clinical Hypnosis: Principles and Applications.* New York, Grune and Stratton, 1975.

Crile GW: *Autobiography.* Philadelphia, JB Lippincott, 1947, p 197.

Erickson EH: *Childhood and Society.* New York, WW Norton, 1950.

Ewin DM: Clinical use of hypnosis for attenuation of burn depth, in Frankel FH, Zamansky HS (eds): *Hypnosis at its Bicentennial—Selected Papers from the Seventh International Congress of Hypnosis and Psychosomatic Medicine.* New York, Plenum Press, 1978.

Faithful NS: Awareness during anaesthesia. *Br Med J* 1969;2:117.

Freud S: Three essays on the theory of sexuality, *Standard Edition of the Complete Psychological Works of Sigmund Freud* vol 7. London, Hogarth Press, 1953, p 135.

Gaal JM, Goldsmith L, Needs RE: The use of hypnosis, as an adjunct to anaesthesia, to reduce pre and post operative anxiety in children. Presented at the annual meeting of the American Society of Clincal Hypnosis, Minneapolis, November 1980.

Gale EM, Ayer WA: Treatment of dental phobias. *J Am Dent Assoc* 1969;79:1304-1307.

Golan HP: Control of fear reaction in dental patients by hypnosis. *Am J Clin Hypn* 1971;13:279.

Gershman J, Reade G: Hypnosis and dentistry, in Burrows G, Dennerstein L (eds): *Handbook of Hypnosis and Psychosomatic Medicine.* New York, Elsevier/North Holland Biomedical Press, 1980, p 443-475.

Hutchings DD: The value of suggestion given under anaesthesia: A report and evaluation of 200 consecutive cases. *Am J Clin Hypn* 1961;4:26.

Kroger WS: *Clinical and Experimental Hypnosis in Medicine, Dentistry and Psychology,* ed 2. Philadelphia, JB Lippincott, 1977.

Lamaze F: *Painless Childbirth.* London, Burke, 1958.

Leckie FH: Hypnotherapy in gynecological disorders. *Int J Clin Exp Hypn* 1964;12:121.

Lederman EI, Fordyce CY, Stacy TE: Hypnosis as an adjunct to anaesthesiology. *Md Med J* 1958;7:192-194.

Levinson BW: States of awareness during general anaesthesia, in Lassner J (ed): *Hypnosis and Psychosomatic Medicine.* New York, Springer Verlag, 1967.

Moll A: *The Study of Hypnosis.* 1889. Reprint. New York, Julian Press, 1958.

Morgan G: *Hypnosis in Ophthalmology.* Birmingham, Ala, Aesculapius Publishing, 1980.

Newman M: Hypnosis in haemophiliacs. *J Aust Dent Assoc* 1974;88:273.

Oystragh P: The use of hypnosis in general and obstetrical practice. *Med J Aust* 1970;2:731.

Platanov K: *The Word as a Physiological and Therapeutic Factor.* Moscow, Foreign Languages Publishing House, 1955.

Read GD: *Childbirth without Fear.* New York, Harper, 1953.

Roig-Garcia S: Report from Pan American Medical Association Special Panel on Clinical Hypnosis, May 1960.

Silverberg EL: Hypnosis in the treatment of warts. *Arch Gen Psychiatry* 1973;28:439-441.

Stolzenberg J: *Psychosomatics and Suggestion Therapy in Dentistry.* New York, Philosophical Library, 1950, pp 21-22.

Van Dyke PB: Some uses of hypnosis in the management of the surgical patient. *Am J Clin Hypn* 1970;12:227.

Wallace G, Coppolino CA: Hypnosis in anaesthesiology. *NY J Med* 1960;60:3258-3273.

Werner W, Schauble P, Knudson M: An argument for the revival of hypnosis in obstetrics. *Am J Clin Hypn* 1982;24(3):143.

Wilson J, Turner DJ: Awareness during caesarean section under general anaesthesia. *Br Med J* 1969;1:280.

Zimmerman D: Hypnotherapy in surgical management: A review. *J R Soc Med* 1980;73:579.

INDEX

Acne, 151, 159
Adjustment disorders, 87
Affective disorders, 117
Afferent sensory pathways in pain, 113–116
Age regression, 214–219
  approaches to use of, 215–216
  case histories with, 216–219
  definition of, 214
  dentistry with, 231
  hypnosis and, 37–38
  psychotherapy with, 183
  views regarding use of 214–215
Agoraphobia, 87, 98–99
Altered state of consciousness
  effects of hypnosis on, 32
  future research on, 15–16
  hypnosis as, 8–9
Amblyopia, 234
American Medical Association, 6
American Psychiatric Association, 6, 223
Amnesia
  multiple personality differentiated from, 212
  posthypnotic, 35, 36
  psychotherapy with hypnosis for, 183–185
Analytic hypnotherapy, 180
Anesthesia
  awareness during surgery of, 228
  dentistry and, 232
  historical developments in, 3
  surgical use of hypnosis for, 225–229
  see also Glove anesthesia
Animal magnetism, 2
Anorexia nervosa, 108
  psychological factors in, 155–156
  treatment of, 109–112, 156
Anorgasmia, 164–172
  case history in, 164–166
  causes of, 166–167, 168–169
  treatment of, 169–172
Anxiety
  asthma and, 158
  autogenic training for, 91–93

  biofeedback and relaxation for, 93–94
  cancer patients and, 138, 141, 142
  death and, 144, 145
  dentistry and, 230–232
  evaluation of, 85–87
  hospitalization and, 127, 128, 135–136
  hypnotic treatment of disorders with, 87–98
  impotence and, 174, 176–177
  incidence of, 85
  meditative training for, 94–96
  obstetrics and, 223
  phobic disorders with, 99, 185–186
  posthypnotic suggestion and, 36
  psychosomatic disorders and, 159
  psychotherapy for, 182
  relaxation techniques for, 88–91
  surgery and, 226
Apollonian personality type, 202, 203
Arthritis, 125
Asthma, 151, 158–159, 160
Atavistic hypothesis of hypnosis, 11–12
Aura stage of induction, 74, 75
Autogenic training
  anxiety treatment with, 90, 91–93
  effects of, 93
  exercises in, 91–92
  peptic ulcer and, 154
  psychosomatic disorders and, 160
Automatic behavior, 54
Automatic handwriting, 13, 37

Barber Suggestibility Scale (BSS), 73
Behavioral approaches to hypnosis, 9, 13–15
Behavior therapy, 199
Bernheim, Hippolyte, 4, 5, 12
Biofeedback
  anxiety treatment with, 93–94
  essential hypertension with, 157
  hypnosis combined with, 94
  psychosomatic disorders with, 160
Body image in hypnosis, 31

237

Body trip, in anorgasmia treatment, 170-171
Braid, James, 3-4
Brain
  gate theory of pain and, 113-116
  hypnosis and pain and, 29
  hypnotism as form of sleep and, 11
Breuer, Joseph, 5, 16
Bronchoscopy, 128-129
Bulimia, 108-112
Burn patients, 229

Cancer patients, 137-149
  application of hypnosis to, 137-138
  case histories in, 138-140, 142, 147-148
  chemotherapy side effects and, 141-144
  denial in, 145-146
  imagery used by, 147-148
  influencing disease process itself by, 147-148
  management of cancer symptoms in, 138-140
  psychological adjustments in, 137-138, 144-147
  relationship between pain and anxiety in, 138
  techniques in, 140-141
Capacity for hypnosis
  individual differences in levels of, 67
  personality traits and, 202-204
  rating scales for, see Rating scales
Cardiovascular system
  autogenic training and, 92
  hypnosis and changes in, 25-26
  hypnosis for disorders of, 156-157
Case histories
  age regression, 216-219
  cancer patient, 138-140, 142, 147-148
  ego state theory, 190-192
  grade 5 syndrome, 206-209
  hypnosis in hospitalization, 128-129, 132-134
  meditative training in anxiety treatment, 97-98

pain control, 120-124
sex therapy, 164-166
psychotherapy with hypnosis, 181-183, 183-189, 190-192
short-term therapy, 199-201
Central nervous system, and hypnosis, 9, 27-28
Charcot, Jean-Martin, 4-5, 10, 12
Chemotherapy side effects, 137, 141-144
Child abuse, and age regression, 216-218
Childbirth methods, see Obstetrics
Children
  dentistry and, 233
  hospital hypnosis with, 133-135
Children's Hypnotic Clinical Scale (SHCS-Child), 71, 72
Cognitive restructuring, 199
Cognitive techniques, 18
Communication
  capacity of hypnotherapist for, 50-51
  Ericksonian approaches to psychotherapy and, 193
  hypnosis and intensification of, 31
Concepts of hypnosis, 7-15
  as altered state of consciousness, 8-9
  as atavistic phenomenon, 11-12
  behavioral approaches to, 13-15
  ego state theory on, 15
  as form of sleep, 10-11
  physiological theories of, 9-12
  psychoanalytic theories of, 12-15
Consciousness
  Ericksonian approach to, 193
  future research directions on, 15-16
  posthypnotic suggestion and, 36
Control, fears involving, 45-46
Conversion reactions, 152
Countertransference, 50
Counting method, in anxiety treatment, 90
Creative Imagination Scale, 73-74
Creativity
  clinical applications of hypnosis to, 18-19
  definitions of, 17-18

Daydreams, 33, 53
Death
  hypnotherapist philosophy of, 144–145
  psychological adjustment of patient to, 144–147
  stages of dying in, 144–145
Decrement profile configuration, in Hypnotic Induction Profile (HIP), 80, 83
Deep relaxation techniques, *see* Relaxation techniques
Defenses, in Ericksonian approaches to psychotherapy, 194–195
Deleuze, J.P.F., 3
Denial, and cancer patient hypnosis, 144, 145–146
Dentistry, 229–233
  control of bleeding in, 232–233
  historical note for, 229–230
  hypoanesthesia in, 232–233
  indications for hypnosis with, 230–232
  pediatric hypnosis in, 233
Depression, hypnosis for, 41–42
Dermatological disorders, 151, 159
Desensitization, for chemotherapy-induced nausea, 143
Diabetes mellitus, 151, 160
Diagnostic and Statistical Manual of Mental Disorders (DSM-III), 87, 151, 210
Diagnostic Rating Scales (DRS), 74
Dionysian personality type, 202, 203
Dissociation
  chemotherapy-induced nausea and, 143–144
  hypnosis and, 6, 13, 37
  pain control and, 121–122
  trance states and, 54
Dream induction, in phobia treatment, 186–188
DSM-III, 87, 151, 210

Eating disorders, 108–112
  anorexia nervosa, 108, 109–112, 155–156
  bulimia, 108–109
  hypnotic treatment of, 110–112
  simple obesity, 109
Ebers Papyrus, 1, 20
Ego, and creativity, 18
Ego state theory of hypnosis, 15
Ego state therapy, case history of, 190–192
Ego strengthening, for cancer patients, 146
Electrocardiogram (ECG), meditative training on, 95
Electroencephalogram (EEG) anxiety treatment with biofeedback with, 94
  hypnosis and changes in, 9, 27–28
Electromyogram (EMG), in anxiety treatment, 94
Emotions, and hypnosis, 34
Endocrine functions, 26–27
Endorphins, 117
Erectile dysfunction, *see* Impotence
Erickson, Milton, 6, 192–193
Ericksonian approach to psychotherapy, 192–195, 198
Essential hypertension, 156–157
Evaluation of patient, *see* Examination of patient
Evoked potentials, and hypnotic changes, 9, 27
Examination of patient, 41–51
  anorgasmia in, 165–166
  anxiety in, 85–86
  conceptions and misconceptions of patient in, 44–47
  decision to use hypnosis as treatment and, 41–42
  explaining hypnotic process during, 48–49
  goals of treatment and, 47
  hypnotherapist and, 49–51
  motivating patient for change and, 47–48
  patient selection for, 41–44
  smoking control treatment and, 104–105
  symptoms explored in, 42–43
Eye movements, and hypnosis, 28
Eye-roll sign
  capacity for hypnotic trance and, 28
  Hypnotic Induction Profile (HIP) with, 76–79

measurement of, 77–79
physiological theories of hypnosis and, 10
use of, 80, 81

Family habits, 102–103
Fantasy, in anorgasmia treatment, 170
Faria, Abbe, 3
Fears
  dentistry and, 230–232
  of patient about hypnosis, 44, 45–47
Flooding, 231
Franklin, Benjamin, 2
Free association, 5
Freud, Sigmund, 5, 12, 16, 152, 230
Fugue, 54, 211
Future directions for hypnosis, 15–21

Gagging, 231–233
Galvanic skin response (GSR) biofeedback in anxiety treatment, 94
Gassner, Johann Joseph, 2
Gastrointestinal disorders
  hypnosis in treatment of, 153–155
  psychological factors in, 153, 154, 155
Gastrointestinal functions, and hypnosis, 26
Gate theory of pain, 113–116
Generalized anxiety disorder, 87–93
  diagnostic criteria for, 87–88
  hypnotic treatment of, 88–93
Genitourinary functions, and hypnosis, 26
Glaucoma, 234
Glove anesthesia
  cancer patient hypnosis with, 140
  pain control with, 122–123
Goals of treatment, 47
Grade 5 syndrome, 204–209
  case history of, 206–209
  treatment considerations in, 206
Gynecology, 234

Habit disorders, 101–112
  basic approach to, 111–112
  development of habits and, 101–103
  eating disorders treatment and, 108–111
  restructuring of habits in, 103–104
  smoking control treatment in, 104–108
Hair pulling, 199–201
Hallucinations, 29
Handwriting, automatic, 13, 37
Harvard Group Scale of Hypnotic Susceptibility, Form A (HGSHS:A), 73
Hearing hallucinations, 29
Heart, *see* Cardiovascular system
Hemispheric laterality, and hypnosis, 20–21, 198
Highway hypnosis, 53–54
HIP, *see* Hypnotic Induction Profile (HIP)
Historical aspects
  dentistry and hypnosis, 229–230
  development of hypnosis, 1–6
  obstetrics and hypnosis, 221–222
  psychosomatic disorders, 152
  surgery and hypnosis, 225
Hospital hypnosis, 127–136
  case histories of, 128–129, 132–134
  children in, 133–135
  indications for, 135–136
  motivation of patient in, 132–133, 136
  principles of, 130
  rehabilitation medicine with, 131–134
  special procedures in, 128–134
  touch in, 131
  see also Cancer patient
Hunger, as antidote to chemotherapy nausea, 142–143
Hypermnesia, 35
Hypertension, 156–157
Hypoanesthesia
  dentistry and, 232
  historical developments in, 3
  surgical use of, 225–229
  see also Glove anesthesia
Hypnobiofeedback, 94
Hypnoreflexogenic method, 222

Hypnotherapist, 49-51
  in Ericksonian approach, 193-195
  explanation of hypnotic process to patient by, 48-49
  patient fears about hypnosis and, 44-47
  patient selection and preparation by, 41-44
  pediatric hypnosis and, 134-135
  philosophy of death of, 144-145
  qualities of, 50
Hypnotic Induction Profile (HIP), 76-83
  decrement profile configuration in, 80, 83
  eye-roll sign in, 76-79
  grade 5 syndrome with, 204-205
  hypotheses associated with, 76
  intact profile configuration in, 80, 81
  psychotherapy and use of, 201-204
  scoring of, 79
  self-hypnosis induction and, 66
  soft profile configuration in, 80, 82
Hypnotizability, see Capacity for hypnosis; Rating scales

Imagery
  anxiety treatment with, 90
  cancer patient hypnosis with, 138, 141, 143, 147-148
  choosing individual preferences for, 33
  hypnotic effects on, 32-33
Impotence, 26, 172-177
  causes of, 173
  definition of, 172
  treatment of, 174-176
Induction techniques, 74-83
  aura stage in, 75
  definition of, 74
  Hypnotic Induction Profile (HIP) in, 76-83
  modification to specific patient needs in, 81-82
  personality style of patient and, 43
  preparation for, see Preparation for hypnosis

  psychological enhancement in, 75
  self-hypnosis instructions for, 54-66
  stages in, 74
  surgery and, 227
  trance entry stage in, 75
Intact profile configuration, in Hypnotic Induction Profile (HIP), 80, 81
Interview of patient, 41-51
  anorgasmia in, 165-166
  anxiety in, 85-86
  conceptions and misconceptions of patient in, 44-47
  decision to use hypnosis as treatment and, 41-42
  explaining hypnotic process during, 48-49
  goals of treatment and, 47
  hypnotherapist and, 49-51
  motivating patient for change in, 47-48
  patient selection for, 41-44
  smoking control treatment and, 104-105
  symptoms explored in, 42-43

Jacobson's method of relaxation, 93, 98
Janet, Pierre, 5, 6, 13

Lamaze method, 221-222, 225
Laterality, hemispheric, 20-21, 198
Low-back syndrome, 125

Magnetic resonance imaging (MRI), 9
Magnetism, 4, 10
  first use of, 2
  introduction to North America of, 5-6
Manic-depressive illness, 21
Medicine
  future research directions in, 16-17
  space travel and, 19-20
  see also Hospital hypnosis; Surgery
Meditation and meditative training
  anxiety treatment with, 94-96
  case history of, 97-98

demands of, 97
essential hypertension with, 157
hypnosis and, 96-98
indications for, 97
peptic ulcer and, 154
Memory
  age regression and, 37-38, 218-219
  dissociation and, 37
  fears of patient regarding loss of, 46
  hypnotic effects on, 35-38
  posthypnotic suggestion and, 35-36
Mental illness
  hemispheric laterality and, 21
  see also specific conditions
Mesmer, Franz Anton, 2, 7
Migraine headaches, 124-125
Mime techniques, in pediatric hypnosis, 135
Mind cure, 6
Motivation
  after beginning treatment, 47-48
  goals of treatment and, 47
  hospital hypnosis and, 132-133, 136
  for seeking hypnotic treatment, 43
Multiple personality, 212-214
  features associated with, 211-212
  psychotherapy with hypnosis for, 212-214
Multiple sclerosis, 207-209, 234
Muscle tension disorders, 125

Natural childbirth methods, 225
Nausea
  chemotherapy-induced, 143-144
  obstetrical hypnosis for, 224
Neurodermatitis, 151, 159
Neurological applications of hypnosis, 234
Neurophysiology, see Physiological changes in hypnosis; Physiological theories of hypnosis
Neurotransmitters, 10, 16
Nonstate theories of hypnosis, 13-15
Nonverbal communication, 11-12

Obesity, 109-112
Obsessive compulsive disorders, 87

Obstetrics, 221-225
  advantages of, 222-223
  historical note on, 221-222
  natural childbirth methods in, 225
  objections to, 223-224
  practical considerations in, 224-225
Odyssean personality type, 202, 203-204
Oedipal situation, 12-13
Ophthalmological applications of hypnosis, 234
Optokinetic nystagmus, 28
Orthopedics, 234
Otolaryngeal applications of hypnosis, 234
Overweight control treatment, 109-112

Pain control, 113-125
  cancer patient hypnosis for, 138, 140-141
  case histories in, 120-124
  complex interaction in perception of, 117-118
  dentistry and, 232
  dissociation in, 121-122
  gate theory of, 113-116
  glove anesthesia in, 122-123
  historical developments in, 3
  hypnosis and effects in, 28-29
  individual methods in, 125
  insensitivity to pain in, 116-117
  migraine headaches in, 124-125
  muscle relaxation and distraction in, 119-121
  nature of pain and, 113
  obstetrical hypnosis and, 222
  rewarding versus nonrewarding pain in, 118-119
  sensory alteration of pain in, 123-125
  subjective variation to pain and, 116
  surgery and, 225, 226
  techniques in, 119-123
Panic disorders, 98-99
Paracelsus, Theophrast, 1-2
Paranoia, 41, 43
Parkinsonism, 234

Pediatric hypnosis
  dentistry with, 233
  hospital hypnosis in, 133-135
Peptic ulcer, 151, 153-155
Perception, hypnotic effects on, 33-34
Personality
  Apollonian type, 203
  Dionysian type, 203
  ego state theory of hypnosis with, 15
  Ericksonian approaches to, 193
  hypnotizability and, 202-204
  interview of patient for, 43
  Odyssean type, 203-204
Phobic disorders
  case history of, 185-188
  dentistry and, 230-231
  evaluation of, 87
  psychotherapy with hypnosis for, 185-188
Physiological changes in hypnosis, 25-29
  induction techniques and, 75
  rating scales with, 68
Physiological theories of hypnosis, 9-12
  future research in, 16
  hypnosis as atavistic phenomenon in, 11-12
  hypnosis as form of sleep in, 10-11
Plastic surgery, 234
Positron emission tomography, 9
Posthypnotic suggestion, see Suggestion
Posttraumatic stress disorders, 87
Pregnancy, see Obstetrics
Preparation for hypnosis, 41-51
  anorgasmia and, 165-166
  anxiety in, 85-86
  conceptions and misconceptions of patient in, 44-47
  decision to use hypnosis as treatment and, 41-42
  explaining hypnotic process during, 48-49
  goals of treatment and, 47
  hypnotherapist and, 49-51
  motivating patient for change and, 47-48
  patient selection for, 41-44
  smoking control treatment and, 104-105
  symptoms explored in, 42-43
Psychoanalysis
  Freud's use of hypnosis and, 5
  future research directions in, 16
  theories of hypnosis based on, 12-15
Psychogenic amnesia, 183-185, 212
Psychological factors
  anorexia nervosa and, 155-156
  cancer patient and, 137-138, 144-147
  essential hypertension with, 157
  gastrointestinal disorders with, 153, 154, 155
  hospital hypnosis and, 127, 132
  impotence and, 173
  multiple personality and, 211-212
  respiratory disorders and, 158
Psychological phenomena of hypnosis, 29-34
  emotions and, 34
  imagery and, 32-33
  perception and, 33-34
  subjective experience of hypnosis and, 30-32
  variations in individual reactions in, 30
Psychomotor slowdown in hypnosis, 31
Psychosomatic medicine, 151-160
  anorexia nervosa and, 155-156
  anxiety in, 86
  cardiovascular disorders and, 156-157
  definition of, 151
  dermatological conditions in, 159
  gastrointestinal disorders in, 153-155
  historical note on, 152
  illnesses included in, 151-152
  mind-body interaction in, 152-153
  psychological factors in, 152-153
  respiratory disorders in, 157-159
  treatment considerations in, 159-160
Psychotherapy, 179-195
  age regression in, 214-219
  anorexia nervosa and, 156

anorgasmia in, 165
case histories of, 181-183, 183-189, 190-192
catharsis of repressed effect in, 185
clarification of presenting issues in, 181-183, 188-189
early use of hypnosis with, 4
ego state therapy based on, 190-192
Ericksonian approaches to, 192-195, 198
essential hypertension with, 157
future research directions in, 17
grade 5 syndrome in, 204-209
highly hypnotizable individual in, 198-219
hypnosis applications to, 179-180
Hypnotic Induction Profile (HIP) and, 201-204
multiple personality in, 210-214
panic disorders with, 99
phobic disorders with, 185-188
practical issues in, 181
psychogenic amnesia with, 183-185
psychosomatic disorders with, 160
stages of, 181
supportive measures in, 185
ulcerative colitis and, 155

Quadriplegia, 132-134

Radiation therapy, 137
Rapid eye movements (REM), 28
Rating scales, 68-74
see also specific scales
Regression
psychoanalytic theories of hypnosis with, 13
see also Age regression
Rehabilitation medicine, 131-134
Relaxation techniques
anxiety treatment with, 88-91, 93-94
cancer patient hypnosis with, 146
chemotherapy for cancer patient and, 143
creativity and, 18
essential hypertension and, 157
hospitalization and, 128, 129
hypnosis and effects in, 32
Jacobson's method of, 93, 98
pain control with, 119-121
panic disorders with, 99
peptic ulcer and, 154
phobic treatment with psychotherapy and, 186-188
psychotherapy with, 182
space travel and, 20
Repression, in cancer patient hypnosis, 146
Resistances, in Ericksonian approaches to psychotherapy, 194-195
Respiratory disorders
hypnotic treatment of, 157-159
psychological factors in, 158
Respiratory system
autogenic training and, 92
hypnosis and changes in, 26
meditative training and, 95
Responsibility in treatment, 48
Restructuring habits, 103-104
Revivification, and hypnosis, 37-38

Scales, *see* Rating scales
Schizophrenia, 41
anxiety in, 86
hemispheric laterality and, 21
insensitivity to pain in, 117
multiple personality differentiated from, 212
Schultz, J.H., 91
Screening interview, *see* Interview of patient
Self-hypnosis
anorgasmia treatment with, 169
cancer patient and, 146
early use of, 6
emerging from, 60-62, 65-66
illustrated method for, 54-66
impotence treatment with, 174, 176-177
meditative training for anxiety treatment with, 94-96
multiple personality with, 213
pain control with, 120-121, 122, 124

quick reference for induction of, 63–66
short-term therapy with, 199–200
space travel with, 20
Sex therapy, 163–177
  anorgasmia in, 164–172
  case history in, 164–166
  impotence in, 172–177
Short-term therapy
  case history of, 199–201
  hypnosis with, 17, 199
  personality traits and, 203
Skin, hypnosis and changes in, 27
Skin disorders, 151, 159
Sleep
  EEG studies of correlation of hypnosis and, 27
  fears of patient concerning, 46
  hypnosis as form of, 4, 10–11
  induction technique model with, 28
Smell hallucinations, 29
Smoking control treatment, 104–108
  interview in, 104–105
  posthypnotic discussion in, 106–108
  trance strategy in, 105–106
Social habits, 103
Social phobias, 87
Soft profile configuration, in Hypnotic Induction Profile (HIP), 80, 82
Space medicine, 19–20
Spiritualism, 6
Stanford Children's Hypnotic Clinical Scale (SHCS-Child), 71, 72
Stanford Hypnotic Clinical Adult Scale (SHCS-Adult), 71, 72
Stanford Hypnotic Susceptibility Scales
  Form A (SHSS:A), 68–71, 72, 73
  Form B (SHSS:B), 68–71
  Form C (SHSS:C), 69
Stanford Profile Scales of Hypnotic Susceptibility, Forms I and II (SPS:I and SPS:II), 70
State theory, 8, 9
Stress
  cardiovascular disorders with, 156, 157
  hospitalization and, 127
  multiple personality and, 211
  psychosomatic disorders with, 152
  ulcerative colitis and, 155
Stress disorders, posttraumatic, 87
Suggestion
  anxiety treatment with, 89–90
  atavistic hypothesis of hypnosis and, 12
  behavioral theories of hypnosis with, 14
  burn patients with, 229
  cancer patient hypnosis with, 140
  dentistry and, 231
  eating disorders treatment with, 110–111
  historical developments using, 4
  hypnotic effects on memory and, 35–36
  obstetrics with, 222
  smoking control treatment with, 105–108
Surgery, 225–229
  anesthesia awareness in, 228
  historical notes on, 3, 5, 225
  hypnosis used during, 228–229
  patient selection in, 226–227
  postoperative hypnosis in, 229
  preoperative preparations in, 227
Systematic desensitization, with chemotherapy-induced nausea, 143

Taste hallucinations, 29
Temperature, and hypnosis, 26, 27
Thermal biofeedback in anxiety treatment, 94
Thinking, hypnosis and changes in, 31
Time sense, 31
Touch, hypnosis and effects on, 28–29
Touch in hypnosis
  anxiety treatment with, 90–91
  hospital hypnosis with, 131
Trance logic, 8–9, 205
Transcendental meditation (TM), 95–96
Transference, 12, 13, 50
Trichotillomania, 199–201

Ulcerative colitis, 151, 154–155
Unconscious
  Ericksonian approach to, 193
  fears of unconscious patient
    regarding, 46
Urology, 234
Urticaria, 151, 159

Visual hallucinations, 29
Visualization
  cancer patient hypnosis with, 148
  creativity and, 18
  pediatric hypnosis with, 135
Vomiting reactions, 153

Warts, 151, 159
Weight disorders, 108–112

Yoga, in psychosomatic disorders, 160